Applied Public Relatio

Applied Public Relations provides readers with the opportunity to observe and analyze how contemporary businesses and organizations interact with key groups and influences. Through the presentation of cases covering a wide variety of industries, locations, and settings, authors Kathy Brittain McKee and Larry F. Lamb examine how real organizations develop and maintain their relationships, and offer valuable insights into contemporary business and organizational management practices.

McKee and Lamb place special emphasis on public relations as a strategic management function that must coordinate its planning and activities with several organizational units—human resources, marketing, legal counsel, finance, and operations, among others. A commitment to the ethical practice of public relations underlies the book, and students are challenged not only to assess the effectiveness of the practices outlined, but also to understand the ethical implications of those choices.

This second edition includes the following key features:

- New and updated cases.
- Additional Professional Insight commentaries.
- Expanded use of charts and photographs.
- An appendix with the PRSA Member Code of Ethics and the IABC Code of Ethics for Professional Communicators.
- A companion website with resources for the student and the instructor.

With its practical orientation and scope, *Applied Public Relations* is a useful text for courses on public relations management, public relations cases and campaigns, and integrated communication management.

Kathy Brittain McKee is a professor of communication at Berry College. She is the co-author of *Media Ethics: Cases and Moral Reasoning*, which is now in its 8th edition.

Larry F. Lamb has managed public relations at Fortune 500 companies, served international clients of a communications consulting business, and taught at two public universities.

Applied Public Relations
Cases in Stakeholder Management

Second Edition

Kathy Brittain McKee
Berry College

Larry F. Lamb

Routledge
Taylor & Francis Group

NEW YORK AND LONDON

First edition 2005
by Lawrence Erlbaum Associates, Inc.

This edition published 2009
by Routledge
270 Madison Ave, New York, NY 10016

Simultaneously published in the UK
by Routledge
2 Park Square, Milton Park, Abingdon, Oxon OX14 4RN

Routledge is an imprint of the Taylor & Francis Group, an informa business

© 2005 Lawrence Erlbaum Associates, Inc.
© 2009 Taylor & Francis

Typeset in Minion by
HWA Text and Data Management Ltd, London
Printed and bound in the United States of America on acid-free paper by
Walsworth Publishing Company, Marceline, M0

Library of Congress Cataloging in Publication Data
Lamb, Larry F.
  Applied public relations : cases in stakeholder management /
  Larry F. Lamb, Kathy Brittain McKee. – 2nd ed.
      p. cm.
  Includes index.
  1. Public relations – Case studies. I. McKee, Kathy Brittain. II. Title.
  HD59.L36 2009
  659.2–dc22   2008054734

ISBN10: 0-415-99915-4 (hbk)
ISBN10: 0-415-99916-2 (pbk)
ISBN10: 0-203-87154-5 (ebk)

ISBN13: 978-0-415-99915-1 (hbk)
ISBN13: 978-0-415-99916-8 (pbk)
ISBN13: 978-0-203-87154-6 (ebk)

Contents

Figures

Preface

Applied Public Relations: Cases in Stakeholder Management offers readers the opportunity to observe and analyze the manner in which contemporary businesses and organizations interact with key groups and influences. A basic assumption of the text is that principles of best practice may best be learned by examining how real organizations have chosen to develop and maintain relationships in a variety of industries, locations and settings.

We seek to offer insights to readers into contemporary business and organizational management practices. Some of the cases detail positive, award-winning practices, while others provide an overview of practices that may have been less successful. Some target specific public relations campaigns, while others offer evidence of broader business and organizational practices that had public image or public relations implications. Readers should be prompted not only to consider the explicit public relations choices but also to analyze and assess the impact of all management decisions on relationships with key stakeholders, whether they were designed or implicit or even accidental.

Pre-professional programs in schools of business, law, and medicine commonly include case-study courses because they encourage students to use both deductive and inductive reasoning to sort through the facts of situations, propose alternatives, and recommend treatments or solutions. For the same reason, academic programs in public relations usually offer courses that teach reputation and relationship management through the case-study method. In fact, the Commission on Public Relations Education specifically recommends the use of case-study teaching to provide undergraduates with a bridge between theory and application.

The strategic use of public relations is expanding in business, government, cultural institutions, and social service agencies. According to the U.S. Bureau of Labor Statistics, public relations continues as one of the fastest growing professional fields in the nation, and its practice is spreading rapidly throughout the rest of the world as well. Paralleling this growth, the complexity of public relations has increased with globalization of corporate enterprise and the application of new communication technologies. Social movements and activist organizations now cross borders easily by using public relations strategies to influence a public that is connected by satellites and the Internet. Through case studies throughout the book, readers can examine these changing stakeholder relationships from several perspectives.

This book is appropriate for use as an undergraduate text for courses such as public relations management, public relations cases and campaigns, business management, or integrated communication management. A commitment to the ethical practice of public relations underlies the book. Students are challenged not only to assess the effectiveness of the practices outlined but also to consider the ethical implications of those choices. We have placed special emphasis on public relations as a strategic management function that must coordinate its planning and activities with several organizational units—human resources, marketing, legal counsel, finance, operations, and others.

The first chapter provides a review of the public relations landscape: the basic principles underlying effective practice. It also offers a method for case analysis, pointing to an understanding of the particular case and leading students to assess the more comprehensive implications for best practices and ethical practices.

This chapter is followed by nine chapters, each of which offers an overview of principles associated with relations with the particular stakeholder group and supplemented with suggestions for additional readings. Then, within each chapter, four or five case studies are presented, to offer sufficient information for analysis and to provide opportunities for students to engage in additional research that would support their conclusions. Reflection questions are offered to help prompt thinking and focus discussion.

Chapter 2 examines relationships with employees, posing such questions as why is employee satisfaction vital to customer service, financial results, recruiting, and what are the most important predictors of employee satisfaction? How do high-performing organizations use employee communications?

The third chapter explores relationships with community stakeholders. What obligations or duties do organizations have to act as good citizens? What are the appropriate means of publicizing organizational activities as a community citizen?

Relationships with consumers are probed in chapter four. What are the most effective means of communicating with this group? How are new fusions of marketing, public relations, and advertising working together to reach this group? What duties do businesses owe their customers?

What is news and what motivates reporters to cover it are some of the concerns raised in chapter 5, which deals with media relations. Cases explore both planned and unplanned interactions with reporters and raise issues of traditional and emerging media formats.

Chapter 6 focuses on a priority stakeholder group for public companies: shareholders and investors and those who offer advice to them. Examining the cases presented in this chapter yields insight into issues such as the importance of timely and truthful material disclosure and the implications management decisions have on subsequent stock values.

In contrast, chapter 7 focuses on building and maintaining relationships with the stakeholders of nonprofit organizations, their members, volunteers, and donors. The unending need to raise funds is addressed, as is the ongoing need to keep members and volunteers satisfied and to attract new members and volunteers.

Relationships with government regulators are addressed in chapter 8. Cases examine how governments seek to influence their constituents and how organizations seek to influence regulation.

Chapter 9 examines activist stakeholder groups and how they use public relations strategies to grab attention, win adherents and motivate change. It also considers how targeted organizations may establish and maintain effective communication with them. The impact of public demonstrations and of media coverage is examined. Principles of cooperation are explored.

The final chapter looks at relationships in the global community, focusing on the ways in which media practices, cultural mores, and political differences may affect relationships that cross borders and languages.

Eleven guest commentaries are included, each answering a question about the best practices in contemporary public relations. We thank Dr. James Grunig, professor emeritus of public relations at the University of Maryland; Ron Arp, president, Amplify Group, Inc.; Lisa Owens, vice president of public relations, Regnier Valdez; Anne Sceia Klein, APR, Fellow PRSA, president, Anne Klein Communications Group, LLC; Richard D. French, president and chief executive officer, French/West/Vaughan; David Henderson, author, *Making News: A Straight-shooting Guide to Media Relations*; Linda Kelleher, executive vice president, National Investor Relations Institute; James E. Moody, president, Construction Suppliers Association; Gene Rose, communications director, National Conference of State Legislatures; Larry Pfautsch, vice president, corporate communications, American Century Investments; and Julie Freeman, ABC, APR; president, International Association of Business Communicators, for their thoughtful reflections based on years of expertise and experience.

Three guest case studies are also included. We thank Dr. Krishna Dhir, Henry Gund professor of management, Campbell School of Business, Berry College, and Dr. Marcie L. Hinton, assistant professor, Middle Tennessee State University, for their thorough analyses of these public relations situations.

Professors may approach the cases within the book in several ways. A focus on specific stakeholder groups would be easily possible, using the chapters as presented. However, one might also focus on particular issues, such as labor relations or crisis management, by selecting cases from within several chapters. One might highlight the operations of agencies, corporations, and nonprofits in the same manner. One might also select cases that contrast campaigns with ongoing programs or managerial behaviors.

The authors acknowledge the contribution of Dr. Carol J. Pardun of the University of South Carolina to the inception of this project.

PROFESSIONAL INSIGHT

THE MANAGEMENT CHAMPION
OF SOCIAL RESPONSIBILITY

James E. Grunig, professor emeritus, University of Maryland

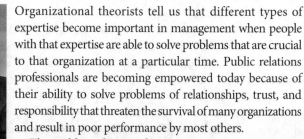

Organizational theorists tell us that different types of expertise become important in management when people with that expertise are able to solve problems that are crucial to that organization at a particular time. Public relations professionals are becoming empowered today because of their ability to solve problems of relationships, trust, and responsibility that threaten the survival of many organizations and result in poor performance by most others.

The public relations function provides a voice for publics when management makes critical, strategic decisions. Too often, management makes decisions without considering the consequences of those decisions on publics who have no say in the decisions. When management makes such decisions, many publics develop into activist groups who actively oppose the organization. Opposition typically results in litigation, legislation, regulation, and negative publicity that cost the organization a great deal of money.

Even if publics do not organize to oppose decisions, management has a responsibility to alleviate negative consequences of its actions, such as pollution, risky products, discrimination, economic hardship, or a dangerous workplace. Recognizing and alleviating these consequences is the essence of social responsibility, and the public relations function is the management champion of social responsibility.

Public relations managers are the voice of management to explain its decisions, but, more importantly, they are also the voice of publics. I have described this relationship between public relations, other managers, and publics as two-way symmetrical public relations. Others have called it collaborative advocacy. Still others have called the public relations professional an in-house activist. All of these terms suggest that the public relations professional has a duty to the organization that employs him or her, a duty to the publics that make up society, and to himself or herself. Increasingly, public relations professionals are the chief ethics officers of their organizations. This role is a challenging one, but it makes public relations one of the most relevant and interesting professions today.

James E. Grunig is an emeritus professor of public relations in the Department of Communications at the University of Maryland. He holds a Ph.D. in mass communication from the University of Wisconsin. He has written or edited five books and over 225 articles and chapters about public relations.

1

Public Relations
Maintaining Mutually Beneficial Systems of
Stakeholder Relationships

No formal organization is an island. Each is composed of an internal system of social networks, and each exists within a framework of interrelated systems of relationships with key stakeholders such as competitors, donors, consumers, regulators, the media, and so on. Some organizations may prefer to think of themselves as islands, however, or floating battleships equipped with all the resources necessary for their own sustenance. In reality, such a view is too shortsighted for success.

PRACTICING PUBLIC RELATIONS

The effective practice of public relations is integrally bound to the health of an organization or institution. As such, it provides the avenue for the organization to effectively monitor, interact, and react with other key groups in the organizational environment. Public relations is thought of here as *the communication and action on the part of an organization that supports the development and maintenance of mutually beneficial relationships between the organization and the groups with which it is interdependent.* This text is written overtly from a systems theory perspective, which suggests that without such adaptation, units in an environment will wither and fade as they will not be able to exchange vital information with other units in the environment. Such a balanced flow of information creates an *open system*, one that is responsive and adaptive to changes within the environment and its internal and external systems and subdivisions. In public relations terms, we think of this exchange as occurring through the building of mutually beneficial relationships based on a balanced flow of information from and to the organization and its key publics. Thus, effective public relations practice underlies the maintenance of an open system. Conversely, when public relations is not an integral part of the organization and balancing internal and external communication with the environment and other systems and subsystems is not a basic function for the organization and its management, then the system is described as closed, one subject to restriction and perhaps even death because it will not change or respond to its environment.

Clearly, for the practice of public relations to ensure openness, it requires the support and involvement of management. To use a crude human systems example, the nervous system within one's leg or arm cannot truly function without support and direction from the brain. Some movement or reaction may occur, but the functioning of the limb is dependent on coordination with all other internal systems that is triggered by the brain through the central nervous system. Public relations practitioners may be assigned duties or activities, but unless these are coordinated with the "management brains" of the entire organization, these actions may produce little that is truly functional for the organization or its interrelated systems.

PUBLIC RELATIONS PROCESSES WITHIN SYSTEMS

With the assumption that effective public relations promotes a healthy, open system for an organization and its interrelated systems and environment, comes certain other suppositions. First, an organization must be able and willing to identify who or what these key interrelated systems are. Because the health of other units within a system is also dependent on a mutually beneficial relationship and exchange, as is that of the central unit, they have a mutual stake in each other's well-being. Thus, these groups are often identified as *publics* or *stakeholders*. The process of coming to know and continuing to understand the concerns, needs, priorities, media habits, communication patterns, and social commitments of those key stakeholder groups requires effort, resources, and knowledge. And, although it may be sometimes frustrating, such research is an ongoing process; one never can "know" all one needs to know about a stakeholder. Thus, the practice of public relations requires continuing efforts at research, planning, executing, and evaluating in order for organizations to remain open for new input and output. This text seeks to explore how the relationships with those stakeholders may best be managed through appropriate public relations practices.

Stakeholder theory takes a similar approach in understanding how business and corporate "firms" relate to their stakeholders—defined as those with the power to affect or be affected by a firm's performance. From this theoretical standpoint, the relationships between and among stakeholders and the organization are metaphorically described as "contracts," which "can take the form of exchanges, transactions, or the delegation of decision-making authority, as well as formal legal documents" (Jones, 1995, p. 407). Managers within firms make decisions that may not necessarily be the most efficient in advancing the interests of all stakeholders, and some decisions or contracts may be more ethical than others. Stakeholder analysis, then, seeks to understand how the contracts can become more efficient, ethical and effective in advancing the interests of the firm and its stakeholders.

Although different writers and organizations may describe the process differently, systems theory suggests that the practice of public relations requires systematic, ongoing environmental monitoring. Plans should be based on solid and thorough research that explores the internal and external situation of the organization and its systems. Effective public relations departments or firms lead their businesses and clients to engage in *issues management*, a systematic environmental analysis that helps identify potential problems and potential ways of responding to or avoiding them. Such research should guide organizations to define carefully the problem or opportunity within the environment that should be responded to. Setting a goal or goals that relate to the problem or opportunity establishes the environment for planning. In turn, plans are only as good as their execution, and systems theory again would suggest that such execution should be carried out at the same time environmental monitoring is maintained. Finally, input regarding successes and weaknesses should be sought out deliberately at the end of a program and plan. That way, important feedback may become part of the next system action or program and perhaps shared with other linked systems as appropriate to help foster their health.

On occasion, however, organizations may find themselves in crisis situations, some anticipated through scenario planning, others because of sudden internal or external changes in the environment. Public relations practitioners have important responsibilities in helping organizations craft solutions and communications in those instances. While particular responses may vary, organizations that continue to communicate clearly, carefully, compassionately, and accurately with their stakeholders usually find those relationships endure beyond the crisis.

It should be acknowledged that effective analysis, planning, executing, and evaluating of both the environment and relationship management may be approached from other theoretical perspectives. Additionally, other theories and constructs may inform the assumptions of systems theory. Persuasion theory suggests that the motivations and needs of those communicating—both the speaker and the receiver—should be considered when shaping strategies. Members of different publics judge the credibility of the communicator differently, based not only on the communicator's perceived characteristics, but also on their own social and psychological attributes.

Practitioners and managers within organizations would be well advised to attend to the other dominant communication and social-psychological constructs, such as Maslow's hierarchy of needs and the theories and assumptions of social exchange, social learning, agenda setting, behaviorism, diffusion of innovations, classical rhetoric, and the elaboration-likelihood model. Knowledge of traditional business fields such as marketing and management provides a solid underpinning for effective communication within and throughout organizations. An understanding of contemporary media practices is also a vital tool for practitioners.

ETHICAL AND LEGAL PERSPECTIVES

A plethora of laws, regulations, and torts may govern the relationships of organizations with various publics. Within the United States, the framework of the First Amendment to the Constitution provides for the free practice of public relations, yet certain practices may be either restricted or required by statute or regulation. For example, businesses and organizations are as affected by concerns regarding libel and privacy as any individual or media group. Copyright and trademark regulation may, in fact, promote and protect the interests of organizations over the interests of individuals. Publicly traded companies face specific regulation of communication activity, ranging from required speech dealing with quarterly and annual statements, to prohibited or premature information sharing among insiders. Clearly, the practitioner must consider the legal environment as a key component that affects relationships with stakeholder groups.

The social and economic power of public relations practices today should also be grounded in a foundation of social ethics. Professional associations such as the Public Relations Society of America (PRSA) and the International Association of Business Communicators (IABC) have endorsed principles that should underlie practice: advocacy of free speech and communication; commitment to disseminating truthful and accurate information; respect for the dignity and value of all individuals; and the maintenance of independence from undue conflicts of interest or allegiance. Again, systems theory suggests that the good of the whole is supported by the good of the parts, so behaviors that promote mutual benefit are not only ethical but even essential for the ongoing growth and success of an organization or business. Practitioners must discern what is the best choice for behavior—that which most effectively promotes the principles of human dignity, social responsibility, and truth telling. As the communications conduit between and among systems that may have competing interests, determining what choices offer the most effective ethical alternatives requires reflection and introspection, rather than just reaction and response.

CASE-STUDY ANALYSIS

This book addresses nine key stakeholder groups with which many businesses and organizations interrelate and proffers contemporary case studies for analysis. Some of these cases exemplify the very highest standards of public communication, mutual benefit, and business savvy. Others may raise questions about performance and benefit. Chapter 2 investigates relationships and communication with employees as exemplified by national and international firms such as General Motors, Southwest Airlines, UPS, and Sun Microsystems. Chapter 3 presents examples of community stakeholders from the perspective of for-profit corporations such as Avon or the Chicago Bulls basketball team, and nonprofit groups such as Habitat for Humanity. The ways in which corporations seek to foster healthy relationships with consumers may be examined through cases in chapter 4 involving crisis communication, branding, and product publicity.

The important role played by media relations is explored in chapter 5 where health care, economic, religious, and social issues arouse media coverage to which organizations had to react and respond. Chapters 6 and 7 address special stakeholder groups, investors, members, and volunteers. From crises of financial reporting to efforts to diversify memberships, these cases raise issues for publicly traded and nonprofit organizations.

Chapter 8 investigates the relationships between governmental organizations and their publics or organizations and regulatory agencies. Critical questions about the role of public relations within public affairs are explored. Chapter 9 addresses critical questions from another perspective—those raised by activist groups seeking to affect change in environmental or social practices. Last, chapter 10 raises the issue of the expanded international environment in which organizations and businesses now operate. How does one successfully build and maintain relationships in varied settings with diverse stakeholders?

Although there are many ways to approach case studies as a learning tool, we suggest the following as one method that may prove helpful. It suggests three layers of analysis that might be used:

- *Analyze the Problem*: How fully do you understand the situation described here? Note the various stakeholders that may be involved in each case, and how they are being affected by the issue raised in the case. Through additional research you might conduct, what more can you learn about the organization in question, its stakeholders and publics, this situation, or other organizations that have faced similar situations? Articulate the public relations problem or opportunity faced by the organization and/or its key stakeholders in one or two sentences.
- *Understand the Practices*: Critique the actions or reactions undertaken by the organization and its publics described here. Identify the phases of the communication or campaign cycle—the research, the strategies, the actions and communication tools, and the evaluation processes—and judge the strengths and weaknesses of the plan and actions. Are they in line with accepted best practices? In your opinion, were actions taken that were not necessary? Were other appropriate actions not included? Were there factors of timing and budgeting that affected actions, or that could have been exploited to better advantage?
- *Identify the Principles*: What long-term principles seemed to underlie the decisions made by the organizations and groups in each case? What did each value? What are the implications of this case for developing, maintaining or restoring mutually beneficial relationships with the key stakeholder identified, or with other strategic stakeholders? How does this

case illustrate, either positively or negatively, common ethical principles for effective practice? What does this case suggest in terms of effective principles for public relations practitioners in other situations with the same stakeholder or others?

The following questions may help you to clarify aspects of the cases as you analyze these levels:

- What is the environmental situation for the organization in this case? Is it economically healthy? Is the organization in a stable or changing environment?
- What goal(s) and objectives do you think this organization is attempting to achieve through its actions or reactions?
- What communications or actions would characterize a mutually beneficial relationship with this public or stakeholder? What would motivate members of that stakeholder group to enter into or to maintain a relationship with this organization? What might be a liability or caution about an ongoing relationship?
- Do this organization's actions demonstrate open- or closed-system practices and philosophies? What type of research do you believe was used to develop this plan of action? What more should the organization have known to more effectively plan and execute its communication program or campaign?
- What ethical philosophies or precepts are demonstrated by the organization in this case?
- Are there other examples you can cite of organizations that have faced similar challenges? What do those examples tell you about how this organization might have improved its relationships and its outcomes?
- What style of internal management does this case illustrate? Does it appear that public relations practitioners within the organization are taken seriously? Is public relations a management function within this organization?

SUGGESTED READINGS

Ault, Philip H., Warren K. Agee, Glen T. Cameron, & Dennis L. Wilcox. (2002). *Public relations: Strategies and tactics* (7th ed.). New York: Pearson, Allyn & Bacon.

Caywood, Clarke L. (Ed.). (1997). *The handbook of strategic public relations & integrated communication*. Boston: McGraw-Hill.

Cutlip, Scott M., Allen H. Center, & Glen M. Broom. (2000). *Effective public relations*. (8th edn.). Upper Saddle River, NJ: Prentice Hall.

Freeman, R.E. (1984). *Strategic management: A stakeholder approach*. Boston: Pitman.

Grunig, James E. (Ed.). (1992). *Excellence in public relations and communications management*. Hillsdale, NJ: Lawrence Erlbaum Associates.

Heath, Robert L. (Ed.). (2000). *Handbook of public relations*. Thousand Oaks, CA: Sage.

International Association of Business Communicators Code of Ethics. Accessible at www.iabc.com/about/code.htm (accessed January 21, 2009).

Jones, Thomas M. (April 1995). Instrumental stakeholder theory: A synthesis of ethics and economics. *The Academy of Management Review*, 20(2), pp. 404- 437.

Lattimore, Dan, Otis Baskin, Suzette T. Heiman, Elizabeth T. Toth, & James K. Van Leuven. (2004). *Public relations: The profession and the practice*. Boston: McGraw-Hill.

Ledingham, J.A., & Stephen D. Bruning. (Eds.). (2001). *Public relations as relationship management: A relational approach to the study and practice of public relations*. Mahwah, NJ: Lawrence Erlbaum Associates.

Moore, Roy L., Ronald T. Farrar, & Erik L. Collins. (1999). *Advertising and public relations law* (2nd ed.). Mahwah, NJ: Lawrence Erlbaum Associates.

Newsom, Doug. (2003). *This is PR: The realities of public relations*. New York: Wadsworth.

Public Relations Society of America Code of Ethics. Accessible at www.prsa.org/aboutUs/ethics/preamble_en.html (accessed January 21, 2009) .

Toth, Elizabeth L., & Robert L. Heath. (Eds.). (1992). *Rhetorical and critical approaches to public relations*. Hillsdale, NJ: Lawrence Erlbaum Associates.

PROFESSIONAL INSIGHT

THE CASE FOR CHARACTER

Ron Arp, president, Amplify Group, Inc.

A North Carolina real estate appraiser once approached me seeking a definition of what communications people actually do. We discussed differences between advertising and PR: "Ads you pay for, PR you pray for." Then, we spent an hour describing how communications explains, positions, accelerates, differentiates, protects.

Testing his viewpoint, I asked if he saw value in communications. "Of course I do," he affirmed. Then, I asked him to play back what he thought communications professionals do: "Well, it seems like you shovel an awful lot of smoke."

We laughed. However, his point was not lost on me.

Perhaps the greatest challenge for communications professionals has nothing to do with writing poetically, designing stunning four-color reports, or hosting standing-room-only press conferences. Instead, it is to explain what we do and why.

So, what is communications?

In short, I view it as character expression. It is a process of helping people understand who you are, what you stand for, and why you do the things you do. Character is anchored in honesty, integrity and trust. It is the essence of your brand.

It is not to be confused with reputation management. This is a notion of attempting to manage what others think of you. It deserves the disparaging handles of "spin," "fluff," and "flak."

Abraham Lincoln contrasted the two: "Character is like a tree and reputation like its shadow. The shadow is what we think of it; the tree is the real thing."

Character is enduring: it is who you are and it rarely changes. Reputation is fleeting: it is what others think of you and it changes constantly.

So, what is your job? To use every opportunity, good and bad, to help people understand the character of your organization.

Johnson & Johnson twice set the tone in the 1980s with its $100 million decision to clear the shelves and restock after evidence of product tampering. It is what you'd expect from a company that makes great health care products.

Nautilus received letters of praise when it communicated a recall offering free repair parts, and told people it was setting a new standard for safety and quality. It's what you'd expect from a leading fitness brand.

In 1996, NFL quarterback Brett Favre chilled the Lambeau faithful by checking into treatment for six weeks because he was addicted to painkillers. Less than a year later, the future Hall of Famer took the Packers to a Super Bowl victory. It's what you want to see from an athlete role model who stumbled into an addiction.

Why is character so important? Because it is a guiding compass for you, and for those around you. Character is the bedrock upon which communications programs must be built to assure they endure the harshest of storms. People want to know whether they can count on you. They want to see your feet match your lips.

Contrast the earlier examples with those where reputation is king.

An apparel company suddenly backed away from funding a controversial non-profit organization. Facing a storm of controversy from the group's sympathizers, the company reversed course and reinstated the funding. Guess what happened? Critics from the other side took aim at the company. The company chased its reputation like a dog its tail.

Imagine if Martha Stewart had quickly acknowledged an error in judgment after trading in ImClone stock. She knew better. She used to be a stockbroker! Instead, she became ensnared in obstruction of justice that sent her down the 'perp walk' and damaged a rising brand.

Perhaps the most disingenuous of all efforts to manage reputation is the Hollywood apology: "I'm sorry if I may have offended someone." What? Your character is not situational. You either are sorry, or not. You're going to change, or not.

Bad things happen. Things break. People err. How we respond in those times is when our character becomes obvious.

Abraham Lincoln was quick to point out that character is revealed in difficult times. "Character cannot be developed in ease and quiet," he said, "Only through experience of trial and suffering can the soul be strengthened, ambition inspired, and success achieved."

Take time to understand the character of your organization—what you stand for and why. Present it in ways that resonate with your audiences. Prove it in times of crisis. Communications need not be any more complicated.

Always communicate true to your character. I can assure you that people will have a high respect for what you do, even if they can describe it only as shoveling smoke.

Ron Arp is president of Amplify Group, Inc., a strategic communications consultancy. Previously, he served as senior vice president, corporate communications, for Nautilus and as senior partner and general manager of the Portland, Ore, office of Fleishman-Hillard.

2
Stakeholders: Employees

The first day of a new job often includes an employee's initial contact with the public relations department, though the employee may not realize it. Part of the day is spent in the human resources office, completing paperwork and an orientation program, and part is spent with the employee's new supervisor. During these visits, a new employee may receive printed material about the organization, see an orientation video, and learn how to use the intranet to get news and information. The printed, visual, and online materials very likely were prepared by or with help from a public relations professional. Through a variety of media channels, this connection to public relations will continue, directly and indirectly, until the individual retires or leaves the organization.

Employee relations responsibilities cut across many departments. Human resources focuses mainly on recruiting, pay and benefits, training programs, employee appraisal systems, and similar concerns affecting all jobholders. The marketing department wants to keep employees up to date on products and services offered to customers. In every department, individual supervisors handle employee relations needs that are specific to the people in their work groups, such as linking an organization's overall mission and goals to the everyday reality of the job.

Public relations professionals work in close partnership with these human resources managers, individual supervisors, and others to foster good employee relations. In fact, public relations professionals seldom undertake employee relations programs without input from human resources and other departments. This partnership aims to create conditions where all employees, individually and as a group, can get the greatest reward from the human capital they invest in the job and where the organization can gain the highest value from the resources it uses to reach its goals.

All of us invest varying amounts of *human capital* in work. Human capital is the combination of talents and skills, knowledge, behavior, effort, and time that an individual commits to the job. In turn, an organization pays its workers for their human capital and also provides capital of its own—machinery, office space, computers, and so on—for each of us to use on the job.

EMPLOYEE SATISFACTION PAYS MEASURABLE RETURNS

Everyone, individuals and the organization, will get the most from an enterprise when all commit as much human and hard capital to the endeavor as they can. And employees are most likely to invest more human capital when they are satisfied with their jobs. Satisfied employees care more about customer satisfaction, cooperate more with each other, and apply more effort. They are more productive.

Employee satisfaction has tangible benefits for all organizations, but the results may be most easily measured in for-profit businesses. Satisfied employees are associated with higher revenues (the dollars that businesses receive from their customers), lower costs (the dollars that businesses spend to provide customers with products or services), and greater profitability (the revenues that remain after all costs are met). The reasons for the positive payback from employee satisfaction are self-evident. Not only do they appeal to our common sense, but they also have been examined by researchers and found valid. Here are a few examples:

- *Employee retention*: Satisfied employees are less likely to look for or accept new jobs with other organizations, which might be competitors. As workers stay longer at one employer, they become more proficient, building up their human capital in ways that benefit both employee and employer. Turnover, replacing employees who quit, is expensive; some say it costs between 100% and 200% of an individual's base pay. It entails not only the visible costs of recruiting new workers but also the invisible costs of a lower level of human capital offered by a new employee.
- *Customer satisfaction*: Each of us, as consumers, has encountered unhappy employees, surly or slow or sour. They can make a sales transaction or a meal away from home an experience to remember, which we vow never to repeat. On the other hand, satisfied employees create a detectable climate of care to which customers respond. It may lead to a bigger purchase and to repeat business. Similarly, customer satisfaction appears to have a reciprocal effect on employees. Imagine how much more pleasant a job can be when customers are happy.
- *Productivity*: Employees generally must interact with coworkers and managers to make a product or provide a service; few create output entirely on their own. When individuals actively cooperate with each other, more work gets done in less time, often using fewer resources. Similarly, satisfied employees put more "discretionary effort" into the job, making the difference between average and superior performance.

Considering the payoff that is available to employers from taking steps to assure employee satisfaction, what's surprising is how many organizations neglect the things they could be doing, big and little, to make employees happier.

EFFECTIVE LEADERS INSPIRE TRUST AND CONFIDENCE

Some things that might improve employee satisfaction are beyond the influence of public relations professionals, for example, better pay and benefits. Yet, there are many areas where public relations professionals, in partnership with others, can and should apply their expertise. These areas include feedback mechanisms that give employees a voice and an opportunity to raise questions, open-book management that shares details on current results, reports on goals and plans that are expressed in language everyone can understand, and more.

Perhaps the best place to begin is employees' desire to know where the organization is going, how it's going to get there, and when it will arrive—goals, strategies, and timetables. These subjects constitute leadership responsibilities, and there may be nothing more important to employees. Coincidentally, these subjects also give public relations professionals the opportunity to make their greatest contributions.

Research shows that employee satisfaction depends on the qualities of trust and integrity that bind individuals to organizations. Yet, investigators have learned that workers are most disappointed in employers' efforts to achieve open and honest communication. Also high on the list of disappointments are clarity of goals and directions, trust and respect, and management competence.

The Hay Group, international consultants on human resources, says that its studies have shown that trust and confidence in top leadership constitute the single most important predictor of employee satisfaction. Moreover, a Hay study found that leaders can get trust and confidence through effective communication programs that:

- Help employees understand the overall strategy of the organization.
- Help employees see their role in achieving key objectives.
- Update employees regularly on progress that's made toward the objectives

SOURCE OF SATISFACTION: OPEN AND HONEST COMMUNICATION

Because key indicators of an organization's success depend on employee satisfaction and, in turn, satisfaction depends on trust and confidence in leadership, public relations professionals should develop programs that help leaders win trust and confidence as well as show respect and appreciation for employees. In some cases, these programs will involve giving employees valid reasons to extend trust; in others, programs will help leaders earn it. In all cases, trust cannot exist without open and honest communication.

Of course, communication should be two-way—not simply the top-down, here's-what-you-need-to-know approach used in too many employee relations programs. Instead, it should provoke a dialogue that will help employees gain satisfaction from their work life and support the overall goals of the organization.

When Watson Wyatt Worldwide, a global human resources consulting firm, examined 914 companies to learn which communication policies typify successful organizations, they found that the high-performing companies integrated communications into business strategy. Working with the IABC and the IABC Research Foundation, Watson Wyatt found that employees in high-performing firms understood overall goals better and the employees' roles in reaching them. The study learned that the high-performing organizations:

- Provide channels for upward communication and use employee input in decision making.
- Focus on helping employees understand the business, its values and culture, goals and progress, and ways for employees to improve performance.
- Give communications professionals a strategic role in business planning rather than pigeon-holing them as facilitators.
- Do better in explaining major changes to employees and winning support for change.

MEDIA CHANNELS FOR EMPLOYEES

Organizations use a variety of media to reach employees, including newsletters and employee newspapers, posters, bulletin boards, voice-mail announcements, e-mail messages, closed-circuit TV newscasts, kiosks, intranets, blogs and more.

Intranet communication has been growing fastest because it offers the advantages of speed, flexibility, color, interactivity, and ease in updating. However, experts advise public relations professionals to use intranet communication for its special capabilities rather than treat it as if it were print projected on a screen. Intranets can offer multimedia, chats and bulletin boards, previews of ad campaigns and commercials, breaking news, and more, but people don't read intranet screens as if they were the printed page. In fact, the proliferation of office computers has led to a rising tide of electronic communication, but it is unsuitable where employees, such as assembly line workers or outdoor crews, have little or no access to a digital network.

Even with all the advanced technology available today, one of the most effective media channels is an old standby, used in offices and garages and on the plant floor for generations: the small-group meeting where the boss and team get together for a 10- or 20-minute discussion. There are two main reasons for the continued popularity of small-group meetings:

- Face-to-face discussion is the most effective form of communication.
- Employees prefer to get job-related news from their immediate supervisor.

Public relations professionals often play an important role in the success of small-group meetings even though they may not be present when the supervisor and team get together. To introduce major policy changes and the like, materials for small-group meetings are prepared in advance by public relations practitioners. The materials take the form of what is often called a meeting-in-a-box that includes a meeting outline, skeleton remarks for the supervisor to adapt, perhaps a short videotape, DVD or PowerPoint presentation, handouts for participants, feedback forms, and similar items. The purpose is to give the supervisor useful materials, minimize preparation time, keep the message consistent, and achieve communications objectives. Proving that everything old is new again, each supervisor may obtain the PowerPoint presentation or visual portion of the meeting-in-a-box by downloading it from the intranet or receiving it as an e-mail attachment.

The cases in this chapter provide opportunities to discuss some of the opportunities and challenges faced by practitioners communicating with or about employee stakeholders. As you consider these cases, seek to identify the public relations problem or opportunity, the methods and tools used to resolve the situation, and how one might evaluate the success or failure of the public relations efforts. Ask yourself: What are the issues employees care about in this case? How might management communicate its goals, strategies and progress more effectively? How might employee viewpoints be sought out and responded to in a timely manner?

ADDITIONAL READINGS

Becker, Brian E., Mark A. Huselid, & Dave Ulrich. (2001). *The HR scorecard: Linking people, strategy, and performance*. Boston: Harvard Business School Press.

Beitler, Michael A. (2003). *Strategic organizational change*. Greensboro, NC: Practitioner Press International.

Catlette, Bill, & Richard Hadden. (2001). *Contented cows give better milk: The plain truth about employee relations & your bottom line*. Germantown, TN: Saltillo Press.

Koys, Daniel (2001). "Effects of employee satisfaction, organizational citizenship behavior, and turnover on organizational effectiveness," *Personnel Psychology*, 101-114.

CASE 1. GENERAL MOTORS TRIMS ITS WORKFORCE AND OPERATIONS

Increasing international competition. Changing fuel technologies. Higher gas prices. Costly employee benefits. General Motors faced a variety of challenges to its once dominant position as the world's largest car manufacturer.

Managing its employee relationships was a priority. In 2005, GM reported losses of $8.6 billion, with $5.6 billion in the United States. The company announced it would lay off 30,000 workers, about 17% of its 173,000 employees, and begin to close 12 factories. United Auto Workers Union official Bob Alexander was quoted as saying: "It's hard because there are no jobs in the area, let alone the country. We've sat back and watched all these jobs leave the country."

On November 22, 2005, "Good Morning America" interviewed two GM employees at the GM plant in Oklahoma City about their reaction to the announcement of the layoffs. Employee Dave Fleming described the reaction in the plant: "The whole crowd just turned around. They just turned around. They didn't say nothing, they didn't do nothing, they just like, were just like a bomb had went off, like they were shell shocked and they just turned around and walked away." His wife, Rena, said: "Well, 26 and a half years, that's a long time. I wasn't ready to walk out the door yet."

GM ended the job banks program, established in 1984, that had allowed some 7,500 employees to replace others who would then participate in other activities, from taking online courses to doing crafts while being paid. According to the Associated Press, each of these employees cost GM from $100,000 to $135,000 annually.

The cutbacks continued. In February 2006, pension benefits for salaried employees were frozen, and health care benefits for retirees who held salaried positions were cut.

In March 2006, GM announced it would offer buyouts to all its hourly factory workers, seeking to reduce its workforce by 7% during the year. White-collar jobs were also being cut through layoffs and attrition; the former employees would maintain their health insurance and wages for a short period. GM also offered a job-search assistance program.

Later that year, the U.S. Labor Department announced it would make available job retraining funds of $3,000 for individuals who had been laid off by automakers in Georgia, Michigan, Minnesota, Missouri, and Ohio by matching $1.5 million in grant money with state funds. Workers could use the money for tuition, books and fees.

UAW Seeks to Protect Worker Benefits

Members of the United Auto Workers held a two-day strike in September. In a release announcing the strike, UAW President Ron Gettelfinger said employees had worked with GM to address its economic challenges. "Since 2003 our members have made extraordinary efforts every time the company came to us with a problem: the corporate restructuring, the attrition plan, the Delphi bankruptcy, the 2005 health care agreement. In every case, our members went the extra mile to find reasonable solutions."

UAW vice president Cal Rapson said: "This is our reward: a complete failure by GM to address the reasonable needs and concerns of our members. Instead, in 2007 company executives continued to award themselves bonuses while demanding that our members accept a reduced standard of living."

After the short strike, a majority of union members ratified a new contract that covered more than 73,000 active workers at GM and more than 269,000 retirees and 69,000 surviving spouses through September 2011. Under the contract, active workers were to receive two 3% lump sum payments and a 4% lump sum payment. The UAW also asked for a moratorium on plant closings. The contract did not guarantee an overall general wage increase, but it maintained comprehensive health care and prescription drug coverage for active employees.

GM agreed to contribute $24.1 billion to a new Voluntary Employee Beneficiary Association that would establish a trust fund to pay retiree health benefits; additional funds would be invested, and an estimated $5.4 billion would be used for direct payments for retiree healthcare. The contract also provided for an increase in basic retiree pension benefits. GM also agreed to provide $15 million in initial funding to help establish a National Institute for Health Care Reform, a joint labor-management funded center.

Problems continued, and GM negotiated with the United Auto Workers to develop an additional attrition program. The news release, released February 12, 2008, at 7 a.m., reported:

DETROIT: General Motors Corp. (NYSE: GM) and the United Auto Workers (UAW) union have reached an agreement on a comprehensive special attrition program that will be offered to all of GM's 74,000 UAW-represented employees.

The special attrition program offers a choice of several pension and buyout incentives. It is offering retirement pension incentives of $45,000 for production employees or $62,500 for skilled trades. Eligible employees can select from a variety of ways to receive their incentive:

- One-time, lump-sum cash payment.
- Direct rollover into their GM 401(k) or into an Individual Retirement Account.
- Monthly annuity.
- Combination of partial lump-sum payment and direct rollover into their GM 401(k).

The other retirement and buyout options available are similar to those offered employees in 2006. These options include:

- *Mutually Satisfactory Retirement (MSR)* for employees who are at least 50 years old with 10 or more years of service. This option provides a pension payment with full benefits.
- *Pre-Retirement Program* in which employees with 26, 27, 28 or 29 years of service can grow into a "full and out" retirement. Until they reach 30 years of credited services, participating employees would receive a fixed monthly payment with full benefits.
- *Cash Buyout* for employees who agree to voluntarily quit and sever all ties with GM.
  - $140,000 buyout incentive is offered to employees with 10 or more years of credited service or seniority.
  - $70,000 buyout incentive to employees with less than 10 years of credited service or seniority.

In December 2007, GM and the UAW reached an agreement on what the company was calling the first phase of a comprehensive special attrition program. Details of this program were rolled out to employees at select locations last month. Those employees are now eligible for the enhanced provisions of this new agreement.

"We've worked with our UAW partners to ensure our employees have a variety of attractive options to consider," said Rick Wagoner, GM Chairman and CEO. "The special attrition program is an important initiative that will help us transform the workplace."

General Motors Corp. (NYSE: GM), the world's largest automaker, has been the annual global industry sales leader for 77 years. Founded in 1908, GM today employs about 266,000 people around the world. With global headquarters in Detroit, GM manufactures its cars and trucks in 35 countries. In 2007, nearly 9.37 million GM cars and trucks were sold globally under the following brands: Buick, Cadillac, Chevrolet, GMC, GM Daewoo, Holden, HUMMER, Opel, Pontiac, Saab, Saturn, Vauxhall and Wuling. GM's OnStar subsidiary is the industry leader in vehicle safety, security and information services. More information on GM can be found at www.gm.com.

In April 2008, GM announced one shift would be cut at truck and sport-utility vehicle plants in Flint and Pontiac, Michigan; Janesville, Wisconsin; and Oshawa, Ontario, idling some 3,550 employees. The laid-off workers were to receive unemployment benefits and supplemental pay that would lead to 80% of their normal 40-hour gross pay, according to GM spokesperson Dan Flores.

A corporate news release on May 29, 2008, announced that about 19,000 U.S. hourly employees had committed to the attrition program. Job openings would be filled with other current employees, and any new hiring would be with entry-level wages and benefits. Troy Clarke, group vice president and president of GM North America, said: "This attrition program gives us an opportunity to restructure our U.S. workforce through the entry-level wage and benefit structure for new hourly employees. Participation in the attrition program was an important, personal choice for employees and their families."

Another Plan is Announced

Yet, despite the cutbacks, the corporate losses continued. During the second quarter of 2008, GM experienced a loss of $15.5 billion. Slowing sales of its truck-based products and financial charges challenged the corporation, as did the cost of healthcare for its employees and retirees. In a corporate fact sheet released July 15, 2008, GM estimated that its spending for U.S. hourly and salaried legacy pension and healthcare had averaged $7 billion over the past 15 years; under the new agreements, it should be less than $2 billion in 2010.

On July 16, 2008, GM CEO Rick Wagoner used a conference call to announce the corporation's plan for recovery. Additional job cuts were possible. U.S. salaried retirees over 65 would lose their company healthcare coverage in January, and a $1.7 billion payment for the new union retiree health care trust would be delayed. Base pay for U.S. and Canadian salaried employees would be frozen until 2010, and executive cash bonuses for 2008 would be eliminated. Truck-manufacturing capacity would be cut, and work on next-generation pickups would be cut back. The Hummer brand would be reviewed.

In a corporate news release, Wagoner said, "While some of the actions, especially the capacity reductions, are very difficult, they are necessary to adjust to changing market and economic conditions and to keep GM's U.S. turnaround on track and moving forward." Increased production of fuel-efficient cars and an electric vehicle, the Chevy Volt, was planned.

QUESTIONS FOR REFLECTION

1. Analyze the GM news release provided in this case, and identify the ways in which it seeks to bolster confidence in its actions.
2. Evaluate other communication efforts undertaken by GM. What are the issues associated with communicating what may be perceived as negative news? What challenges have management changes and federal financial support posed for GM communicators?
3. Employee relations are particularly important during times of change. How can corporations seek to sustain effective communication with employees during reductions, cutbacks and labor negotiations?

Information for this case was drawn from the following: Associated Press (3 March 2006), "GM temporarily lays off 400 workers at Saturn plant," www.lexisnexis.com; Carty, S.S. and Healey, J.R. (16 July 2008), "GM hopes $15B boost to bottom line adds stability." *USA Today*, B1; General Motors (12 February 2008), "General Motors and the UAW reach agreement on comprehensive special attrition program," *General Motors News Release.* www.media.gm.com; General Motors (29 May 2008), "Approximately 19,000 GM hourly employees participate in attrition program; Program enables company to restructure workforce," http://media.gm.com; "GM layoffs in their own words," *Good Morning America*, (22 November 2005), www.lexisnexis.com; "GM Fact Sheet: GM Turnaround: Actions and Accomplishments," (15 July 2008), News Release. http://media. gm.com/servlet/GatewayServlet?target=http.//image.emerald.gm.com/gmnew...; Krisher, T. (29 April 2008), "GM to lay off 3,550 at 4 pickup truck and SUV factories," Associated Press. www. lexisnexis.com; Peters, J.W. (29 March 2006), "G.M. lays off hundreds of white-collar employees," *The New York Times*, C5; Thomas, K. (26 October 2006), "Labor Department announces retraining program for auto industry layoffs," Associated Press; Vlasic, B. (2 August 2008), "Automakers race time as their cash runs low," *The New York Times.* www.nytimes.com/2008/08/02/business/02gm.html; U.S. Fed News. (26 November 2005); www.voanews.com/mediaassets/english/2005_11/Audio/rm/ randle_GM_Layoffs_Communities_22nov05.rm; "UAW members ratify new collective bargaining agreement with General Motors," (10 October 2007), UAW News Release. www.uaw.org/news/ prn_article.cfm?ArtId=428; "UAW sets strike deadline at GM for Monday," (24 September 2007), UAW News Release. www.uau.org/news/prn_article.cfm?ArtId=423.

CASE 2. "YOU CAN'T BUY THAT KIND OF PR": SOUTHWEST AIRLINES EMPLOYEES STAR IN REALITY TV

Perhaps the most telling evidence of the relationship between Southwest Airlines and its most important publics lies in the capitalized words within the corporate mission statement:

> The mission of Southwest Airlines is dedication to the highest quality of Customer Service delivered with a sense of warmth, friendliness, individual pride, and Company Spirit.

To Our Employees

> We are committed to provide our Employees a stable work environment with equal opportunity for learning and personal growth. Creativity and innovation are encouraged for improving the effectiveness of Southwest Airlines. Above all, Employees will be provided the same concern, respect, and caring attitude within the organization that they are expected to share externally with every Southwest Customer.

Employees, Customers and Company: Integral relationships for the consistently profitable airline.

The commitment to emphasize these relationships was evident in the low-cost airline's participation in the reality program, "Airline," that aired for three seasons, 70 episodes, on the cable TV A&E network. The episodes typically followed multiple story lines as employees interacted with customers. Some customers were happy; others complained or coped with personal or travel issues.

Figure 2.1 Southwest's emphasis on customer service has contributed to years of profitability for the airline (Photo courtesy of Southwest Airlines)

On Air and In the Air

The idea for the series was sparked by the success of a similar show that ran for more than six years in the United Kingdom, which had featured easyJet, a London-based airline, A&E officials told the Associated Press (AP, 2 January 2004). Colleen Barrett, then president and CEO of Southwest, said she approved the participation after consulting the British airline. "I started thinking…it's basically 18 hours of free publicity. You can't buy that kind of PR."

The series focused on the interactions of customers with customer service employees in the various airports. Episode titles describe the nature of the customer and employee interactions. "You Can't Take It With You," "Stormy Weather," "A Hard Day's Flight," and "Love at First Flight" illustrate the many stories captured by the television crew, who would show up at airports—Los Angeles International, Baltimore-Washington International, Houston Hobby and Chicago Midway—and film what they found of interest. Some customers also suggested story lines.

A&E's Web site described the episode "Spirit Party" in this way:

> The FAA rules are clear, alcohol and air travel simply do not mix. In LA, passenger…has been drinking and it's fallen to supervisor Yolanda to tell him he's too drunk to board the flight. It's the night of the Southwest Spirit Party—a vast annual staff gathering—and a huge occasion for supervisor Mike. He's invited a special guest he wants to introduce to his colleagues. Gospel group the Faithway Doves are on their way to Chicago to be honored by the American Gospel Society and surprise their fellow passengers with some remarkable spirituals.

Demonstrating Customer Service

Customer service supervisors and managers at the four airports became de facto cast members. Michael Carr, a customer service supervisor at LAX, told A&E that being a part of the "Airline" cast was "an honor. I feel very fortunate to demonstrate the excellent Customer Service Southwest Airlines prides itself on providing our Customers." The best experience he had filming the series, he said, was "Being able to show the daily challenges all airline employees deal with each day."

According to the Associated Press, the airline received no compensation for participating in the show. Southwest could request a "voice-over narration to give 'context'" or give an explanation of how customer complaints were treated. Producer Chris Carey explained the relationship in USA Today after the first season: "They clearly need to see the shows before they air to make sure we're getting facts right…they have no editorial say…Colleen Barrett only agreed to take part if it was real. They're proud of their airline and had the courage to step up to the plate and expose themselves."

Reactions were positive. Job applications at the airline rose from around 180 to 600 on the days following initial airing of the programs ("Job applications," 18 June 2004).

Southwest Airlines serves more than 60 cities in 32 states. Based in Dallas, Southwest has more than 33,000 employees. The Associated Press reports that Southwest has been profitable since early 1991 and was the only major U.S. airline to earn a profit during the first six months of 2008.

QUESTIONS FOR REFLECTION

1. What were the benefits and risks faced by Southwest as it considered whether to participate in the production of "Airline"?
2. What legal and ethical considerations would impact participation in such a reality program?
3. How has Southwest profited from its trust in its employees? How have the employees benefited?

Information for this case was drawn from: A&E network's Web site: www.aetv.com/airline/airline_ Episode_guide.jsp?/episode=150898) and www.aetv.com/.airline/airline_castcrew_losangeles. jsp?index=1&type=character; Southwest Airline's Web site: www.southwest.com/about_swa/mission. html; Associated Press (2004 January 2), "Southwest Airlines stars in TV 'reality show'," *USA Today*. www.usatoday.com/travel/news/2004-01-02-southwest-tv_x.htm; Associated Press (27 August 2008), "Southwest to cut 196 flights in early 2009," *The Atlanta Journal Constitution*, B3; Hodes, C. (1 April 2004), "'Airline' TV show reflects airports, baggage and all," *USA Today*. www.usatoday.com/travel/news/2004-04-01-airline_x.htm; (18 June 2004), "Job applications for Southwest Airlines increase due to TV series," *Airline Industry Information*. Accessed on June 9, 2008, at www.lexisnexis.com.

CASE 3. TEAMSTERS DELIVER PUBLIC SUPPORT
DURING THE UPS STRIKE

Many businesses and homes that receive or send packages are familiar with the brown vans and brown uniforms of the United Parcel Service (UPS), and many customers have formed friendly ties with their UPS carriers. The power of these ties was demonstrated during the 1997 Teamsters' strike when public-opinion polls showed that two of three Americans sided with the union, rather than with UPS management, during the UPS work stoppage. A *CNN/USA Today* Gallup poll conducted in the second week of the strike found that 55% of Americans backed the Teamsters, whereas only 27% backed UPS. *Business Week* writers concluded on September 1, 1997: "For the first time in nearly two decades, the public sided with a union, even though its walkout caused major inconveniences."

UPS employs some 370,000 workers and handles 3 billion packages each year, an average of 12.2 million per day delivered by drivers. Some 185,000 UPS employees belonged to the Teamsters union. In its 90-year history, UPS had never before faced a national strike by its employees.

"How Could This Happen?"

Before the 1997 strike, relations between the Teamsters and UPS had traditionally been positive, according to *HRMagazine*. Quoting Lea Soupata, the senior vice president for human resources at UPS headquarters in Atlanta, the magazine reported: "It was two weeks that felt like two years. Whether you were management or union, you were wondering, 'How could this happen to the UPS family?'"

UPS had adopted what it believed to be an effective labor-dispute plan, including creating a strike crisis manual. Media lists were updated, and

Figure 2.2 UPS drivers use a fleet of vans, tractors and other vehicles to serve every address in the United States and more than 200 countries and territories

spokespersons were trained. Yet Kate Miller argued in *Public Relations Quarterly* in summer 1999 that UPS failed to conduct adequate environmental scanning and issues management so it was not fully aware of the changes in labor trends and growing cynicism among the U.S. workforce.

The strike focused on several issues. The Teamsters argued that UPS relied too much on part-time workers. The union asked that more full-time employees be hired and that the wage gap between experienced full-time workers and newly hired part-time workers be reduced. Management had offered a pay raise of $1.50 per hour over 5 years to full-time employees and a $2.50 per hour increase over 5 years to part-timers with seniority. Controlling subcontracting, the practice of allowing UPS to use nonemployee truckers when a company driver was not available, was also a key issue. Pension benefits were also on the table.

Teamsters Communicate Their Views

Ron Carey, then head of the Teamsters Union, used skillful tactics in communicating labor's views. The union had given $2.7 million in political contributions during the 1995-1996 election campaign, 96% to Democratic candidates and another $209,000 in soft money to the Democratic National Committee. In contrast, UPS had given $1.3 million during the campaign season, and 64% of it went to Republican candidates. Carey was confident that President Clinton would not invoke the Taft-Hartley Act to intervene to prevent the strike.

Second, Carey prepared the Teamsters membership for the experience of the strike and for interactions with others about strike issues. He used videos and held rallies to inform members, and members were allowed to take other part-time jobs during the strike. The union also used a media blitz to inform the public about the Teamsters' causes. *The Boston Globe* reported on August 19 that before the strike began, the union had released a "flurry of news releases" and a "report on part-time work at UPS" to major news outlets. The union successfully played upon the familiarity many customers had with their local carrier, whom many saw during daily deliveries. They were skillful in exploiting fears among many Americans about their potential loss of full-time jobs. They were able to establish sentiment of support for these employees against a relatively faceless, large "management" force.

Bill Schneider, a political analyst with the American Enterprise Institute in Washington, was quoted in the August 19 *San Francisco Chronicle*: "The union very skillfully undertook a PR offensive, exploiting the feelings of insecurity many Americans have about corporate downsizing. I don't think it was that people suddenly became champions of unions, but people were sympathetic with the workers. Everyone knows and likes their UPS worker, who does hard, often unpleasant work, and brings people's goodies."

The support of other key U.S. and European labor unions was obtained; Miller's *Public Relations Quarterly* article reports that in May, the Teamsters held a global day of action with the theme "Part-Time America Doesn't Work," and UPS facilities were picketed. The AFL-CIO endorsed the strike action, as did numerous other unions across the country.

UPS Responds Slowly

For its part, UPS did not begin external communications until after the contract expired. Its first press release was issued on July 31, and it did not address the issues of the strike directly. Subsequently, UPS management did not allow its spokespeople to criticize Carey of the Teamsters directly, but instead were to focus on the issue UPS believed had prompted the strike—its threat to pull out of the union's multiemployer pension plan. Though much of the focus of the strike was on the part-time workers used by UPS, UPS did not counter union complaints with information about the pay scale for part-timers and the like.

There was no designated spokesperson for UPS; CEO James P. Kelly was deemed too new to the position, having served for only seven months. Instead of one speaker, responses to the 20,000 daily media inquiries came from a variety of headquarters' sources, including human resources and public relations.

Recovering From the Strike

To end the strike, UPS agreed to increase hourly wages for full-time workers by $3.10 an hour and for part-time workers by $4.10 an hour. The company also agreed to combine part-time positions to create 10,000 new full-time jobs.

After the 15-day strike was settled, UPS worked to regain the confidence of its customers. Representatives of UPS called or visited many customers in the month following the strike. Nevertheless, the company reportedly lost more than $750 million in revenue during the strike, and UPS continued to see a drop in its land-based delivery customers. The strike led UPS to adopt some cost-saving measures including washing the brown vans less frequently and allowing packages to stay on trucks for one additional day if necessary.

UPS also worked to restore communication with employees. A video presentation featuring CEO Kelly was used to communicate the message: "Let's get back to work and do what we know best—deliver packages." Managers also held town meetings with workers and supervisors in the 60 UPS districts. Some workers reported feeling as though some managers were retaliating against strikers, but an anonymous toll-free telephone line was established for employees to use in reporting any retaliation.

Averting a Second Strike

When contract negotiations came due in 2002, UPS wanted to avoid a repeat of the 1997 strike. Discussions began much earlier than in 1997. Negotiations again centered on job security, but this time the two sides were able to agree to terms without a strike being called. The union and UPS agreed upon a series of cost-of-living wage guarantees, banning of supervisors' working to handle packages, and so on.

QUESTIONS FOR REFLECTION

1. Identify the key stakeholders for UPS in this labor situation. What principles should characterize relationships with each?
2. Evaluate the communication strategy of the Teamsters. What public relations principles does the strategy illustrate?
3. How might UPS exploit the strength of the relationships between its carriers and customers?

Information for this case came from the following: Clayborn, S., "UPS vs. Teamsters Union: Why UPS lost and lessons learned for other negotiators," *CMN #37*, www.inionline.com; DeBare, I., & Hoover, K. (19 August 1997), "UPS, Teamsters reach a deal," *The San Francisco Chronicle*, p. A1; Gluckman, A. (21 November 1997), "A contract worth fighting for," *Dollars & Sense*, p. 10; Grossman, R.J. (September 1998). "Trying to heal the wounds," *HRMagazine*, 43(10), 85-92; Harrington, L.H. (March 2002), "High-stakes poker: UPS-Teamsters master contract negotiations are under way," *Transportation & Distribution*, 43(3), 37; Hirschman, D. (30 August 2002), "Teamsters approve UPS contract," *The Atlanta Journal-Constitution*; Lewis, D.E. (19 August 1997), "UPS strike: Massive preparation appears to have aided efforts by Teamsters," *The Boston Globe*, p. D1; Magnusson, P., Harris, N., Himelstein, L., Vlasic, B., & Zellner, W. (1 September 1997), "A wake-up call for business," *Business Week*, p. 28; Miller, K. (Summer 1999), "Issues management: The link between organization reality and public perception," *Public Relations Quarterly*, 44(2), 5-11; Schulz, J.D. (3 March 1997), "'Problem solving' labor talks," *Traffic World*, 249(9), 10ff; (1 February 2002), "UPS and Teamsters in early start," *Fleet Owner*; and (31 July 1998), "UPS has regained most of its customers lost during the strike," *Orange County (CA) Register*, www.Ocregister.com.

CASE 4. SUN SHINES THROUGH EMPLOYEE BLOGS

In 2004, Sun Microsystems encouraged its employees to "tell the world about your work, without asking permission first," by establishing a Web site at Blogs. sun.com to host employee blogs, according to *Computerworld* magazine. Sun's policy, www.sun.com/communities/guidelines.jsp, noted: "Many of us at Sun are doing work that could change the world...You are encouraged to tell the world about your work, without asking permission first, but you are expected to read and follow the advice in this note."

By 2008, almost 6,000 employees were blogging, and almost 120,000 comments had been posted in response to entries. The blogs were posted in English, Spanish and Japanese. Postings included notifications of new files now available for downloading, descriptions of recent professional meetings, white papers, and information on specific products.

More personal postings were also found. Examples? "Sheep, Haggis, Scotch, and More" describes a couple's trip to Scotland, and "Training Update," a brief account of a runner training for a marathon. A September 8, 2008, posting from one employee described his last day at work after completing eight years as a Sun engineer. Former Sun employees were encouraged to participate in an "alumni blog" site.

Jonathan Schwartz, Sun's president and CEO, told *Technology Review*: "Sun's employees are our most passionate evangelists. From where I sit, the more our investors and customers know about us, the better."

CEO Joins the Blogosphere

Schwartz himself has been writing a blog on the company Web site since 2006, becoming what the *New York Times* called the first top executive to blog publicly. He described his rationale for blogging in *IndustryWeek* in August 2006. He said:

> Blogging effectively enables participation in communities you wish to cultivate—employees, partners, the next generation of technology developers and leaders, customers, potential customers, to name but a few. Through my blog, I am able to immediately and directly reach all of these communities to discuss everything from business and operational priorities to technology developments and company culture.

His 2008 postings included "Fanning the Winds of Change in Storage" and "Solaris on Wall Street: Faster and Faster."

Schwartz asked the Securities and Exchange Commission in 2007 to consider blog postings as a form of legitimate public disclosure. No binding judgment was announced, but SEC chairman Chris Cox encouraged further discussion of the issue.

Blogging Within Limits

While Sun encouraged any interested employee to blog, it did revise its "Guidelines on Public Discourse" in May 2008, noting, "By speaking directly to the world, without prior management approval, we are accepting higher risks in the interest of higher rewards." The guidelines warned employees not to share proprietary information, not even on a restricted community site, and not to comment on legal issues faced by Sun. Bloggers were encouraged to be respectful, honest and interesting.

Employee bloggers were also told to acknowledge their affiliation as a Sun employee and note, in the blog, whether they were offering their views only or were representing the corporation. The guidelines also reminded employees that the corporation's Standards of Business Conduct and other policies remained in effect. Advising employees to "Think About Consequences," the guidelines say: "Once again, it's all about judgment. Using your public voice to trash or embarrass the company, our customers, your co-workers, or yourself is not only dangerous, but not very smart."

Blogging Opportunities and Risks

Employee blogs are not confined to Sun. Employees and executives at organizations ranging from Microsoft to Google to Marriott to Coca-Cola are blogging on corporate-supported Web sites. The Blog Council, a forum for executives who use blogging as a communication tool, was formed in December 2007, with members from corporations such as Wells Fargo, Kaiser Permanente and AccuQuote.

Encouraging employees or CEOs to blog does present some risks for organizations. An employee of Google was reportedly fired after posting critical comments about his employer on his blog. A posting on a Wal-Mart corporate intranet site for managers by CEO H. Lee Scott Jr. was leaked to *The New York Times* in 2007. A blog published by an in-house counsel at Cisco was cited in a defamation suit against the blogger and the corporation. Pseudonymous postings by John P. Mackey, the CEO at Whole Foods, which advanced his company's worth and seemed to disparage a chief rival, sparked an investigation by the Federal Trade Commission after his identity was revealed.

QUESTIONS FOR REFLECTION

1. Allowing employees to blog on a corporate Web site creates opportunities and risks. What benefits do such blogs offer?
2. Sun uses published guidelines to help reduce risk. What other strategies or tools might they employ to help employees maximize the impact of their blogs while protecting corporate interests?

3.   Some employee and management blogs have led to negative publicity. What advice would you have offered Whole Foods or Wal-Mart, for example, when their CEOs' blogs were criticized?

4.   Identify some of the legal and ethical issues faced by corporations with sanctioned employee or management blogs.

Information for this case was drawn from blogs at http://blogs.sun.com; (6 December 2007), "Corporate bloggers launch the 'Blog Council' organization," Business Wire; Martin, A. (12 July 2007), "Whole Foods Executive Used Alias," *The New York Times*. Accessed at www.nytimes.com; McMillan, R. (6 July 2004), "Sun blogs show uncensored public face," *Computerworld*. Accessed at www.computerworld.com.au/index.php/id;1075854301;fp;;fpid;;pf;1; Orey, M. (7 April 2008), "Busting a Rogue Blogger; Troll Tracker has been unmasked as a patent lawyer for Cisco. Now they're both facing litigation," *Business Week*. Accessed at wwww.lexisnexis.com; Pinedo, A.T., & Tanenbaum, J.R. (January 2007), "The danger of blogging," *International Financial Law Review*, p.1; Purdum, T. (1 August 2006), "Sun Microsystems' CEO Blogs," *IndustryWeek.com*; Roush, W. (April 2005), "Sun Microsystems: Blog Heaven," *Technology Review*. Accessed at www.technologyreview. com; "Sun Guidelines on Public Disclosure," posted at www.sun.com/communities.guidelines.jsp; Zeller, T. (18 April 2005), "When the Blogger Blogs, Can the Employer Intervene?" *The New York Times*. Accessed at www.nytimes.com.

CASE 5. THE CASE OF THE MISFIRED MEMO

Fortune magazine's list of the 100 Best Companies to Work for in America ranked Cerner Corporation at No. 54 in January 2001, a repeat appearance for the Kansas City-based developer of health care software. Within days, the company added to its laurels with news of a record-setting fourth quarter, which capped a successful year. Cerner employees had plenty to be proud of.

Two months later, the company grabbed national attention again, but this time it was for a bad-tempered e-mail message that the company's chief executive expected only Cerner managers would see. In the memo, he threatened to trim jobs and benefits if productivity did not rise. Someone anonymously posted the message on a public Internet site, and alarm spread not just through the Cerner workforce but also into the investment community. The stock market's valuation of Cerner dropped by $270 million in two days, prompting a *New York Times* article that was headlined "A Stinging Office Memo Boomerangs."

An Unhealthy Environment?

Here is what the CEO, Neal Patterson, put in the e-mail that he sent to some 400 managers. The message's unusual capitalization, from Mr. Patterson's original, draws attention to the Cerner custom of referring to the company's 3,100 workers as "associates."

> We are getting less than 40 hours of work from a large number of our K.C.-based EMPLOYEES. The parking lot is sparsely used at 8 a.m.; likewise at 5 p.m. As managers, you either do not know what your EMPLOYEES are doing; or you do not CARE. You have created expectations on the

Figure 2.3 Cerner Corporation's CEO drew criticism when he complained that the headquarters' parking lot had too many empty spaces early and late on weekdays and on Saturdays, too

work effort which allowed this to happen inside Cerner, creating a very unhealthy environment. In either case, you have a problem and you will fix it or I will replace you.

NEVER in my career have I allowed a team which worked for me to think they had a 40-hour job. I have allowed YOU to create a culture which is permitting this. NO LONGER.

Emphasizing his expectation of long workdays, Mr. Patterson noted, "The pizza man should show up at 7:30 p.m. to feed the starving teams working late." He said that the employee parking lot should be "substantially full" at 7:30 a.m. and 6:30 p.m. on weekdays, and on Saturday mornings it should be half-full. "You have two weeks. Tick, tock," his e-mail message warned.

Offensive or Aggressive?

Some employees were shocked and offended by the CEO's unusually harsh language, but others simply chalked it up to his bluntly aggressive leadership style. After earning a master of business administration degree from Oklahoma State University, Mr. Patterson had worked for the Arthur Andersen auditing firm for six years. With two colleagues, he founded Cerner in 1979 to develop automated health care information systems, particularly for application in clinical laboratories. All three founders stayed active in the business, and Mr. Patterson received credit for leading the company's remarkable growth and innovation over its first 20 years.

In information for investors, the company explained, "Cerner Corporation is taking the paper chart out of healthcare, eliminating error, variance and unnecessary waste in the care process. With more than 1,500 clients worldwide, Cerner is the leading supplier of healthcare information technology."

Outside the company, management experts pointed out that Mr. Patterson's e-mail memo to managers did not say what—besides long hours—he was expecting from employees. They also noted that his threats could lead to higher turnover and difficulty in recruiting.

Financial Uncertainty

In the financial markets, many investors were not sure what to make of the e-mail message. Some wondered if Cerner was experiencing performance problems that would affect first-quarter results, and so they reacted to the uncertainty by hurriedly selling shares and driving down the price of the stock.

A business columnist in Cerner's hometown newspaper, *The Kansas City Star,* said the stock price might recover quickly, "but there is no denying that the harm done to company stakeholders has been as grave as it was unnecessary. As such, Patterson's misstep offers an important lesson for top execs everywhere."

Patterson himself was surprised by the firestorm that he had ignited, and he soon followed up with an apology to employees and with a message that was posted on the company's Web site. The message acknowledged that his original complaint applied only to "a small number of associates."

"My intent with the e-mail," he wrote, "was to issue a direct challenge to our front-line managers to set a minimum level of work effort for every one of their team members. And that I, as the CEO, would hold them accountable for this result...My biggest concern was that it had been distributed beyond the list of managers to many, if not all, of our Cerner associates."

Success Uninterrupted

In what most might see as a happy ending to an unhappy episode, Cerner again achieved record results in the first quarter of 2002. Only five weeks after Patterson's blistering e-mail message, the company issued a glowing report on revenues and earnings and commented positively on opportunities for the remainder of the year. Nowhere in the company's earnings announcement was there a hint of any productivity problem.

Cerner's revenues for 2002 were $752 million, an increase of 39% from the $542 million of the preceding year. Net earnings (before nonrecurring items) were $52 million in 2002, an increase of 51% from the $34 million earned in 2001.

Although the company's financial results continued to improve after the misfired memo, *Fortune*'s list of the 100 Best Companies to Work for in America did not mention Cerner again. However, Fortune cited Neil Patterson's e-mail as the corporate world's worst of 2001 in a year-end roundup of miscellaneous "Bests and Worsts" in business.

For public relations professionals, Cerner's experience offered lessons in both employee relations practices and investor relations sensitivities. Moreover, it showed that successful management of different public relations functions is often highly interdependent: Material intended for employees may affect investors, and vice versa.

QUESTIONS FOR REFLECTION

1. What are the benefits and risks of using e-mail to deliver a confidential message to a group of individuals? Would a traditional memo distributed on paper pose the same risks?
2. What should you do if you know that a key message aimed at one important group will disturb or alienate another?
3. How should senior managers tell rank-and-file employees that organizational performance is not satisfactory?
4. How should rank-and-file employees express concerns to senior managers?

Information for this case was drawn from the following: the Cerner Web site at www.cerner.com/aboutcerner/newsroom_3a.asp?id=783; Burton, T., & Silverman, R. (30 March 2001), "Lots of empty spaces in Cerner parking lot get CEO riled up," *The Wall Street Journal*, p. B3; Hayes, D., & Karash, J. (24 March 2001), "Harsh e-mail roils Cerner," *The Kansas City Star*, p. A1; Heaster, J. (28 March 2001), "Executives, heed lesson from Cerner," *The Kansas City Star*, p. C1; Stafford, D. (29 March 2001), "Shattering the illusion of respect," *The Kansas City Star*, p. C1; Wong, E. (5 April 2001), "A stinging office memo boomerangs," *The New York Times*, p. C1.

PROFESSIONAL INSIGHT

YOUR *REAL* JOB DESCRIPTION

Lisa Owens, vice president of public relations, Regnier Valdez

Oh, the glamour, the excitement to be a real public relations professional.

Whether in an agency setting, or within a corporation, as a public relations officer, you will be challenged daily to take a message, tailor it to a specific audience, deliver it to that audience effectively, and do all this using innovative strategies.

It's really fun, I can tell you.

But there is a reality that you need to understand going in. The reality is that you will often sit across the desk from people who don't understand the value of public relations; people who don't understand the process of public relations. And sometimes these people are your bosses.

So now, as you jump into the deep end of the pool, here is some advice on how to be the best PR professional you can be in the real world.

1. Be the most respectable, responsible and credible professional you can be. Represent, every day, what it means to be a PR professional.

2. Say no when you need to. If your client wants to be on the cover of Fortune magazine, but doesn't have a story to tell, be straightforward and tell him so.

3. Know when to give in. Here is the three times rule: offer your recommendation at least three times, and if your boss insists on doing the wrong thing, accept her decision gracefully.

4. Keep learning. As our media world gets more and more fractured, our training and experience becomes more and more valuable. Internet. Tivo. Blogs. Second Wind. And by the time this textbook is published, several of these will likely be obsolete. Know the options that might be right for your challenge.

5. Take personal responsibility. If you goof up, own up. Everyone learns by making mistakes, but it's the professionals who choose to take responsibility and learn from their mistakes who also earn the most respect.

6. Understand the business side of things. Businesses don't approve public relations campaigns because they're fun—they green light them because they have a goal to achieve. Know the business goals and objectives of your client and deliver PR strategies that support those.

7. Build relationships for life, not for projects. You will work with a huge variety of people through your different public relations endeavors, and

each of those relationships has value to you as a professional. Stay in touch, and nurture relationships.

8. Educate your colleagues about what you do. People don't understand how we do what we do, and if we educate them about the rules, the processes, and the essential tenets of PR, they will be more likely to support you in times of need.

Being a public relations professional can be one of the most rewarding jobs, especially if you are passionate about what you do. Good luck out there!

Lisa Owens is vice president of public relations at Regnier Valdez, a full service marketing, advertising and public relations firm in San Antonio, Texas. She has been implementing successful public relations programs on a regional, national and international platform for nearly 20 years.

3
Stakeholders: Community

What characterizes a good neighbor? In your neighborhood it may be someone who maintains a tidy lawn, or someone who has friendly children. It may be the homeowner at the end of the street with the beautiful garden or backyard pool. Yet what constitutes good neighborliness may also be conditional or contextual. The homeowner with the tidy lawn may also have a dog in the backyard that barks ferociously whenever anyone approaches its fence, or she may drive you to distraction during the holidays with an unapproachable standard of decorating. You may wish the friendly children were occasionally less so when you find their toys and playthings scattered across your yard or when their teenage son's car stereo wakes you up each Friday night when he comes home from a date. The level of familiarity you have with your neighbors may be based as much on your willingness to engage in a relationship as on their willingness to accept the responsibility of your friendship, and your satisfaction with the relationship may fluctuate depending on time and context.

COMMUNITY RELATIONSHIPS MAY FLUCTUATE

Although community relationships for an organization or business may not exactly parallel your neighborhood example, there are some similarities. Effective relationship building and maintenance with community stakeholders may also be variable and contextual. Many communities welcome the financial investment and opportunities a new manufacturing plant brings with it, but they may also decry the increased traffic, noise, and waste produced at the plant. A corporation may seek locations that are quiet and relatively inexpensive, and then find transportation limitations and zoning restrictions a nuisance. As economic situations change, communities may find themselves faced with closing plant sites or empty "big-box" stores, even as businesses and corporations seek to adjust to the costs of modernization or environmental adaptation.

Frequently, the basic premises for community relationships are somewhat contradictory in that they mix altruism and self-interest in many interwoven layers. Practicing good community citizenship through environmental consciousness, cultural support, and civic engagement helps develop and support a higher quality of life for an organization's employees and members, thereby making it easier to attract and retain quality employees. However, such behavior may also generate goodwill that makes it possible for tax incentives, abatements, and zoning decisions that may support the most bottom-line of all business motives. Clearly, community relations may also overlap other key areas of practitioner behavior, including management of employee relations, public affairs, consumer relations, and activist groups.

CHANGING DEFINITIONS OF COMMUNITY

Another challenge and opportunity for practitioners and executives may come in defining their organization's community. For one-site locations, this is simple. But consider the questions facing regional, national, or international organizations. The community may be the area around headquarters, or it may include all of the sites where there are major facilities. Community might also include all of the market areas from which employees, donors, or consumers are drawn. In a global economy, businesses and corporations may even be held publicly accountable for the community-based behaviors of their subcontractors or suppliers in areas far away from their headquarters, as well as for their own. Practitioners and executives must work together to define their communities and then to prioritize the publics within them.

RESULTS OF COMMUNITY RELATIONS

Why engage in community relationship building? Organizations and businesses that seek to be known as good neighbors may have different objectives. Some of those may include:

- *Enhanced quality of life for employees and residents*: Contributing to the cultural, recreational, and artistic life of a community may enhance an organization's ability to attract and retain high-quality employees. It may also foster positive relationships among all those who benefit from programming and mitigate future complaints about liabilities of being located in a given area, such as traffic, noise, and so on.
- *Equipped and available labor force*: Supporting local educational systems, from PreK-12 through higher education, may further contribute to the employees' satisfaction as well as to the availability within the community of future employees equipped for the workforce. Technical colleges and schools, for example, often closely work with industries and businesses to ensure that their curricula match the needs of the potential employers.
- *Regulatory intervention*: From the extensive tax breaks and incentives offered for building new facilities in a community to more commonplace requests for easing zoning or noise restrictions, businesses often need help

from communities if they are to carry out their primary functions. These interventions may reflect the need for a mutually beneficial relationship. For example, plant sites may need traffic signals to be placed strategically or better highways built to accommodate shipping; governments may need cooperation from plant sites about shift changes to better regulate traffic flow around peak hours. Businesses that receive tax exemptions during a specific time period may need to offer public infrastructure support in other ways, such as using local vendors whenever possible so that funding is circulated throughout the community.

What benefits may communities receive from these public relations practices? Some of these may include:

- *Increased resources for community activities*: Community-based national organizations such as the United Way are dependent on the cooperation of area businesses to help secure donations and volunteer leadership to support their network of social services. Employees who are encouraged by their businesses or organizations to volunteer also provide staffing and service help to agencies, schools, and cause organizations. Arts and cultural organizations may also find that businesses and corporations are a primary means of grant support, whether locally or through their foundations. Facilities may be made available for civic meetings and celebrations or for public tours.
- *Increased fiscal support*: The financial contributions through taxes, payrolls, and purchases may be enormously important to local, or indeed regional, national, or international, economies. Small businesses within a community may succeed or fail based on the "turnover" of such dollars in local commerce.
- *Growth of related industries*: Having a major manufacturer locate in one's community may sharply increase the likelihood of attracting other similar large industries or even more industry-related small businesses, thereby increasing the economic health of the community. Chambers of commerce within communities often point to this interlocking impact of industrial and business growth as they participate in recruitment efforts for individual and business relocation.
- *Enhanced sense of local pride*: Being known as the headquarters of a major company or organization or being known as a plant site for a national or international brand may offer communities "bragging rights" that instill pride and raise morale throughout a community. The combination of factors that contribute to an overall improvement in the quality of life for area residents manifests itself in this contagious enthusiasm, which in turn may lead to more growth and development.

COMMUNICATING WITH COMMUNITY PUBLICS

Practitioners may use a variety of tools to send and receive messages from community publics. Local media may be important tools. Face-to-face contacts, meetings, and special events may also be utilized in building relationships with key opinion leaders. It is important for organizations to publicly explain their views and positions and to create opportunities for members of publics to react and respond to them.

However, effective community relations practices demand more than just communication through word or image. Practicing social responsibility—using the resources of an organization to promote ethically positive results for key stakeholder groups—may be the most effective public relations tool of all. Volunteering and donating are potent methods that demonstrate real commitment to enhancing and maintaining relationships.

There is also the practice of what some have called "strategic giving" whereby the good works of an organization or business directly tie into the branding of its products, goods, or services. Consider the book dealer who provides a free book voucher for every child who reaches the reading goal of his or her elementary grade level. Promoting reading? Yes. Stimulating traffic and building loyalty among families and potential customers at the same time? Yes.

Can businesses and organizations be good neighbors? Yes. When their behavior and communication supports the general well-being of their neighborhood, something that is defined by the organization in its dynamic 21st-century environment.

The cases in this chapter will explore the neighborhood for community relationships, looking at how corporations and nonprofits are working together through philanthropy, direct action and employee support. As you consider these cases, seek to identify the public relations problem or opportunity, the methods and tools used to resolve the situation, and how one might evaluate the success or failure of the public relations efforts. As you review the cases, ask yourself: In what ways do these groups define their communities? Who is their neighbor?

ADDITIONAL READINGS

Burke, Edmund M. (1999). *Corporate community relations: The principle of the neighbor of choice.* New York: Quorum.

Sagawa, Shirley, Eli Segal, and Rosabeth Moss Kanter. (2000). *Common interest, common good: Creating value through business and social sector partnerships.* Boston: Harvard Business School Press.

CASE 6. 'THE COMPANY FOR WOMEN' PLEDGES SUPPORT

Avon Co., in business for more than 100 years, offers beauty and health products in 143 countries, and has long been associated with the sound of a doorbell ringing to welcome a representative into homes to sell products directly to women. However, in recent years, Avon has achieved fame for more than its line of beauty and clothing products. In 2003, the National Association for Female Executives rated it as the top company for executive women, and it has become known as the largest corporate partner in the fight against breast cancer.

Since 1992, Avon has been influential in raising more than $525 million in funds in 50 countries for cancer research, education and early-detection programs, clinical care, and support programs for breast cancer patients. Many of the funds raised locally are then spent locally. Avon especially targets use of its funds for those who are medically underserved, including low-income, elderly, and minority women, and women without adequate health insurance. Its efforts, working with Patrice Tanaka & Company (PT&Co.), won it a 1997 Silver Anvil award for public service. When announcing the 2000 awards of $14 million to breast cancer causes, Avon president and chief executive Andrea Jung told *Women's Wear Daily* on March 10 that this was "the best part of the job."

Take the Avon Pledge

Avon teamed with the National Alliance of Breast Cancer Organizations (NABCO), the Centers for Disease Control and Prevention (CDC), the National Cancer Institute, and the YWCA to communicate the need for early detection and to provide access to services for underserved women. Research conducted in 1996 showed that, although the National Cancer Institute announced a 5% drop in the breast cancer death rate, Black women still had a higher mortality rate and a lower median age of death than White women. Fewer than half of the respondents to the American Cancer Society's (ACS) 1995 Mammography Attitudes and Usage Study reported mammography that complied with ACS guidelines.

The objectives of the 1995 Breast Cancer Awareness Crusade and the Crusade Online were: to enhance awareness of Avon Products as a corporate leader in the fight against breast cancer and the crusade itself as a model of corporate/governmental/nonprofit partnership; to motivate women to respond to the message that early detection of breast cancer saves lives; to support sales of Avon's Pink Ribbon Pin and Pen as fund-raising products; and to raise money to fund grassroots breast cancer programs across the United States. The crusade won 15 awards and citations from the White House, the federal government, and health and philanthropic communities.

The awareness crusade employed a variety of strategies. Using the theme, "Take the Avon Pledge for Better Breast Health," sales of a pen adorned with a pink ribbon were promoted. Women were asked to use the pen to sign a pledge to follow the three-step recommendation to early detection of breast cancer. To support this strategy, a "Take the Avon Pledge" flier and brochure were distributed by more than 440,000 Avon sales representatives. Women were given a pledge card they could sign and keep, and a direct-mail campaign sought to have key opinion leaders sign the pledge. A shopping mall program invited women to sign giant pledge walls and to purchase the Avon fund-raising products. Advertising supported the October National Breast Cancer Awareness Month.

The pledge theme helped support Pink Ribbon pen sales. In the fourth quarter of 1995, $6.5 million was raised. More than 700 media placements generated more than 150 million media impressions. Influential women offering support included Rosalynn Carter, Olympia Snowe, Barbara Mikulski, and Dianne Feinstein. More than 16 million Pledge fliers were distributed. First Lady Hillary Rodham Clinton taped a message played at the shopping-mall events.

New media were important tools. In 1995 PT& Co. helped Avon establish a Web site devoted to the issue of breast cancer. Online events, conferences, chats, and "virtual support groups" were promoted through the site. An online initiative invited women to e-mail pledges.

Building Partnerships for Outreach

In 1996, Avon continued its emphasis, expanding its fund-raising product line to include Pink Ribbon earrings and a Pink Ribbon phone card. The Avon Breast Cancer Leadership Initiative was created to highlight the leadership of educators, patient advocates, doctors, volunteers, and Avon representatives in offering messages and services to under-reached women. A national teleconference and satellite media tour with the theme of "Building Partnerships for Breast Health Outreach" were created with the CDC and funded by Avon to promote the exchange of ideas about how to increase the number of women who receive screening.

The Avon Breast Cancer Leadership Awards were created to provide an unrestricted grant of $100,000 to 10 individuals who had made major contributions to breast cancer prevention and treatment. The director of the Office of Research on Women's Health from the National Institutes of Health chaired the awards committee. Avon worked with NABCO on a national survey to investigate the factors that motivated women to have mammograms and clinical examinations.

More than 350,000 women were reached with the early-detection message, and more than 60,000 of the women said they sought mammograms as a result. More than 300 million media impressions were achieved, including a cover story on breast cancer awareness in the New York Times magazine that quoted the crusade director. The campaign again won numerous awards.

Kiss Goodbye to Breast Cancer

Avon continued to develop Pink Ribbon fund-raising products, including mugs, candles, and bears. All crusade products were priced at $4 or under; they came gift-boxed with an enclosed "Guide to Better Breast Health." The "Kiss Goodbye to Breast Cancer" campaign used a special fund-raising lipstick collection and an awards event to raise money and awareness. In October 2001, Avon partnered with "The Rosie O' Donnell Show" to give away a "Thanks for the Mammaries" T-shirt to the first 200,000 women who sent in a receipt for a mammogram. Avon held an e-Bay auction of dresses worn by celebrities such as Elizabeth Taylor and Sharon Stone; the "Little Black Dress Against Breast Cancer" campaign coordinated with a new Avon fragrance, Little Black Dress.

An "Avon Kiss Goodbye to Breast Cancer" concert was planned for September 2002. The concert, held in Avery Fisher Hall in New York's Lincoln Center, featured an awards ceremony to honor companies and persons who had contributed to the breast cancer fight. A portion of the proceeds from ticket sales went to the Avon Breast Cancer Crusade.

Avon Walks for Breast Cancer

One of its best-known means of partnering in the fight involved partners walking long distances as they raised money. Avon has sponsored "Avon Walks for Breast Cancer" in communities across the country, including Washington, D.C., California, Colorado, North Carolina, Texas, Florida, Georgia, New York, Illinois, and Massachusetts. In practice, walks occur during a three-day period where walkers are challenged to conquer 39 miles over two-days, or 26 miles the first day of walking and 13 miles the second day—the equivalent of one and a half marathons. Walkers are provided with tents and hot food during the overnight event. The 2008-2009 walks were scheduled in San Francisco, Los Angeles, New York, Charlotte, Houston, Washington, D.C., Boston, Chicago and the Rocky Mountains.

The Rocky Mountain walk in June 2008 involved more than 1,500 participants who raised more than $3.3 million. Each participant raised at least $1,800 in donations. The 2008 walk in Chicago involved about 4,000 participants who raised more than $9 million.

Other Initiatives

The AVONCares Program for Medically Underserved Women provides funds directly to the patient or her health care provider for diagnosis and then funding for such necessary expenses as transportation and child care during treatment. Through a variety of programs, fellowships and grants are given to individuals and centers across the country to support research, screening and imaging, educational seminars, and advocacy training.

Through the Avon Breast Care Fund, grants are given to local community programs that will identify women who need help, and offer education and assistance to them to obtain screening and necessary care. Avon also provides an expert Coordinating Center to work with the community-based programs to ensure that personnel understand the latest in education and care techniques. Since its inception, women in almost 50 countries have been helped. More than 600 nonprofit community programs have received grants totaling more than $37 million.

The Avon-National Cancer Institute Progress for Patients program was created with a $20 million gift in 2001 to offer grants to cancer researchers and others seeking to identify new ways to detect and treat breast cancer. Recent recipients include cancer research centers at the New York-Presbyterian Hospital and Columbia University Medical Center, St. John's Health Center, Northwestern University, Johns Hopkins Medical Center, UCLA, Emory University and Grady Memorial Hospital, and the University of California-San Francisco.

Dr. Marc Hulbert, scientific director for the Avon Foundation, said, "The Avon Foundation's goal is to foster collaboration and bring the latest results from the laboratory to those who are on the front lines of educating the public about breast cancer early detection and treatment options."

Hello Tomorrow Fund

Avon's support for women's causes extends beyond cancer research and education. In March 2007, marking International Women's Day, Avon announced the creation of the Hello Tomorrow Fund. Beginning in April 2007, the fund gave $5,000 a week for one year to an individual in support for a program, project, or idea to empower women in community service, business development, or awareness and outreach. The fund would support efforts of various types in 18 countries, from the Ukraine to Argentina. The fund's Web site, http://shop.avon.com/HelloTomorrowFund, provides information about other resources and organizations that support these causes.

Chairman and CEO Andrea Jung, in a news release announcing the new program, said: "The Hello Tomorrow fund is the latest realization of Avon's profound commitment to empowering women around the world. Given the resources, women can impact their lives, families and communities in meaningful ways. Women can change our world."

In 2008, Avon committed $1 million in support of the United Nations Development Fund for Women. A new product, the Women's Empowerment bracelet, was created. Net profits from sales of the $3 bracelet were to be donated to the fund.

QUESTIONS FOR REFLECTION

1. What is the public relations problem or opportunity that drives Avon's involvement in the breast-cancer crusade? What are the implications of this problem for its key stakeholders? Evaluate its development and use of partner stakeholders.

2. What are some of the extrinsic and intrinsic outcomes of this ongoing campaign? What are some of the potential liabilities?

3. Breast cancer research, prevention, and treatment are a cause that evokes strong empathetic responses from consumers and donors. What are the advantages and disadvantages when a corporation aligns its cause-related sponsorships with such an emotion-laden topic?

4. Avon uses special events such as conferences and walks to build awareness and raise funds for the campaign. What are the advantages and risks of using such events?

Information for this case was drawn from the following: Avon Web site at www.avoncompany.com, http://walk,foundation.org; http://shop.avon.com/HelloTomorrowFund/press_03072007.html; Patrice Tanaka & Co. Web site at www.ptanaka.com, and Crusade support sites at www.avonwalk.org. Additional information came from the following: (November 2001), "Avon's breast cancer crusade," *Happi-Household & Personal Products Industry*, 38(11); Avon Foundation (29 June 2008), "More than $3.3 million raised in first-ever Avon Walk for Breast Cancer Rocky Mountains," Release at www. avoncompany.com/women/news/press20080629.html; Avon Foundation (5 February 2008), "Avon Foundation brings together breast cancer experts in Houston to report significant new data," Release at www.prnewswire.com; "Choose causes that resonate with women when considering sponsorship opportunities," *About Women & Marketing*, 11(12); L.K. (10 March 2000), "Avon donates $14M," *Women's Wear Daily*, 179(48), 7; Jacobson, T. (26 August 2002), "Avon vows to continue 2002 3-day walks," Release at avoncrusade@avon.com; Nugent, K. (20 April 2003), "3-day Cancer Walk Revived" (Worcester, MA), *Telegram & Gazette*, p. B1; and Yoon, L. (6 February 2003), "Survey shows women making gains in corporate world; Avon rated the best employer for female executives," CFO.com.

CASE 7. CHARITABULLS HELP OTHERS WIN AT LIFE

Mention the Chicago Bulls, and fans across the world think of sports superstars, NBA championships, and exciting competition. But the team is using its celebrity status to win more than championship rings. The nonprofit organization, CharitaBulls, was formed in 1987 with the motto, "Helping Others Win. At Life." The charitable foundation has contributed to local and regional causes, and its Bulls Scholars program that funds supplemental enrichment education for middle-schoolers won a Golden Trumpet for Community Relations from the Publicity Club of Chicago in 2002.

Bulls Scholars Program Supports Student Retention and Enrichment

The Chicago Bulls Scholars Program was born in 1998 with a $3.5 million grant from the Bulls to the Children First Fund: The Chicago Public Schools Foundation. The program was developed after the 1997-1998 season when Jerry Reinsdorf and the Bulls community-relations staff asked the Chicago Public Schools (CPS) to identify academic needs. The Bulls Scholars program was designed to help students make a successful transition between middle school and high school.

In the program, about 1,000 students in Chicago public middle schools are chosen by their teachers to participate in after-school classes in English or algebra, which are taught by certified middle and high school teachers. By attending the course, completing assignments, and scoring well on the Chicago Academic Standards Examinations (CASE) at the end of the year, students may receive a high school credit in the subject area. The program is based on enrichment, rather than remediation.

The funding from the Bulls, which is managed by the School Partners Program, supports the costs of the teachers, texts, and technology. All of the participating middle schools received wireless technology for use in the program.

Bulls players and office staff visit the participating schools regularly, and each school is invited to a game during the season. Rallies are held at the United Center to encourage and reward the students who are involved in the program. At the May 29, 2002 end-of-the-year rally, Bulls head coach Bill Cartwright, players Eddy Curry and Marcus Fizer, and former Bulls John Paxson and Bob Love appeared, along with the CEO of the Chicago Public Schools. The rally was emceed by Tom Dore, the Bulls TV announcer. A Chicago-based brother quintet, STRONG, performed. The Bulls' fan interactive team, the IncrediBulls, also entertained the student group.

On Thursday, May 22, more than 530 seventh- and eighth-grade CPS students who completed the 2002-2003 program attended the Bulls Scholars Jam. The event, held in the arena, featured addresses from former Bull Bob Love, current

Bulls guard Roger Mason, Jr., and broadcaster Dore, along with entertainment by the Bucket Boys, the IncrediBulls, Benny the Bull, and live music.

Bulls Scholars Score Well on Exams

Results of the program have been impressive. In 1998-1999, the average Scholar scored higher than 49% of their high school counterparts in English and 79% of their counterparts in algebra on the CASE exam. On the national Test of Achievement and Proficiency, 53% of the Scholars scored at or above grade level in reading, compared to 35% of other ninth-grade students. In math, 69% of the Bulls Scholars scored at or above their grade level, compared to the 44% of other ninth graders who did so.

In 1999-2000, 62.5% (366 of 586) of the students earned the credit. In the first year, 90.3% of the 390 students earned the credit. The Scholars in the program scored higher on achievement tests than other students in their schools, and nearly 75% earned high school credits before they were out of middle school.

Teaming Up For Other Community Programs

The Bulls also cooperate in other educational-relations programs, such as the NBA's "Read to Achieve" program where books are given to children, and players and family members assist with reading initiatives throughout the year. Scholarships are awarded to area seniors to attend college. Through an Adopt-A-School program, incentives are offered to encourage students to attend school and improve their grades. Financial assistance helps fund equipment for area schools. The Bulls also sponsor an annual art contest for elementary schools in area counties, and winning art appears in Bulls publications. The Bulls also support the Newspaper in Education program of the *Wall Street Journal*.

The Bulls' primary objective is to create positive educational and recreational opportunities for children and young people. Other CharitaBulls beneficiaries have included Special Olympics Illinois, City Year Chicago, James Jordan Boys & Girls Club, Chicago Park District, and the Chicago Public Library. During the holidays, the Bulls sponsor food drives, a party for underprivileged children, and participate in MLK and Black History Month activities.

The organization has given more than $1 million over five years to repair and restore 140 damaged city basketball courts and has donated more than $700,000 to fund the Men's and Women's Chicago Bulls/Chicago Park District Late-Night Basketball Leagues that are operated at parks throughout the city. More than 1,000 players age 18 to 26 participate. Working with the Chicago Police Department, the group sponsors the Chicago Bulls/Chicago Park District Inner City Hoops League and Citywide Championships, a basketball league for children ages 9 to 12.

CharitaBulls donated $4.5 million in 1994 to build a 40,000 square-foot building housing a computer center, art studio, science lab, clinic, gym, day-care center, dance and game rooms, classrooms, and more two blocks from the United Center. The building was named in memory of James Jordan, Michael Jordan's father. The Boys & Girls Clubs of Chicago operates the center as one of its units and serves about 1,500 neighborhood children and families annually. The foundation also supports other efforts to help renovate the neighborhood around the United Center.

Perhaps not surprisingly, focus is also given to basketball programs. The Bulls work with corporate sponsors to donate more than 200 tickets for each home game to local groups to provide a way for underprivileged children and adults to attend a game. Official instructional youth summer camps were begun in 1999. Children ages 6 to14 attend camps in more than 150 community locations, working through local park districts. The camp runs more than three hours a day for a week. The Bulls and the White Sox worked together in 2001 to establish a player development facility that offers private instruction, traveling teams, leagues, and tournaments for young players.

Local park districts throughout Illinois cooperate with the Bulls to offer "2ball," a youth skills competition played on a half-court. The one-minute competition puts two players at different locations on the half-court in a shooting competition. Some 9,000 young people participate each year.

Sports-Related Events and Activities Support the Foundation

Funds for the CharitaBulls Foundation come through contributions to the Bulls and from special events and programs including a Tip-Off Luncheon, held each October l, and FestaBulls, a sports memorabilia auction held every spring, which raises nearly $200,000 annually. Other events, such as online memorabilia auctions and in-game auctions, help support the foundation.

Sponsors also donate to the foundation in response to a variety of game-based achievements, including the number of wins, dunks, free throws, points, steals, rebounds, and so on. Fees for personal scoreboard messages have also been donated to the foundation.

QUESTIONS FOR REFLECTION

1. Why would a successful sports franchise invest time and fund-raising efforts to support education or other local community projects?
2. How do the fund-raising efforts, such as those previously described, support relationships with key stakeholders? Why would sponsors be motivated to cooperate?
3. Why would children be among a key stakeholder group for a professional sports franchise or other entertainment company?

4. Evaluate the importance of local community-improvement projects as part of ongoing community relations for a for-profit enterprise.

Material for this case was drawn from the following: the Chicago Bulls' Web site at www.nba.com/bulls/community/communities.html, www.sportsphilanthropy.com; the Publicity Club of Chicago's Web site at www.publicity.oprg/trumpets2000.htm, and the Web site of Public Communications Inc. at www.pcipr.com/newsroom_archive/Chicago Bulls. Other background was provided through fact sheets and releases by Public Communications Inc. of Chicago.

CASE 8. "WALKING THE TALK": DUPONT'S LAND LEGACY PROGRAM DONATES 16,000 ACRES TO THE CONSERVATION FUND

In August 2003, DuPont announced it would donate 15,985 acres of land adjacent to the Okefenokee National Wildlife Refuge in southeast Georgia to The Conservation Fund. The Conservation Fund then was to transfer ownership of the 16,000 acres to federal and state agencies or to local community groups, which would manage the land as a protected area. Some 5,000 of the acres became part of the Okefenokee refuge. The donation was the largest in the history of the DuPont Land Legacy program and may reflect the corporation's response to what *The Atlanta Journal-Constitution* called a "national uproar" of protests about its original plans for using the land.

DuPont chairman and CEO Charles O. Holliday, Jr. said in an August 27, 2003, press release:

> We believe that our donation of DuPont land in and near Okefenokee National Wildlife Refuge is a concrete example of "walking the talk" with regard to our company's commitment to sustainable growth and social responsibility. The refuge is an ecological treasure. Through the good work of our partner, The Conservation Fund, we are confident that the land we are donating will be properly and permanently protected. We are also grateful to all the stakeholders who participated in the collaborative process that helped us reach this very positive outcome.

Collaborating on Land Management

The 396,000-acre Okefenokee National Wildlife Refuge was established in 1937 to protect the 438,000-acre swamp. In 1974, the interior 353,981 acres of the refuge were designated a National Wilderness Area. International Paper holds the land's wood fiber and recreational rights, which it will retain through 2080. International Paper will maintain a working forest on the property. The corporation cooperated with DuPont to protect the land by relinquishing acquisition rights permanently, which will prevent mining of the property in the future.

Responding to the announcement, Georgia Gov. Sonny Perdue told *The Atlanta Journal-Constitution*, "This is a great gift for Georgia, the local community and the entire nation."

Plans for a Titanium Mine Arouse Protests

The corporation had purchased the land in 1991 and 1996 in order to mine titanium ore from the site. Titanium is the key ingredient in titanium dioxide, a white pigment used in paint, plastics and paper. In 1997, DuPont announced plans to mine three-mile-wide pits along a 30-mile ridge that bordered the Okefenokee, the world's largest and purest freshwater wetland area. It contains more than 1,000 species of plant, bird, and aquatic life and connects to the headwaters of the Suwannee and St. Mary's rivers.

Almost immediately after the mining plan was announced, protests began. Environmentalists said the ridge, the site of Native American burial grounds and a remnant of a prehistoric seashore, acted as a natural dam that causes rain to flow into the Okefenokee. U.S. Secretary of the Interior Bruce Babbitt visited the land site to announce his opposition, and Georgia Gov. Zell Miller also protested the proposed mining activities. The Georgia Board of Natural Resources passed a resolution opposing the mining unless DuPont could demonstrate "beyond a reasonable doubt" that the operation would be safe for the swamp.

In response, DuPont announced it would suspend its plans and would instead form a collaborative to discuss the project. DuPont established a Collaborative Process Core Group of landowners, mining, tourism, and wood-fiber interests, local community officials and politicians, local nongovernmental organizations, landowners, and Native Americans. The corporation agreed to accept the recommendation of the collaborative.

At its shareholder meeting that April, a proposal to bar the company from mining at the site was voted down, although enough votes were cast to require revisiting the resolution at the next year's shareholders' meeting. About 3.4% of the shareholders, representing about 50 million common shares, voted in favor of the proposal. The proposal had come from a coalition of shareholders and environmentalists, including the Sisters of St. Francis of Philadelphia, the Missionary Oblates of Mary Immaculate in Silver Spring, Maryland, the Community of the Sisters of St. Dominic of Caldwell, and Jean A. Reisman of East Boston, Massachusetts, part of a nationwide network of about 300 institutions belonging to the Interfaith Center on Corporate Responsibility.

The second shareholder consideration would not be needed. In 1999, the collaborative group endorsed a "no mining" option and recommended that public and private funding be sought to reimburse DuPont and others for their anticipated profit if the mining had been allowed.

DuPont then sought $90 million in compensation, for the actual cost of the land and estimated profits it might have earned over the 40-year life of the mine. The Atlanta Journal-Constitution, in a February 11, 1999 editorial, opposed the compensation, arguing that the price was too steep and that recovering $20 million in actual costs of the mining project and the collaborative would be a more equitable settlement. However, the newspaper reported on August 27, 2003, that DuPont's title to the land was being transferred to The Conservation Fund without compensation except for a tax write-off.

The Conservation Fund and DuPont received awards from the Natural Resources Council of America in 2004 for working together on the project.

International Paper agreed to permanently retire all mineral rights on the donated land, and it then received the "Forest Conservationist of the Year" award from the Georgia Wildlife Federation in 2004.

DuPont Establishes a Land Legacy Program

DuPont had been involved in land management for more than 200 years, but has been offering this type of protection to certain lands for about a decade. Since 1802, DuPont has owned property that has been used for plants and offices, but some land holdings were undeveloped or were no longer in use by the corporation. The undisturbed lands became prime areas for preservation, and DuPont's Land Legacy Program has placed nearly 18,000 other acres of company land into protected status since 1994.

In 1994, DuPont donated the 1,000-acre Willow Grove Lake property to the Nature Conservancy of New Jersey. In 1997, DuPont gave 7,700 acres near Brevard, North Carolina, to The Conservation Fund to create what is now North Carolina's DuPont State Forest. Monds Island in the Delaware River estuary near Gibbstown, New Jersey, was donated to the New Jersey Audubon Society in 1998 and is now part of Twin Islands Sanctuary, a nesting site for great blue herons and bald eagles. In 2002, DuPont gave 855 acres in Louviers, Colorado, to The Conservation Fund and Douglas County to offer a habitat for such species as elk and black bear.

The Wildlife Habitat Council, a Maryland-based nonprofit dedicated to increasing the quality and amount of habitats on corporate, private, and public lands, has certified 23 DuPont sites in Mexico, Ireland, Spain, Luxembourg, and the United States where the corporation has developed or protected such wildlife-friendly habitats as wetlands, tree and wildflower plantings, and nesting platforms for various bird species.

Mr. Holliday explained the corporation's environmental philosophy in a statement on DuPont's Web site:

> At DuPont we are proud of a decade of reducing our environmental footprint. We have come a long way, certainly in reductions of waste and emissions, but also in recognizing the impact of our operations on global issues such as climate change. However, there are still enormous challenges…As a company that is owned by thousands of investors, our challenge is to address these issues in a way that makes business sense. We define this direction as sustainable growth—the creation of shareholder and societal value while decreasing our environmental footprint along the value chains in which we operate.

DuPont operates in more than 70 countries, offering a wide range of products and services in agriculture, nutrition, electronics, communication, safety and protection, home and construction, apparel, and transportation.

⌒〜

QUESTIONS FOR REFLECTION

1. As an out-of-state neighbor, DuPont had to establish communication with a number of stakeholders within the swamp's region and beyond. What strategies did it employ?

2. It is not uncommon for corporations to encounter concerns about environmental issues when they seek to build or expand operations in a locale. Apart from the donation of the land, what other actions could DuPont have taken to help address those concerns?

3. What does this case illustrate about the benefits and risks of building public and private coalitions?

4. How do DuPont shareholders benefit from its environmental philanthropy?

Material for this case was drawn from the following: the DuPont Web site at www.dupont.com; (29 September 2004), "DuPont recognized for Okefenokee land donation."; M2 Presswire; Editorial (11 February 1999), "Mining buyout looks like gouging," *The Atlanta Journal-Constitution*, p. A22; Mack, M. (1 January 1998), "The State of Georgia: The environment. On the edge of the Okefenokee," *The Atlanta Journal-Constitution*, p. A16; Ouellette, R. (2 June 2005), "Georgia Wildlife Federation names International Paper Forest Conservationist of the Year," PR Newswire; Reuters (11 April 1997), "DuPont suspends Georgia mine plan," Reuters Business Report; Seabrook, C. (30 April 1998), "Mining proposal still alive: DuPont shareholders leave the door open for extracting titanium dioxide from land next to Georgia's Okefenokee Swamp," *The Atlanta Journal-Constitution*, p. D1; Seabrook, C. (27 August 2003), "16,000-acre gift to swamp," *The Atlanta Journal-Constitution*, pp. A1, A12; Sissell, K. (17 February 1999), "DuPont will forgo mining to protect Okefenokee Swamp," *Chemical Week*, 161; Spangler, T. (29 April 1998), "DuPont shareholders reject proposal to retire Okefenokee mining rights," AP Online.

CASE 9. HABITAT FOR HUMANITY: BUILDING CORPORATE BRIDGES AND AFFORDABLE HOUSES

Habitat, a nonprofit Christian ministry based in Americus, Georgia, has united volunteers in an effort to build affordable decent housing for low-income residents across the globe. Founded by Millard and Linda Fuller in 1976, Habitat for Humanity International and its affiliates in more than 3,000 communities in 89 nations have built and sold more than 150,000 homes to partner families with no-profit, zero-interest mortgages. In 2007, some 49,000 homes were built worldwide.

The Foundation Is Laid

Habitat for Humanity International has more than 1,900 active affiliates in 83 countries, all 50 states, the District of Columbia, Puerto Rico, and Guam and works with many other nonprofit partners. Habitat saw a dramatic increase in growth after former U.S. President Jimmy Carter and his wife, Rosalynn, took their first Habitat work trip, the Jimmy Carter Work Project (JCWP), to New York City in 1984. Their personal involvement in Habitat's ministry brought the organization national visibility.

The former president's work continues to bring media, corporate, and volunteer attention to Habitat. An article in *The Atlanta Journal-Constitution* on May 16, 2008, noted the 25th anniversary of the Carters' involvement in builds. The Carters have participated in Habitat builds not only in many locations in the United States but in eight nations, from South Africa to the Philippines.

The Structure Is Developed

Habitat houses are affordable to low-income people because they are sold at no profit, with no interest charged on the mortgage. Using volunteer labor and donations, Habitat builds and/or refurbishes houses with the help of the homeowner (partner) families. The houses are then sold to partner families at no profit, financed through affordable, no-interest loans. A down payment and mortgage payments are required, and partners are required to put "Sweat Equity" into building their house and the houses of others. Prices of homes range from $800 in some countries to almost $60,600 in the United States. Mortgages run 7 to 30 years, and the monthly mortgage payments are used to build other houses.

Habitat for Humanity International's headquarters provides information, training, and a variety of other support services to Habitat affiliates worldwide. Habitat for Humanity's work is accomplished at the community level by affiliates, independent, locally run, nonprofit organizations. Each affiliate coordinates all aspects of Habitat home building in its local area: fund-raising, building site selection, partner family selection and support, house construction, and mortgage servicing.

All Habitat affiliates are asked to "tithe"—to give 10% of their contributions to fund house-building work in other nations. Tithing provides funds for international building, and it gives affiliates the opportunity to demonstrate the spirit of partnership. In 2001, U.S. affiliates tithed $9.04 million to support Habitat's work overseas.

Corporate Partners Donate, Blitz, and Build

Habitat for Humanity International's Corporate Sponsorship program challengescorporations to work to ensure that all people have decent, affordable shelter. Corporate partnerships address the problem of poverty housing while offering benefits to corporations, including tax deductions, effective public relations, and a positive effect on company morale.

Companies form partnerships with Habitat in a variety of ways, through product donations, financial support, and/or encouraging employees to work as Habitat volunteers. The Habitat Web site encourages partners to become involved. "United in the goal of helping those in need, employees at every level get to see each other at their best on a Habitat build. It's an opportunity to grow, to bond and to experience good feelings that get carried back to the workplace." The corporate and foundation partners noted on Habitat's Web site range from the National Hockey League Players Association to Delta Airlines.

Habitat regularly sponsors building blitz events, where volunteers are challenged to build a certain number of houses in one week. The Jimmy Carter Work Projects are the most visible of the blitzes, and sponsorships during that week are reserved for corporations who have made considerable contributions to Habitat. The Nobel Peace Prize Laureate and former president and his wife have led work projects across the globe, from South Africa to South Korea and from Hungary to Houston.

Although numerous corporations and businesses have joined in partnership with Habitat, examine just a few.

The "Do It Yourself Network" (DIY), a how-to cable and digital network, has partnered with Habitat to produce and air workshops about Habitat builds. In 2008, it produced a one-hour special featuring the 24th annual Carter Work Project. Titled "Hollywood Habitat for Humanity," the program highlighted the celebrities who worked with the former president to build 100 homes in Los Angeles. Featured celebrities included Dustin Hoffman, Trisha Yearwood and Oscar Nunez

Nissan has donated more than $3 million to Habitat in house sponsorships and truck donations; employees have donated 40,000 volunteer hours. In 2008, Nissan committed itself to sponsoring seven houses specially fitted with energy-saving features such as low-flow toilets, faucets and showerheads, efficient lighting and recycled carpeting. Following the 2005 hurricane season that devastated the Gulf Coast, the auto manufacturer donated 50 Titan trucks to support rebuilding efforts.

Schneider Electric is a Cornerstone Society member of Habitat's "More Than Houses" campaign and has donated almost $6 million of electrical equipment for homes. The corporation is committed to donate $7 million more of Square D residential electrical equipment through 2010. In 2007, the corporation also committed to funding nine Habitat houses in North America. Their Web site reports, "We share in Habitat for Humanity's commitment to helping people in need everywhere secure decent, affordable shelter."

Thrivent Financial for Lutherans has worked with Habitat since 1991 to build more than 500 homes, donate more than $25 million and provide almost 1.5 million volunteer hours.

Whirlpool Corporation donates a range and a refrigerator to every new Habitat home built in North America—donating more than 73,000 appliances since 1999—and has announced plans to support every new Habitat home globally by 2011. Whirlpool has created a program called "Building Blocks," which its Web site says is "designed to raise awareness and recognize an outstanding Habitat affiliate every year with a blitz build in their area and volunteers from all over the country."

Lowe's serves as the national underwriter of the Women Build program of Habitat. Since 1994, the corporation has provided more than $10 million in donations and encouraged volunteer support. In 2005, Lowe's was an event-wide sponsor of the Jimmy Carter Work Project in Michigan, giving grants or store credits to support each of the 231 houses built during the project.

The Honeywell CEO Blitz Build 2000 involved more than 400 Honeywell volunteers from locations worldwide. Honeywell contributed more than $1 million to Habitat between 1995 and 2000 and donated 6,000 home security systems and 8,600 home thermostats. Over 3,400 Honeywell employees and retirees have built more than 50 Habitat homes in the United States and in Australia, Canada, and Hungary.

Dow Chemical has been named a Lifetime Cornerstone Society Member of Habitat. It provided a four-year $1 million donation to Habitat in 1997 and extended its partnership in 2001 with another four-year $2 million pledge. In September 2000, at the JCWP in Plains, Georgia, Dow pledged a $5 million donation of its Styrofoam brand insulation for the next 25,000 homes to be built in North America through 2005. The corporation also sponsored one Habitat home at the Ed Schreyer Work Project in Ottawa, Canada; the JCWP in Durban, South Africa, and nine others in Africa; and in Indianapolis, Indiana, and Plaquemine, Louisiana. Several crews of Dow employees have volunteered on builds around the world, including more than 60 employees and customers who participated in the JCWP 2002 in Durban.

Dow president and CEO Michael D. Parker, quoted in a company news release, said, "From both a business and a human perspective, Habitat's philosophy of giving a hand up, not a handout, is simply one of the best acts of humanity I can imagine."

QUESTIONS FOR REFLECTION

1. Habitat partnerships offer corporations and businesses a variety of philanthropic options. What objectives might be addressed through different types of involvement?
2. What are the strategic motivations for corporations and foundations to become involved with an international social service agency? What are the potential liabilities of such involvement?
3. Habitat celebrates the involvement of Jimmy and Rosalynn Carter. What are some opportunities and threats presented by celebrity involvement or identification with a charitable or social-service organization?
4. How do group service opportunities improve employee morale?

Information for this case was drawn from the following: the Habitat Web site at www.habitat.org; news releases including Roeder, S. (22 January 2003), "Andersen Corporation to donate $5 million in cash and windows and thousands of employee volunteer hours to construct 100 Habitat for Humanity homes nationwide," PR Newswire; Vallentine, R. (6 June 2002), "Dow employees and customers lend a hand to former president Jimmy Carter in Durban," PR Newswire; Vincent, C. (3 November 2002), "America's community bankers help build tallest Habitat for Humanity house during annual convention," PR Newswire; Webber, B. (14 November 2002), "Habitat for Humanity announces PSA campaign, Ladies' Home Journal partnership," PR Newswire; Webber, B. (12 February 2003), "Lowe's and Whirlpool join forces as 'premier sponsors' of the Jimmy Carter Work Project 2003," PR Newswire; Webber, B. (15 May 2003), "Nobel Peace Prize winner joins thousands of volunteers for Habitat for Humanity's Jimmy Carter Work Project," PR Newswire; and corporate Web sites at www.asia.citibank.com; http://content.honeywell.com/das /releases/6_9_00.htm; www.diynet.com/ DIY/pressRelease/0,1031,325,FF.html; www.dow.com/styrofoam/na/habitati/20011219a.htm; www. squared.com/us/ squared/corporate_infor.nsf; www.vinylinfo.org/humanity/whatispartnership. html; www.whirlpoolcorp.com/social_responsibility/habitatforhumanity/default.asp. Other sources include Attrino, T. (13 July 1998), "SAFECO helps build low-income homes," *National Underwriter Property & Casualty*, 102(28), 9; Buchoiz, B.B. (September 1996), "Building morale off-site," *Crain's SmallBusiness-Chicago*, 4(7), 18; and Gunsauley, C. (1 September 2001), "Charity projects improve employee motivation, morale," *EBN*, 15(10), 63-64.

CASE 10: COMMUNITY SERVICE CONSTITUTES CORE COMPETENCY OF TIMBERLAND

The message on the volunteers' gray T-shirts captured the spirit of the day. In black block lettering, it said: "Pull on your Boots and Make a Difference." The Timberland Company's offices around the world closed May 30, 2002, so that more than 2,000 employees and local partners could earn their regular pay by working on civic projects.

Near Timberland's headquarters in Stratham, New Hampshire, volunteers tackled improvements to park and playground equipment. About 60 Timberland employees in Lawrence, Massachusetts, focused on cleanup and landscaping around an elementary school attended by 375 inner-city children. On the slopes of Maine's Mount Agamenticus, more than 50 employees and Timberland business partners cleared brush from trails used by hikers and cross-country skiers.

By the time the New England projects got under way, the day of activities was half over. It had started shortly after sunrise in Japan when 25 Timberland employees showed up at the Chiyoda Volunteer Center to clean and repair wheelchairs for the elderly. Later, Timberland volunteers in Singapore did fix-up/paint-up work at the Yishun Family Service Centre for disadvantaged families. Still later, some 30 Timberland employees in Milan worked to raise funds for materials that would give disabled children a chance to participate in individual and team sports.

A Record of Serving

Timberland closed its headquarters offices for the first Serv-A-Palooza, the company's name for the day-long community service event, in 1998. All international offices were shuttered to join the annual Serv-A-Palooza for the first time in 2002. Although the global Serv-A-Palooza is a major commitment to community service, it is simply a new entry in the company's long record of paying wages—rather than lip service—to employees whose civic efforts demonstrate corporate social responsibility.

The company that became Timberland, under the ownership of the Swartz family, began as the Abington Shoe Company in Boston. In 1973, the name Timberland was first applied to the company's innovative waterproof leather boot, and the boot became so popular so fast that the name Abington was dropped in 1978 in favor of Timberland. Soon, casual shoes and boat shoes were added to the product line, and the company entered the international market, starting with Italy.

By the time Timberland sponsored its first global Serv-A-Palooza in 2002, the company had 5,400 people in 20 countries around the world and was operating its own retail and factory stores, including 77 stores in the United States, 35 in Europe, and 93 in Asia. In addition, Timberland products—expanding beyond footwear to include apparel and accessories—were sold through independent retailers, department stores, and athletic specialty shops. Shares in the company were originally offered to the investing public in 1987 and have been listed on the New York Stock Exchange (symbol: TBL) since 1991. Revenues in 2002 were $1.2 billion and grew to $1.4 billion five years later. In 2003, the Swartz family controlled about 82% of ownership voting power.

The Service Spirit Sinks In

For years, the company supported community causes and cultural life, as corporations customarily do, through financial contributions. In 1989, the Timberland custom was altered—in a small way at first. Writing in *The Brookings Review*, Timberland's chief executive officer, Jeffrey Swartz, described what happened:

> I received a letter one day, the standard, well-intended plea for charity from yet another worthy nonprofit. This one, City Year, was an urban peace corps of sorts, starting up in Boston, near where I live. The letter described 50 young people, out to save the world, lacking only boots for their feet. Would I send along the boots?
>
> Who knows why I did or why the cofounder of City Year decided to come to my office and challenge me to spend four hours doing community service with him and a small group of young leaders near our headquarters in New Hampshire. But I sent the boots, Alan Khazei paid the visit, and I accepted the challenge to serve. And I found myself, not a mile from out headquarters, face to face with the stories you read in the newspaper, face to face with a vision for America not unlike the one that drew my grandfather to leave Russia in steerage so many years ago. I spent four hours with the corps members from City Year and some young recovering drug addicts in a group home. I painted some walls and felt the world shaking under my feet.

City Year Partnership

Moved and inspired by the experience, Mr. Swartz looked for ways to make community service an integral element of the corporate culture at Timberland. Initially, the company strengthened its involvement with City Year, a nonprofit program that enlists college-age young adults in a year-long commitment to civic improvement efforts. The nonprofit calls itself an "action tank."

Alan Khazei, the City Year CEO who first hooked Timberland on community service, explained that "An 'action tank' is both a program and a think tank... constantly combining theory and practice to advance new policy ideas, make programmatic breakthroughs, and bring about major changes in society. City

Year is an action tank for national service, working to advance and improve the concept and delivery of voluntary national service so that, one day, giving a year of service will become a common expectation and a real opportunity for millions of young Americans."

In 1992, Timberland launched a program giving all of its employees the opportunity to roll up their sleeves and spend the day working on community improvement without losing a dollar of pay. Under this new Path of Service program, employees could use up to 16 hours of paid time annually for civic service. Three years later, the number of hours was raised to 32 and, not long after, was increased to a total of 40 hours annually.

In the early years of Path of Service, participation was far from universal. Employees shrugged off the opportunity because they were too busy to miss a day on the job, and some supervisors discouraged any excused absence, suspecting that volunteers simply lacked enough work.

Stay the Course

When Timberland posted its first annual loss in 1995, some creditors, investors, and employees suggested that the Path of Service was an expendable distraction, diverting attention from the demands of running the business. Layoffs of some U.S. workers underscored the concerns. Yet, Path of Service was not simply protected but promoted even more energetically, and a loss of 53 cents a share in 1995 became a profit of 91 cents in 1996, which grew to $2.02 in 1997 and $2.52 in 1998. That year, the *Christian Science Monitor* published a flattering feature on the company's voluntarism and included Jeffrey Swartz's comments on a question often raised about costs of civic service and motivations for pursuing it.

"We think that doing well and doing good are inextricably linked in our business," the newspaper quoted him as saying. "There's a skeptical notion out there: is this about business or philanthropy? My answer is that this is how we earn our right to do business."

Employee participation in volunteer efforts has climbed along with the company's success, and Timberland estimates that almost all have been involved in community efforts at some time.

More Opportunities for Service

Path of Service and the global Serv-A-Palooza demonstrate Timberland's commitment to community relations in big ways. Another program, Service Sabbatical, is smaller but just as remarkable. Each year, up to four employees, who must have three years on the company's payroll, receive a three- to six-month paid leave to work full-time at nonprofit organizations that are dealing with civic issues.

Timberland lures its customers into community service as well. For Earth Day each year, the company sponsors projects where Timberland employees, customers, and business partners gather for a day of outdoor work to repair some of the damage that the planet's population inflicts on Mother Earth.

On Earth Day in April 2003, about 4,000 customers, community leaders, and members of the Timberland community from 258 participating stores pitched in to serve and preserve the planet at more than 100 conservation sites worldwide. For example, a task force of 100 in the New York borough of Queens developed green space and a learning garden through a partnership with Public School 19. Along the Thames River in London, a team of 80 restored a stripped stretch of shoreline.

Best Companies to Work For

Acknowledging Timberland's knack for combining community service and employee relations, *Fortune* magazine put the organization on its very first list of "100 Best Companies to Work For" in 1998 and has kept it there since then. The ranking uses results of a random survey of employees as well as information supplied by the company on culture, philosophy, and benefits. The employee survey, accounting for two-thirds of the score, measures trust in leadership, pride in work and in the company, and employee fellowship.

Sharing Information on Good Works

Timberland devotes a great deal of its Web site to sharing information about its Corporate Social Responsibility commitment. Offering a full CSR annual report, quarterly reports and an online community called "justmeans," Timberland invites scrutiny by offering "Transparency & Accountability" tools. With the theme, "Make It Better," Timberland says it has committed itself to three emphases: environmental stewardship, community engagement, and global human rights. The Web site explains the rationale:

> Everything we do at Timberland grows out of our relentless pursuit to make it better—from creating practical, purposeful products for consumers who value the outdoors to delivering strong results for shareholders and forging powerful partnerships that create positive, sustainable impact in our world…Our commitment to corporate social responsibility is grounded in the values that define our community: humanity, humility, integrity and excellence.

In 2008, Timberland announced a new initiative, the Earthkeeper campaign. Its goal is to enlist a million people in an online effort to spark real change in the way people treat the environment. Through social networking, the Earthkeepers would exchange practical ideas to deal with climate change and similar ecological concerns.

For Timberland and all other companies committed to community service, measuring the direct effect of civic programs on relationships with important publics is complex, and results are not uniform or consistent. Consumers and other publics may not learn about community programs unless corporate sponsors talk about them in some way—speakers bureaus, news releases, editor's advisories, advertisements, Web sites, brochures, and so on. Yet, these public pronouncements appear smarmy and self-congratulatory to many people and may do as much harm as good.

In a report on the Harris Interactive/Reputation Institute survey of corporate reputations, the *Wall Street Journal* said:

> Almost unanimously, the public says it wants information about a company's record on social and environmental responsibility to help decide which companies to buy from, invest in and work for. But philanthropy is a tricky facet of corporate public relations. Good deeds can redound to a company's credit...But they can be overlooked if untrumpeted, making the company a target for unfair criticism, and they can backfire if consumers view the purported philanthropy as profiteering or if the company fails to live up to the good-neighbor image it projects. In short, promoting philanthropy is perilous, and companies can find they're damned if they do and damned if they don't.

Because public relations professionals often hesitate to talk up good works, the number of people aware of them remains low. The annual Harris Interactive/Reputation Institute survey measures 20 attributes of corporate reputation, and the one that elicits the largest percentage of "not sure" responses concerned a company's support for good causes.

~

QUESTIONS FOR REFLECTION

1. Are some kinds of business operations more likely to engage in community relations programs than others? Why would Timberland be a prime candidate for community activities?

2. Initially, most employees passed up the chance for a paid day off to work on community projects. Why would they do that?

3. Some critics say "doing well by doing good" is a tired platitude, and for-profit businesses should allocate funds for community activities only if they provide some tangible payoff for the business. Does this view make sense?

4. The *Wall Street Journal* warns that corporate philanthropy can be risky. How can it backfire?

Information for this case was drawn from the following: the Timberland Company Web site at www.timberland.com/cgi-bin/timberland/timberland/corporate/tim_press.jsp; DeConto, J. (23 April 2002), "Helping Earth Day on Mount A," *Portsmouth Herald*, p. 8; DiMassa, C. (10 November 2002),

"Good turns: Being a CEO 'in the tradition of Abraham,'" *The Los Angeles Times*, p. B2; Irwin, N. (20 July 1998), "Giving 'a boot' to community service," *The Christian Science Monitor*, p. B6; Marquis, C. (13 July 2003), "Doing well and doing good," *The New York Times*, p. C2; and Swartz, J. (Fall 2002), "Doing well and doing good," *The Brookings Review*, p. 23.

PROFESSIONAL INSIGHT

A LESSON: ADVERTISING AND PUBLIC RELATIONS *CAN* WORK IN HARMONY

Anne Sceia Klein, APR, Fellow PRSA; president, Anne Klein Communications Group, LLC

While earning my undergraduate degree in economics (marketing major), I was taught that marketing was the umbrella that held the advertising, promotion and public relations disciplines together. When I began working, I saw that each discipline competed for resources, attention and primacy, especially advertising and public relations.

I confess I have never obsessed over the two "competing" disciplines...my career and my agency focused on public relations—media relations, community outreach, internal communications, crisis communications, and so forth. I had read many commentaries and attended seminars about integrated marketing communications programs and heard the complaints about advertising's dominance over public relations. Those issues had not affected my public relations practice.

Recently, however, I had the opportunity to lead a campaign that truly integrated the best of advertising and public relations when our client asked us to write a strategic communications plan. Initially, the client—and we—had only public relations in mind.

Our client, a faith-based organization offering a full spectrum of elder care and social services, was formed through a series of mergers and had a new name. The executive leadership felt their employees did not see the connection between what the organization had been and what it had become. And the new organization name was not resonating with them.

Our challenge was to find out what could be done to bring meaning to the new name of the organization, to give the brand an identity, and to reinforce the caring and compassion that had always been its hallmark.

Through research, we learned that the organization also had a mixed image in the marketplace and among its clients and residents. To help with one aspect of the research—one-on-one conversations with executives, employees, residents, clients, and volunteers—we engaged a marketing communications expert with an extensive background in research and advertising.

When it was time to write the plan, our marketing communications expert recommended an advertising component. I was uncertain our client would accept an advertising program, but I kept an open mind.

Thanks to an "outside" point of view and with buy-in from our client, we developed a creative, integrated campaign with strong advertising and public relations components. Our creative team recommended and we trademarked a theme line that our client loved. When we tested the theme with internal staff, they said it evoked just the right tone and feel; it resonated with them.

Rather than employ actors for the advertising elements—print, outdoor, radio, and television—we asked "real" employees, residents, and clients to participate. To complement the advertising, we incorporated a full range of public relations components including leadership training, a train-the-trainer session, a communications tool kit, spokesperson training, internal communications, constituent communications, media relations, and online communications to roll out and sustain the campaign.

Leveraging the investment in producing the television ads, we used the same footage to create three five-minute videos, one aimed at the internal audience, the second for prospective residents and the third for the speakers' bureau.

Feedback from all audiences has been overwhelmingly positive. By keeping an open mind and by recognizing the potential synergy of a campaign with complementary advertising and public relations components, we developed a creative, effective solution to meet our client's strategic communications needs. In this case, by working in harmony, advertising and public relations are achieving greater results than either could have working alone.

Anne Sceia Klein, APR, Fellow PRSA, is president of Anne Klein Communications Group, a national public relations firm based in the Philadelphia market and the Philadelphia office of Pinnacle Worldwide.

4
Stakeholders: Consumers

Think about your last trip to a shopping mall. You may have visited stores such as Abercrombie & Fitch, The Gap, or Victoria's Secret that have established brand strength for themselves. Inside other stores you may have sought certain brands of clothing or accessories—Nike, Levi's, Russell, Sony, Timex, or Fossil—and avoided others you don't like or don't recognize. You may have completed some purchases after extensive research and others on an impulse. Similar stories may be told of your latest car purchase or trip to a grocery store or pharmacy. When you visit your mailbox, you may find it crammed full of catalogs, and when you visit your electronic mailbox, it, too, may be filled with promotional messages from retailers whom you've visited or purchased from online.

THE CONTEMPORARY CONSUMER

Consumers—those who buy the products and goods or use the services businesses provide—are likely the most voluntary of all stakeholders. In the U.S. marketplace, consumers may be the most jaded of all stakeholders, as well, constantly provided with a variety of options, bombarded with messages and reminders of the merits, real or hyped, of the goods available. Conversely, sometimes they comprise the most loyal group of stakeholders—bound to certain brands by memories of in-home use from decades ago or allied because of features and benefits derived from brands they enjoy. They are the ones who remember slogans and jingles better than their multiplication tables, and they are the ones who willingly become walking billboards for the logos and brands emblazoned on the hats, T-shirts, jackets, and bags they carry.

Consumer groups also reflect the rapid changes in national demography. Practitioners should remain knowledgeable about the growing racial and ethnic diversity of their key consumer publics and be able to strategize with management personnel about the most effective ways to reach these consumers. Similarly, changes in the age patterns or social-role patterns of consumer groups should be noted and researched. Stereotypes about the needs of varying groups among consumers should be replaced with sound research into needs, desires, and capabilities of key publics.

Contemporary consumers are also protected by a variety of national, state, and local regulations promoting their safety, as well as a growing slate of civil torts that enable them to sue when they assert that a product, good, or service was delivered in a deceptive or injurious manner. Maintaining a 1-800 help line or a product-information e-mail and Web site may become the full or partial responsibility of the public relations department, perhaps working in concert with customer service representatives. Well-publicized consumer-related crises of the past 20 years should remind practitioners of the need for extreme care during initial or reactive product-related communications. Practitioners must be aware of the need for clarity when communicating with various consumer groups and particularly conscious of the varied abilities of groups to understand technical or product-related communication.

KEY OBJECTIVES

Maintaining a relationship with a satisfied consumer is far easier than trying to rebuild a relationship that has been hurt by poor service, pricing disagreements, or product failure. Building and maintaining brand loyalty may be a central objective for the practice of consumer relations. Other key objectives may include:

- Providing clear and timely information about products, goods, or services so that consumers may make good decisions.
- Providing avenues for feedback so that consumer questions and complaints are handled in an efficient and cordial manner.
- Supporting the introduction of new products, goods, or services through coordinated media relations, advertising, and product publicity efforts.
- Celebrating successes of branded products or services through special events and other publicity efforts.
- Developing relationships with emerging consumer groups, such as those found in new cultural or ethnic communities, new age or gender demographic groups, and so on.

INTEGRATED COMMUNICATION

Developing relationships with consumers is a multidimensional affair that often requires cooperation across departments or personnel within a business or corporation. The practice of integrated marketing communication may better describe how organizations can reach and hear from these stakeholders. For example, consider an American automaker that is introducing a new high-performance model to its line. Certainly, the product should be introduced at the annual car shows for automotive beat journalists and critics to assess and comment. Vehicles should be made available for test drives by these same media opinion leaders. Releases about the new line and its features and benefits should be disseminated. An advertising campaign geared to begin with the actual release of the line would be essential. Yet even that may not be enough. What about brokering use of the car as the central vehicle in a major motion picture due for a Labor Day release, or using it as the grand prize in a national contest geared at high school and college students, or working with local distributors to link sales of the unit to a sales competition? The manufacturer may also use its national clout to offer buyers a zero-percentage car loan for purchases within its first month on the market. The public relations, advertising and marketing efforts would all work together to target key consumers and to establish the new brand as one with a distinct image and personality attractive to those consumers.

This multiplicity of messages is even more necessary in a crowded media marketplace, where consumers receive messages about products, goods, and services from all forms of mass media, including the Internet, where persuasive messages may be found in obvious places, such as a constant stream of pop-up ads, and more subtle venues, such as chat rooms and national lists where browsers find open, frank, and sometimes staged discussions of the merits and drawbacks of particular brands and suppliers. Canny consumers have at their fingertips the ability to search for reviews of products, multiple price comparisons, and deep background on corporations and businesses. No longer are shoppers merely comparing prices between competing grocery ads in the Thursday newspaper. Among the plethora of tools available to practitioners seeking to disseminate information about products, goods, and services are direct mail, broadcast advertisements, print ads, Internet ads, movie theater ads, product inserts, packaging, catalogs, brochures, trade shows and exhibits, displays, outdoor ads, specialty products, product placements, spokespersons, logos, personal appearances, and media placements—and the list changes with each new technology. Certainly, the need for veracity and constancy in messages grows in this environment.

BUSINESS-TO-BUSINESS COMMUNICATION

Similarly, public relations may form the conduit for communication between businesses and industries. Vendor-to-vendor relationships, supplier-to-supplier relationships, and wholesaler-to-retailer relationships may all depend on the ability of public relations practitioners to identify needs or motivations and to supply the type of information and opportunity in a trustworthy manner that would establish a mutual ground for business exchange. From the production of clear catalogs and brochures to engaging exhibits and demonstrations at trade shows, the practitioner may need to facilitate communication between businesses hungry for profitable advantages.

As you consider these cases, seek to identify the public relations problem or opportunity, the methods and tools used to resolve the situation, and how one might evaluate the success or failure of the public relations efforts. Ask yourself questions such as: How have these corporations and businesses emphasized the importance of their consumer stakeholders? In what ways do these organizations communicate with their consumers and build opportunities for consumers to communicate with them? Could the communication patterns be improved? If so, how? How do these cases illustrate the importance of planning for crisis communication?

ADDITIONAL READINGS

Argenti, Paul A., & Janis Forman. (2002). *The power of corporate communication: Crafting the voice and image of your business.* Boston: McGraw-Hill.

Dilenschneider, Robert L. (2000). *The corporate communications bible.* New York: New Millennium Press.

Ries, Al, & Laura Ries. (2002). *The fall of advertising and the rise of PR.* New York: HarperBusiness.

Thorson, Esther, & Jeri Moore (Eds.) (1996). *Integrated communication: Synergy of persuasive voices.* Mahwah, NJ: Lawrence Erlbaum Associates.

CASE 11. "WOULD YOU LIKE YOUR TACO WITH
OR WITHOUT PESTICIDE TODAY?"

Genetically modified foods—called Frankenfoods by critics—have been a hotly debated subject in Europe since the 1990s, but they've barely raised a stir in the United States. Advocates for consumers and environmental causes warned about risks to human health that might result from genetically modified crops, and they tried to get U.S. food processors to disclose the use of these ingredients on product labels. Yet, their pleas were politely rebuffed by some food companies and simply ignored by others.

Corporate giants in agriculture and food set up their own advocacy alliances to counter the skeptics. They trumpeted the promise of biotechnology's genetic engineering, pointing to higher levels of nutrition, lower levels of pesticides, and greater crop yields for the world's undernourished.

Apparently indifferent to the debate, most American consumers paid little attention. Half did not even know, as the decade ended, that supermarkets already were stocking foods made with biotech crops, including baby formula, muffin mix, tortilla chips, and meatless burgers. "There's no evidence that genetically engineered foods on the market are unsafe to eat," said *Consumer Reports* magazine in September 1999. "But, continued vigilance is crucial."

Traces of Biotech Corn

One year later, Friends of the Earth, an international environmental organization, announced that independent laboratory tests of a leading brand of taco shells had found traces of a type of biotech corn that was not approved for human consumption. The taco shells were being sold by Kraft Foods under the Taco Bell label. The corn, named StarLink by its inventors at Aventis SA, had been engineered to offer built-in protection against the European corn borer insect. To create this feature, the scientists transplanted a gene from the *Bacillus thuringiensis* bacterium, a common soil organism, into the corn. The extra gene enabled the corn to produce a protein (Cry9C) that is toxic to the corn borer. In essence, the corn contains its own insecticide, saving farmers time and money.

Biotech corn itself was not the taco shells' problem. In fact, there were eight varieties of similar corn available at the time, and only StarLink had failed to get approval for use in consumer foods. In tests performed for the Environmental Protection Agency (EPA), StarLink had shown properties that are found in human allergens, and allergens can provoke reactions in vulnerable people ranging from skin rash to anaphylactic shock and death. As a result, the EPA told Aventis that StarLink could be used only to make livestock feed and ethanol fuel, but the agency did not determine conclusively that the corn was or was not allergenic.

Friends of the Earth, in its September 18 news release announcing the lab results, called on Kraft Foods to remove the Taco Bell taco shells from supermarkets immediately. The same day, the Union of Concerned Scientists (UCS) issued a statement urging the Food and Drug Administration (FDA) and the EPA to investigate the situation.

The UCS said: "If substantiated, this development would be another indication that the current regulatory scheme for genetically engineered foods is inadequate to protect public and environmental health and would heighten the need for better procedures to identify potential allergens and enforce legal restrictions and prohibitions."

Biotech Advocates Voice Skepticism

However, representatives of the biotechnology industry initially expressed skepticism about the Friends of the Earth report, challenging the reliability of tests used by the independent lab to detect the StarLink corn.

From the outset, Kraft faced an urgent need to respond quickly to the news, address consumers' anxieties, demonstrate leadership, and plan a course of action that would lead the company though a thicket of complications. Consumers are very impatient when questions involving family health remain unanswered. They would want to know, as soon as possible, if the lab results were correct, and if they were, would want information on any harm that might come to people who had eaten the taco shells. They also would want to know if the corn was in other consumer products, what Kraft was doing to get the products out of supermarkets and homes, how livestock corn got into consumer foodstuffs, what precautions Kraft would take to prevent any recurrence, and so on.

Anticipating those concerns, Kraft issued a statement one day after the Friends of the Earth's announcement. In it, the company explained that new independent lab tests were planned to confirm or discredit the earlier results. Kraft said: "It is clear that StarLink corn should not be used in the production of human food. If the presence of the Cry9C protein is confirmed, we will recall the product."

Kraft Issues Q&A

The same day, Kraft issued additional information in question-and-answer (Q&A) format. It included nine Q&A pairs, including these:

Q. How did this Cry9C protein find its way into your product?
A. We don't know if it is indeed in the corn, and if so, how it may have happened. We are working closely with the FDA to investigate this matter further.
Q. Have you had any complaints of illness or adverse reactions to eating this product?
A. No, we have had no confirmed reports of illness or food sensitivities linked to eating Taco Bell Home Originals taco shells.
Q. Are you going to recall the product?

A. No, not at this time. We are continuing to work with the FDA and will take the appropriate actions in consultation with them. Any decision to recall the product must be based on confirmation that the Cry9C protein from StarLink corn is present in the product. If it is found to be present, we will recall the product.

Q. Is it safe to eat this product?

A. Yes, we have no reason to believe it is not safe to eat it. We have seen no evidence that indicates that the Cry9C protein is unsafe, but we are doing everything possible to learn if there are any safety concerns. If the presence of the Cry9C protein is confirmed in our Taco Bell Home Originals Taco Shells, we will recall the product.

In terms of risk communication, the company could provide consumers with few answers to overcome the situation's major unknowns, which were the validity of the lab tests, the source of the unapproved corn, and the potential for allergic reactions. Most consumers would simply avoid the product until the doubts were resolved.

Kraft Recalls Product

Four days after Friends of the Earth first reported the lab results, Kraft announced a voluntary recall of all Taco Bell Home Originals taco shells—2.5 million packages or more—after new tests corroborated the earlier results.

The September 22 announcement quoted the Kraft Foods chief executive as saying: "As soon as we learned that there might be an issue in the supply chain we purchased from, we have been guided by one priority—the safety of our products and their compliance with all regulatory requirements. Testing has now indicated the presence of StarLink, and we are immediately withdrawing all affected products."

The company also said it was suspending production of taco shells, which generated revenues of about $50 million a year for Kraft, until the quality of the finished product could be assured. The shells represented less than 3% of Kraft Foods' North American revenues for the year 2000.

Again, the company offered details for consumers in Q&A format, simultaneous with its recall announcement, including these examples:

Q. Is there a health concern if I've eaten one of these products?

A. Some of these products have been found to contain a variety of corn that is in the process of being reviewed for approval for use in food. This corn, known as StarLink, has been approved for animal use, but not for use in food. On that basis alone, these products should not be eaten. However, at this point there appears to be no evidence of adverse health effects.

Q. What should I do with the Taco Bell products I've purchased?

A. You should not eat any products containing Taco Bell taco shells, and you can return them to the store where you purchased them for a full refund.

Kraft Offers Recommendations

Kraft also presented recommendations for biotechnology. The company suggested that advances in plant biotechnology should be approved only when:

- They are safe for consumer foods as well as livestock feed.
- Valid tests are available to detect them in both crops and finished products.
- Government agencies review them before they enter the market.
- Biotech crop stewardship requirements are stiffened to safeguard the food supply from farm to finished product.

Commenting on the taco shell recall, *Business Week* magazine offered a recommendation of its own. "None of this has led the biotech-food industry to soften its opposition to labeling or to any special regulations for biotech products. But it's time for a change," the magazine said. "Biotech foods are new, they are different, and they deserve special regulations. The industry should drop its opposition to tougher regulations. That could boost consumer confidence and disarm the critics."

QUESTIONS FOR REFLECTION

1. In what ways would Kraft's initial response, provided the day after release of the first lab results, have relieved consumer anxieties?
2. In what ways might you have altered the first response, using only the information that was available at the time? Are there any inconsistencies between Kraft's initial response and the information that it released with the recall announcement?
3. What intermediaries or organizations could help Kraft manage its relationships with consumers who were troubled by the StarLink corn incident?
4. If Kraft wanted to push for adoption of its recommendations on biotech crops, what alliances or coalitions might it try to establish? What could coalition partners do?
5. Taco Bell was somewhat inadvertently drawn into the publicity surrounding this recall. What options would you recommend for its corporate response?
6. *Business Week* seems to suggest that the food industry should give further consideration to labeling that would disclose biotech ingredients. What would be the upside to biotech labeling? The downside? Are there other alternatives?

Information for this case was drawn from the following: the Kraft Foods Web site at www.kraft. com/newsroom/; a Kraft Special Report recall Web site at www.kraftfoods.com/special_report/ special_news.html (no longer available); Brasher, P. (22 September 2000), "Kraft Foods recalls taco shells," The GE Food Alert Campaign Center, www.gefoodalert.org/News/; Carey, J., Licking, E., & Barrett, A. (20 December 1999), "Are bio-foods safe?" *Business Week*, p. 70; (18 September 2000), "Contaminant found in Taco Bell taco shells," Friends of the Earth news release; Ingersoll, B. (2 October 2000), "Aventis to pay for U.S. to buy modified corn," *The Wall Street Journal*, p. B28; Kilman, S., & Lueck, S. (25 September 2000), "Kraft recall focuses on biotech oversight," *The Wall Street Journal*, p. B2; Kilman, S. (27 September 2000), "Aventis halts seed sales of genetically engineered corn," *The Wall Street Journal*, p. B4; Lueck, S., & Kilman, S. (2 November 2000), "Biotech-corn problems lead to recall of 300 products, disrupt farm belt," *The Wall Street Journal*, p. A2; Pollack, A. (23 September 2000), "Kraft recalls taco shells with bioengineered corn," *The New York Times*, p. C1; Raeburn, P., Forster, J., & Magnusson, P. (6 November 2000), "After Taco Bell: Can biotech learn its lesson?" *Business Week*, p. 107; Rissler, J. (18 September 2000), "Illegal, potentially allergenic altered corn found in taco shells," Union of Concerned Scientists news release; (September 1999), "Seeds of change," *Consumer Reports*, p. 10.

CASE 12. WENDY'S RELIES ON REPUTATION TO COMBAT "FINGER" FRAUD

During dinner one evening at a Wendy's restaurant in San Jose, California, Las Vegas resident Anna Ayala claimed she bit into a partial finger that had been served in a bowl of chili. The fingertip was about one and one-half inches long. The woman told health authorities that when she found the finger in her mouth, she spit it out and began vomiting. After investigators arrived, they closed the restaurant that evening and took the remainder of the chili for analysis.

Wendy's employees were asked to show their hands to Department of Environmental Health employees after the March 22, 2005, incident, and all were whole, prompting an investigation into the source of the finger. No hand injuries were found among the suppliers of ingredients to Wendy's, either.

Wendy's conducted its own investigation. A health department inspection found no problems at the restaurant, and suppliers were ruled out as a source after analysis of the chili ingredients turned up no evidence of the finger. Employees completed a polygraph test.

Search for the Finger Leads to Arrests and Convictions

A search for the owner of the finger began, with Wendy's offering a $100,000 reward for information. A hotline was set up for use in offering information about its source. "The only thing we could think of is either somebody played a practical joke that went bad or it's going to be fraud," CEO Jack Schuessler told the Associated Press.

Following a lead, the finger was identified as the finger of one of the men who worked with Ayala's husband. The injured co-worker told him the couple had offered him $250,000 not to report the plot.

Ayala filed suit against Wendy's in April, but then withdrew the suit. On April 21, Ayala was arrested and charged with attempted grand theft. Police suspected she put the finger in the chili herself. The finger, the Santa Clara County coroner's office told the Associated Press, "was not consistent with an object that has been cooked in chili at 170 degrees for three hours."

In September, Ayala and her husband pleaded guilty to attempted grand theft and conspiracy to file a false insurance claim. She was sentenced to at least nine years in prison, and her husband was sentenced to more than 12 years. They were ordered to pay about $170,000 in restitution for the wages lost by employees following the incident. In addition, the judge ordered them to pay almost $22 million to Wendy's International and the local owner of the restaurant; the corporations agreed not to seek the money if the couple never benefited from the hoax.

Wendy's later gave the $100,000 reward to two sources, one of whom was the employer of the man whose finger was used in the hoax. The second reward recipient was anonymous.

Reactions to the Story Vary From Laughter to Layoffs

News of the supposed finger in the chili spread rapidly. Sales at Wendy's declined, leading to dozens of employee layoffs and a reduction in hours the restaurants were open. The Associated Press reported that Wendy's lost $2.5 million in sales because of the incident, with the local restaurant losing almost $500,000. The 2005 annual report noted that the incident hurt sales "not only in the Western Region, but also throughout the entire U.S. for months afterward."

Early in the scheme, Ayala and her attorney appeared on "Good Morning America" and described the incident. She said, "Knowing that there was a human remain in my mouth, you know, something in my mouth, it's disgusting." Newspapers around the world recounted the story. Late-night talk show hosts joked about the incident.

Restaurant Chain Relies on the Strength of Its Reputation

Wendy's sought help from the Ketchum agency. During the investigation of the incident, the nation's third-largest burger chain did not alter its public communication strategy. No public apology was offered to customers, and executives were not asked to go on television to defend the restaurant's reputation. National advertisements were not changed. The reputation of Ayala was not attacked. The chain did use daily crisis-management conference calls with eight executives and attorneys to discuss the incident. The results of its internal investigation that cleared its employees and processes were announced only in a brief statement.

However, once Ayala was arrested, the tactics changed. Within one day, Wendy's executives were involved in more than 2,000 national newscasts. Denny Lynch, Wendy's senior vice president for communication, appeared on the *CBS Saturday Early Show* on April 23. He was asked how the restaurant was planning to persuade customers to return. He said it would be the company's reputation that would draw customers:

> A company's reputation is built on the things that it does every day; the food that it serves, the way it treats its customers, its employees in the communities that it is in. And we are hoping that America remembers the Wendy's of a month ago, the Wendy's that is open for business and welcomes them. That is, the strength of our company is our reputation.

To help draw consumers back in, Wendy's sponsored a national Customer Appreciation Free Junior Frosty Giveaway and served 18 million customers over the three-day period.

The crisis-communication campaign won an honorable mention in crisis communication from *PRWeek* magazine in 2006. At the time of the crisis, Wendy's International, Inc. was the third largest burger chain in the world, with more than 6,300 Wendy's Old Fashioned Hamburgers restaurants in North America and more than 300 international Wendy's restaurants. In 2008, shareholders of the company approved a merger with Arby's, known for its roast beef sandwiches.

∿

QUESTIONS FOR REFLECTION

1. Evaluate the communication strategies used by Wendy's during this crisis. What are the advantages and disadvantages of using a restrained approach during bad publicity?
2. Identify the priority stakeholders involved in this case. How did Wendy's seek to protect the interests of those stakeholders during this crisis?
3. Humor such as that used during the late-evening talk shows can be a difficult communication to combat. What tactics might Wendy's or other corporations facing these crises use to counter the effect of the negative jokes?
4. As suspicions of fraud emerged, Wendy's refrained from attacks on the perpetrators. Why?

Information for this story was drawn from the corporate website at www.wendys-invest.com/main/cp.php and the 2005 Annual Report to Shareholders at www.wendys-invest.com.fin/annual/2005/wend05ar.pdf; Chadwick, A., & Burbank, L. (19 January 2006), "Wendy's still smarting from finger-in-chili hoax," "Day to Day," National Public Radio; (20 September 2005), "Chili finger tipster has beef with Wendy's," Associated Press; Curtis, K. (18 January 2006), "Nev. Pair sentenced in chili finger case," Associated Press Online; Curtis, K. (23 April 2005), "Wendy's hopes customers will return after woman who claimed she found a finger in her chili was arrested," Associated Press Worldstream; Curtis, K. (22 April 2005), "Woman who claimed she found a finger in bowl of Wendy's chili arrested, police call it a hoax," Associated Press; Drew, J. (20 May 2005). "Wendy's CEO had to endure the finger-in-the-chili jokes, bide his time." Associated Press; (8 March 2006). (8 March 2006). "Honorable Mention-Ketchum and Wendy's: Wendy's sticks to values to weather chili incident," PRweek, p. 33; McPherson, K. (19 January 2006). "Near maximum sentences in Wendy's finger case." San Jose Mercury News; Norton, J.M. (21 April 2005). "Wendy's closes internal investigation, finds no link between finger in chili and its operations." Associated Press Worldstream; (7 April 2005). "Police search home of Nevada woman who claimed to find a finger in her chili." Associated Press; Reed, D. (22 March 2005). "Woman finds human finger in Wendy's chili," San Jose Mercury News; Ritter, K. (8 April 2005). "Woman claiming finger in chili sues often," Associated Press Online; Sandoval, G. (13 May 2005). "Fingertip traced to man who lost finger in accident," Associated Press State & Local Wire; Smith, T. (23 April 2005). "Denny Lynch of Wendy's and Sheriff Rob Davis of the San Jose Police Department discuss the woman who claimed to have found a finger in her bowl of Wendy's chili," The Saturday Early Show, CBS: Smith, T. and Bowen, J. (14 May 2005). "Police say they found the man who lost the finger said to be found in a bowl of Wendy's chili," The Saturday Early Show, CBS; Skoloff, B. (24 March 2005). "Search continues for origin of finger found in Wendy's chili." Associated Press; (27 September 2005). "Two to share $100,000 reward from Wendy's finger case." Associated Press Worldstream.

CASE 13. BAUSCH & LOMB SEES RECALL

By Dr. Krishna S. Dhir, Henry Gund Professor of Management, Campbell School of Business, Berry College

Bausch & Lomb was founded in 1853 by John Jacob Bausch and Henry Lomb. The company's name is one of the best known and highly respected health care brands in the world. In 2007 it employed about 13,000 people worldwide, selling its products in more than 100 countries. Its revenue in 2006 was about $2.29 billion, and net income was $14.9 million.

The company started by manufacturing vulcanized rubber eyeglass frames and other vision products and produced the first optical quality glass in the United States in the early 1900s. By 1903, it was manufacturing microscopes, binoculars, and camera shutters. Later, it manufactured the lenses for cameras that captured the first satellite images of the moon. Emerging as an eye health company, it dedicated itself to enhancing vision and life for consumers around the world, marketing the first soft contact lens in 1971. In addition to soft and rigid gas-permeable contact lenses and lens care products, its core businesses included ophthalmic surgical and pharmaceutical products.

A Crisis Emerges

Dr. David S. Chu is a doctor specializing in cornea diseases who practices in New Jersey. On March 3, 2006, he informed Bausch & Lomb that three of his patients had been infected by a microbe that could cause blindness. All three had used Bausch & Lomb's popular and lucrative products, ReNu lens cleaners. One of the patients had used ReNu with MoistureLoc, another had used the MultiPlus, and the third patient had used both.

Bausch & Lomb quickly confirmed that Dr. Chu's patients had indeed been infected by Fusarium fungi. However, it did not take any action—neither stopping the sales of the cleaners in the United States nor informing the health authorities. Additionally, the microbe had been causing infections among customers in Hong Kong and Singapore. On March 8, Dr. Chu, not Bausch & Lomb, reported the incidences of infection in his patients to the United States health authorities.

Fusarium Keratitis

Infectious keratitis is an eye condition that can threaten sight. If not treated in a timely manner, it can cause serious scarring of the cornea, decreased vision and in some instances the need for corneal transplant. According to the CDC, general incidence of contact lens-associated microbial keratitis is estimated to be 4 to 21 per 10,000 depending on whether lenses were worn on a daily or overnight wearing schedule. However, the CDC found that nearly all of Bausch & Lomb's MoistureLoc eye care products were linked to severe fungal eye infections.

Fungal infections of the cornea are a subset of all microbial keratitis cases. They are generally associated with some sort of injury to the eye, and occur at a higher rate in the warm and moist environments of the tropics and sub-tropics. According to the CDC, in the United States 35% of all fungal infection cases are reported in the southern-most states, while only 2% are reported in New York.

Several fungi may cause fungal keratitis. The most common of these are Fusarium and Aspergillus. Recent increased incidences of infections reported in Singapore, Hong Kong, Malaysia, and the United States have brought attention to Fusarium. Fusarium is commonly found in soil and decaying organic matter, and is common in drains, sinks, and in plant matter. It produces air-borne and water-borne spores.

Bausch & Lomb's Response

On April 11, 2006, Bausch & Lomb stopped shipping ReNu with MoistureLoc when the CDC cited a high correlation between use of the product and suspected fungal keratitis cases. The MoistureLoc formula was introduced in late 2004. (In 2005, the product had generated sales of about $100 million.)

In a full-page advertisement in the *Atlanta Journal-Constitution* on April 16, 2006, Bausch & Lomb chairman and CEO, Ronald Zarrella, sought to address concerns about the product. Part of the message read:

> We continue to work tirelessly with the Food and Drug Administration, the Centers for Disease Control and Prevention, the Johns Hopkins Wilmer Eye Institute, major eye centers and experts around the world to identify the cause of this infection. We won't stop until we're finished. If there is a problem with our product, we'll find it and we'll fix it. If there's not, when we come back you'll be able to know with absolute certainty that we've taken every possible step to ensure your safety.

The ads also contained a series of questions and answers and referred those with questions to a phone number and a Web site.

According to *The New York Times*, Bausch & Lomb had stopped selling its ReNu products in Hong Kong and Singapore in February, but had failed to inform the United States authorities. In the meantime, the CDC announced that by mid-May, it had confirmed 122 cases of the fungal infection, 15 possible ones and 60 that were under investigation across 33 states and territories. A vast majority of the sufferers involved were using Bausch & Lomb products. Nearly 40 of those infected were candidates for corneal transplants to save their vision.

On Monday, May 15, Bausch & Lomb announced its decision to recall ReNu with MoistureLoc from all markets around the world. While doing so, the company suggested that the consumers who were using ReNu with MoistureLoc may switch to ReNu MultiPlus or ReNu Multi-Purpose.

Mounting Criticism

Unfortunately, the company's critics were not satisfied by this response. Critical of Bausch & Lomb's incremental approach to dealing with the Fusarium outbreaks, some argued that the company had taken too long to respond where swift action was required. Also, they were alarmed by Bausch & Lomb's strategy of increasing production of ReNu MultiPlus, noting that 20% of the Fusarium cases were linked to the MultiPlus solution. The company countered this criticism by pointing out that the actual number of cases reported was minute, about 19 as of early May, compared with about 30 million lens wearers who had used the product since its introduction in 1997.

The crisis was growing and now threatened to spill over to its entire lens-care portfolio. This portfolio accounted for $500 million in revenue, which constituted nearly a quarter of the company's 2005 sales of $2.2 billion. By the end of May, Bausch & Lomb stock was down by about 24%.

Regaining Consumer Trust

After withdrawing ReNu with MoistureLoc, Bausch & Lomb immediately started efforts to rebuild its reputation. In a commercial, Ronald Zarrella emphasized that Bausch & Lomb's first priority had always been the health and safety of its consumers. He admitted that despite exhaustive testing, the company had been "unable to eliminate the possibility of a link to a rare eye infection."

QUESTIONS FOR REFLECTION

1. What should have been Bausch & Lomb's international response in February after it stopped selling ReNu products in Singapore? What should have been its response when Dr. Chu first contacted it?
2. Develop a communication strategy that would have been appropriate for use by Bausch & Lomb. What should have been the central message? What media would have been effective for use in disseminating the message?
3. Identify some of the ethical issues involved in health care communication.
4. How would you expect this incident to affect Bausch & Lomb's relationship with health care regulators, such as the Food and Drug Administration, after the crisis passed?

Information for this case was drawn from the following: (16 April 2006), "An important message from Bausch & Lomb" advertisement, *Atlanta Journal-Constitution*, B7; Bausch & Lomb (15 May 2006),

"Bausch & Lomb voluntarily recalls MoistureLoc® worldwide; Customer safety is our top priority, says CEO,' Rochester, NY: Bausch & Lomb, www.bausch.com/us/vision/about/news/ pressrelease. jsp?pressRelease=2006_5_15_recall.html; Bausch & Lomb (19 May 2006), "Fusarium Keratitis & Bausch & Lomb's Response: An Issue Summary," Rochester, NY: Bausch & Lomb; Bausch & Lomb (19 May 2006), 'CDC report supports Bausch & Lomb's decision to recall MoistureLoc® solution, only product associated with unusual increase in Fusarium infections," Rochester, NY: Bausch & Lomb, www.bausch.com/us/vision/about/news/ pressrelease.jsp?pressRelease=2006_5_19_cdc.html; "Bausch & Lomb," Wikipedia, the free encyclopedia, http://en.wikipedia.org/wiki/Bausch_&_Lomb; Bishop, T. (28 May 2006), "Regaining consumers' trust: Bausch & Lomb comes clean on concerns about ReNu," *Knight Ridder Tribune Business News*, p. 1; Crane, M. (3 May 2006), "More recalls ahead for Bausch & Lomb," *Forbes*, www.forbes.com/markets/2006/05/03/bauschandlomb-recalls-0503markets03.html; Feder, B.J., & Pollack, A. (18 May 2006), "From Asia to America, How Bausch's crisis grew," *The New York Times*, p. C1; Thomaselli, R. (22 May 2006), "Bausch & Lomb shortsighted in crisis," *Advertising Age* (Midwest region edition), *77*(21), p. 3.

CASE 14. TIRE TREAD TROUBLES DRIVE FIRESTONE
INTO CRISIS OF CONFIDENCE

Viewers who watched KHOU-TV's Monday night news on February 7, 2000 saw the first public report on a possible relationship between Firestone tire failures and rollovers of Ford Explorer sport utility vehicles (SUVs). Anna Werner, reporting for the CBS affiliate in Houston, said she had identified more than two dozen accidents involving Fords with Firestone tires that resulted in 30 deaths. Investigators' records said the tread had peeled off Firestone Radial ATX tires on the Explorers.

In her news report, Ms. Werner said that Firestone had expressed full confidence in its tires and that Ford had suggested driver error, perhaps in the form of under-inflation, as a possible cause. Before that first February report aired, correspondent Werner had visited the National Highway Traffic Safety Administration (NHTSA) in Washington, D.C., the federal agency responsible for reducing deaths, injuries, and economic loss resulting from traffic accidents. NHTSA officials told her they had no evidence that Firestones were implicated in a disproportionate number of Explorer rollovers.

Despite the absence of confirming NHTSA data, the KHOU news team decided its figures were strong enough to go ahead with the report.

Letter Condemns False Messages

Three days later, Firestone's vice president of public affairs, Christine Karbowiak, sent a letter of complaint to the station and its owner, pointing out items in the report she claimed were misrepresentations or falsehoods. Subsequently, KHOU posted a copy of the letter on its Web site.

"This series," wrote Firestone's Ms. Karbowiak, "has unmistakably delivered the false messages that Radial ATX tires are dangerous, that they threaten the safety of anyone using them, and that they should be removed from every vehicle on which they are installed. Each of these messages is simply untrue."

The letter noted that tread separation might result from a number of external causes, such as puncture, and would not by itself indicate a defect. The Firestone executive said the company had given the station details that could have balanced the report. Ms. Karbowiak continued: "In fact, I am advised that the failure to report such balancing information when it is in your reporter's hands prior to the broadcast may be grounds for finding of actual malice."

Some people thought they saw the thinly veiled threat of a lawsuit in the Firestone letter, but KHOU continued to follow up on the original report and advised worried Explorer drivers who contacted the station to call NHTSA's toll-free number.

In succeeding months, the federal agency received 90 complaints of tread separation and on May 2, 2000, opened a defect investigation into some 47 million

Firestone tires with the ATX, ATXII, and Wilderness AT model designations. NHTSA issued no news release concerning the investigation nor did it make a public announcement.

USA Today *Brings National Attention*

Not until *USA Today* published a story on August 1, 2000, did most Americans learn about the questions raised by KHOU. *USA Today* said NHTSA had received reports of 30 crashes and four deaths potentially related to tread separation.

Once the *USA Today* story was repeated on television networks and cable news channels, it stayed in the headlines for weeks—not just in the United States but also in South America, the Middle East, and Asia, where problems with Fords and Firestones also had been reported. Some news reports noted that Ford had voluntarily replaced Firestone tires for owners of many Ford pickups and SUVs in Venezuela and elsewhere even before the KHOU-TV report.

As the news media swarmed around the story, no one seemed able to explain what was causing the tread separations and rollovers. Most occurred in the summer months in locales with high year-round temperatures. Maybe heat, a natural enemy of tire life, was involved. Some observers said the Explorer's high center of gravity caused instability, and others suggested tire quality might have suffered during chronic labor strife at Firestone's plant in Decatur, Illinois, which produced many of the suspect tires. Others speculated that the combination of Firestone tires and Explorer engineering created the problem. No one knew for sure, and the mystery remained unsolved for months.

Before the investigation reached a conclusion, the news media's interest warmed and cooled and warmed again as new developments periodically sparked headlines. Before year-end:

- Firestone and Ford would abandon their mutual defense posture and end up accusing each other.

Figure 4.1 More than 2,200 company-owned consumer and commercial stores are operated by BFS Retail & Commercial Operations, LLC and its subsidiaries; the stores include Firestone Complete Auto Care, Morgan Tire/Tires Plus, Expert Tire, Commercial & Farm, and Mark Morris

- Hearings on Capitol Hill would shed more light on the conflict and tempt some members of Congress to make themselves look good by making the manufacturers and regulators look bad.
- NHTSA would confirm that an insurance company researcher had told the federal agency two years earlier about possible tread separation problems on some Firestones.

Firestone began producing Radial ATX tires in 1990 to serve as original equipment on the Ford Explorer, which was introduced in March for the 1991 model year. The tire was redesigned in 1995 and 1996 and given two new model designations, Radial ATXII (pronounced a-t-x-2) and Wilderness AT. Through the 1990s, the tires were installed on millions of new Explorers, Mercury Mountaineers, Ford Ranger and F-Series pickups, Mazda Navajos, and Mazda light trucks. By summer of 2000, Firestone had made about 14.4 million tires in the three models, and an estimated 6.5 million were still in use.

After the first *USA Today* article, Firestone insisted that its tire performance data reinforced the company's contention that the tires were safe and reliable, and Ford did not contradict the tire company. But when Sears Roebuck, the nation's largest tire retailer, announced it would stop selling the Firestone Radial ATX, ATXII, and Wilderness tires on Friday, August 4, the situation began shifting.

On the same day, Ford's chief executive, Jacques Nasser, said "We're clearly very, very concerned about the situation...We have teams that are working around the clock. Once we know exactly what the issues are, we will act, because we feel a responsibility to our customers, for their safety and for the safety of their families."

The following Monday, NHTSA said it had received 270 complaints about the tires, including allegations that they may have been involved in 46 deaths and 80 injuries since their introduction in 1990.

Déjà Vu All Over Again

For many middle-aged drivers, the Firestone story was *déjà vu*. The company had barely survived a crisis in 1978 when the federal government forced it to recall 13 million Firestone 500 steel-belted radials. Though reports in 1978 linked the tires to 41 deaths, the company resisted recalling them for 18 months. Weakened by its drawn-out battle with the government and shunned by many motorists, Firestone—one of the oldest and proudest names in American motoring—was acquired in 1988 by Japan's largest tire company, Bridgestone, which began operating as Bridgestone/Firestone Inc. In 1992, the combined operation closed its headquarters in Akron, Ohio, and moved to Nashville, Tennessee.

After Bridgestone took control, Firestone's fortunes eventually turned around, and the company began gaining on its larger rivals—Goodyear and Michelin. Preparing to observe its 100th anniversary in 2000, Firestone planned a big celebration and created a special Web site tracing company history back to its earliest days and founder Harvey Firestone's close friendship with Ford founder Henry Ford. Throughout most of the 20th century, Ford Motor Company was, in fact, Firestone's most important customer.

The Firestone celebration was quickly overshadowed by the escalating tread separation issue. Eight days after *USA Today* put the problem on the nation's news agenda, Firestone announced a voluntary recall of 6.5 million tires in a single size (P235/75R15) with the Radial ATX, ATXII, and Wilderness AT designations.

Unpopular Recall Plan Compounds Problems

While some public relations experts were criticizing Firestone for waiting too long to address the issue, the recall plan itself created further problems. Like shoes, tires are produced in a variety of sizes, widths, and styles. All of the tire warehouses of all of the tire makers around the world did not contain 6.5 million tires in the size needed. To achieve an orderly replacement process, Firestone planned to complete it in phases, taking nine months or more.

"Because the preponderance of incidents is in the four southern states and given the limited supply of replacement tires at this time, the company will be undertaking a three-phase recall starting in Arizona, California, Florida and Texas," Firestone announced. "The second phase for the recall will be implemented in Alabama, Georgia, Louisiana, Mississippi, Nevada, Oklahoma and Tennessee. The final phase will include the remainder of the states."

The three-phase plan provoked an outcry from Ford owners in all 50 states, who wanted their tires replaced NOW! In response to the howls, Firestone doubled production at its U.S. plants, airlifted replacement tires from Bridgestone in Japan, and purchased tires from competitors. By the end of August, it had replaced more than a million tires. On August 31, NHTSA recommended that Firestone recall another million or so tires in a variety of sizes sold mainly as replacements on pickups and SUVs, but the tire company said it was not necessary.

Congress Holds Hearings

Committees of the U.S. House of Representatives began hearings in September to learn more about the tread separation problems and examine the role of NHTSA in fixing it. As the hearings started, NHTSA said that it had received reports of 88 fatalities related to the tires and 250 injuries.

Appearing before a congressional panel, Ford CEO Jacques Nasser and Firestone CEO Masatoshi Ono testified about product safety and their role in protecting the public. The hearings also produced testimony from a researcher at State Farm Mutual Automobile Insurance Company who had alerted NHTSA in July 1998 to an unusual pattern of tread separation cases involving the Firestones. The early warning apparently got little agency attention at the time it was received.

In December 2000, Firestone announced the results of its four-month investigation into the tread separation problem, and they contained no surprises. John Lampe, who succeeded Masatoshi Ono as CEO, said analysis of 2,500 recalled tires pointed to a combination of factors, acting in concert, as the cause of the elevated failure rate.

Ford and Firestone Quarrel

By the time Firestone reported its findings, the company had replaced more than 5.5 million tires in the recall of 6.3 million. The issue of a wider recall, first raised by NHTSA on August 31, continued to simmer, but Firestone rebuffed new agency requests on the matter. Eventually, Ford took the initiative in May 2001 to replace 13 million Firestone tires on its vehicles at a cost of $3 billion. The automaker said the tires had higher failure rates. Stung, Firestone announced a few days later that it would no longer supply tires to Ford's operations in the Americas and accused the company of clouding the issue.

"We have always said that in order to insure the safety of the driving public, it is crucial that there be a true sharing of information concerning the vehicle as well as the tires. Ford simply is not willing to do that," Firestone CEO John Lampe said in a statement. "We believe they are attempting to divert scrutiny of their vehicle by casting doubt on the quality of Firestone tires."

Brave words but subject to amendment. Firestone yielded five months later and recalled an additional 3.5 million Wilderness AT tires made before May 1998. NHTSA closed the defect investigation it had begun in May 2000, saying that it had received reports of 271 fatalities related to the tires under study.

Of the expanded recall, Firestone's Lampe said, "We recognize that a lengthy confrontation with NHTSA would continue to bring into question the quality of our products and delay our ongoing work of rebuilding the company."

In 2003, Firestone promised to spend $15 million on a three-year consumer education campaign, including the use of national media, with the goal of persuading motorists to take better care of their tires. The campaign addressed tire inflation, tire use, tire maintenance, driving safety, and car maintenance.

Firestone's promise was a major provision in its settlement of a nationwide class-action lawsuit stemming from the recall. The company denied wrongdoing or liability and said it entered the settlement to avoid the burden of protracted litigation. The settlement did not affect hundreds of unresolved personal-injury lawsuits involving allegations about the recalled tires.

QUESTIONS FOR REFLECTION

1. How should Firestone have handled its 100th anniversary celebration after *USA Today* published its first story on the Ford/Firestone rollover accidents?
2. Firestone and Ford attempted to cooperate in the early stages of the crisis. Why did the cooperation evaporate?
3. Considering the high demand for replacement tires and the impossibility of meeting the demand immediately, what alternative strategies might Firestone have considered?
4. Do you think that Firestone has succeeded in restoring its reputation?

Information for this case was drawn from the following: the Firestone Web site at http://mirror. bridgestone-firestone.com/news/media_center_fr.html; the National Highway Transportation Administration Web site at www.nhtsa.gov/cars/problems/Equipment/Tires/index.html; Aeppel, T., Ansberry, C., Geyelin, M., & Simison, R. (6 September 2000), "Road signs: How Ford, Firestone let the warnings slide by as debacle developed," *The Wall Street Journal*, p. A1; Bradsher, K. (1 September 2000), "Local TV uncovered national scandal," *The New York Times*, p. 1; Crock, S., & St. Pierre, N. (16 October 2000), "The tire flap: Behind the feeding frenzy," *Business Week*, p. 114; Eldridge, E. (11 August 2000), "Ford owners demand new tires," *USA Today*, p. 1 (accessed 25 January 2001); "Firestone letter to Belo & KHOU executives," www.khou.com/news/stories/1290.html; Grant, L., & Healey, J. (4 August 2000), "Sears stops selling tires involved in probe," *USA Today*, p. 1; Rutenberg, J. (11 September 2000), "Local TV uncovered national scandal," *The New York Times*, p. C17; St. Pierre, N. (8 September 2000), "The Firestone fiasco: Was the NHTSA 'asleep at the wheel'?" *Business Week*, p. 98; Zimmerman, A. (12 September 2000), "News media get in line to take credit for bring about Firestone tire recall," *The Wall Street Journal*, p. A4.

CASE 15. WAL-MART: SOARING THROUGH SUSTAINABILITY

Wal-Mart was recognized as one of the "5 brands that soared" by *PRWeek* magazine in December 2007, which noted the strength of its sustainability campaign in helping it overcome criticism and in becoming a model for other retailers interested in green issues.

Turning 'Green' in a Sustainability Campaign

The focus on sustainability began in 2005, when the retailer began offering more green products in its almost 4,000 U.S. stores and with a plan to reduce energy use and waste at the stores. A national advertising campaign in April 2007 began introducing the products to consumers; the ads used a woman explaining how purchase and use of certain products could help the environment. The campaign included 30-second broadcast ads and print ads in *USA Today, The New York Times* and Sunday newspaper supplements.

Wal-Mart has done more than just sponsor a campaign, however. The corporation has developed the first heavy-duty hybrid truck and has implemented changes in its buildings. Don Mosely, the manager of experimental projects for Wal-Mart, told Arkansas legislators in September about the changes. The stores are adding skylights and white roofs; they are using the heat generated by refrigeration equipment to heat water they use in the stores. The company has targeted 14 categories for energy efficiency in its buildings and transportation.

Marketing Sustainability through Ordinary Goods

To commemorate Earth Day 2008, Wal-Mart launched a month-long multimedia "green" campaign to inform consumers of the affordable sustainable products

Figure 4.2 Wal-Mart serves more than 100 million customers weekly in 14 nations, including Argentina, Brazil, Canada, China, Costa Rica, El Salvador, Guatemala, Honduras, Japan, Mexico, Nicaragua, Puerto Rico, the United Kingdom and the United States (Photo by Lauren V. Wright)

available at the retail giant. In a release announcing the campaign, Matt Kistler, the retailer's senior vice president of sustainability, said:

> Wal-Mart is uniquely positioned to make sustainable choices a real option for hundreds of millions of Americans—not just the few who until now could afford to choose them. The environment and budgets will be top of mind for our shoppers throughout the month of April, and for those reasons, we are unveiling new product initiatives as well as offering seasonal favorites at unbeatable prices.

The chain featured more than 50 such products in stores and more than 500 on line. Products included T-shirts made from alternative fibers such as recycled plastic bottles and organic cotton, mulch made from recycled rubber, and laundry detergents with fewer chemicals.

Designed by the Martin Agency, *PRWeek* reported, the campaign used a series of seven 30-second TV ads, and radio and online banner ads to reach consumers with its message about sustainability and sales. A 16-page "magalog" titled "A budget-friendly guide to helping the planet" was designed to be used as an insert in selected consumer magazines and as a handout in Wal-Mart stores; circulation of more than 20 million of the magalogs was planned. In-store displays featured information about the environmental benefits of sustainable products, along with tips for simple changes homeowners could make that would be of benefit.

An "Earth Month" Web site linked from Wal-Mart's main site using several URLs. On the sustainability Web site, the retailer provided fact sheets, a sustainability newsletter, news releases, backgrounders, streamed video of corporate speeches, and a statement of mission and of the sustainability goals. Consumers could read or print a variety of informational tools and find information about Wal-Mart's progress toward its goals on follow-up visits.

A Saturday, April 19, promotion event involved Wal-Mart giving away a million reusable shopping bags made of recycled materials. The bags were also available for purchase in the stores for $1.

Tracking Sustainability Through Accountability

Wal-Mart had begun tracking consumer decisions to buy designated green products since April 2007. Using what it called a "Live Better Index," the retailer reported an increase of 66% in such purchases between April 2007 and April 2008. For example, the store noted an increase in the average adoption rate of compact fluorescent light bulbs of 19.7% and an adoption rate of concentrated liquid laundry detergents of 76.3%; Wal-Mart began transitioning to only selling such laundry detergents in October 2007.

In March 2008, the giant retailer announced more goals for efficiency. Among them were pledges to require all their suppliers to demonstrate that factors meet specific environmental, social and quality standards within three to five years.

The company also pledged to work with its suppliers to increase the energy efficiency of all air conditioners and flat-panel televisions they sell by 15 to 30%.

Sustaining Active Communications

Leslie Dach, who had served as a vice chairman of public relations at Edelman Worldwide, was hired by Wal-Mart in August 2006 as its executive vice president of corporate affairs, reporting directly to CEO Lee Scott. Dach talked with *USA Today* reporter Mindy Fetterman about the retailer's public-relations efforts, saying: "We have a great story to tell. We may have spent too much time responding to critics, because when we tell our story on sustainability, on job creation, on $4 generic drugs, it's very persuasive. Our opponents look smaller and shriller. We want to run a relentlessly positive campaign."

Since 2004, Wal-Mart has been diversifying its public communication. Facing criticism from various groups over labor practices and the size of its stores, it expanded television advertising, including underwriting "The Tavis Smiley Show" on PBS. It also became a sponsor on National Public Radio. In January 2005, full-page ads were placed in more than 100 U.S. newspapers to focus on Wal-Mart's benefits and jobs. An annual conference for journalists was begun in 2005, where journalists are invited to Arkansas to hear from corporate leaders.

Its lobbying efforts have also increased, expanding to what the *Washington Post* reported in 2007 was a $2.5 million operation, and it has increased political donations from the $135,750 its political action committee gave in the 1998 elections to $1.3 million in 2006. A Web site, www.walmartfacts.com, was launched in 2005 to provide information about the retailer and its role as a community member and as an employer.

Dr. Andrew Young, civil rights leader and former mayor of Atlanta, was hired in 2006 to chair the national steering committee of Working Families for Wal-Mart, although he resigned a short time later after comments about neighborhood businesses stirred controversy.

Former Vice President Al Gore was invited to speak and to show his documentary "An Inconvenient Truth" at a Wal-Mart conference in July 2006. The Associated Press reported that during his speech, Gore said: "I believe that this kind of commitment is so important that the rest of the world is likely to be listening and learning." He received a standing ovation. Wal-Mart later gave $75,000 to the Climate Project, Gore's nonprofit.

Wal-Mart is the world's largest retailer, registering more than $364 billion in sales for the fiscal year that ended January 31, 2008, according to Web site reports, and has more than 2 million associates working worldwide in the more than 7,200 stores.

QUESTIONS FOR REFLECTION

1. Evaluate the communication plan for promoting Wal-Mart's new sustainability initiatives. What are the advantages and disadvantages of these tactics?

2. As part of the initiative, Wal-Mart has committed to educating shoppers about the need for change and ways change can occur. What advantages does Wal-Mart have in reaching a consumer marketplace? What obstacles will they have to overcome?

3. Is there a danger that some might see the new initiative as intended to create a distraction from negative publicity Wal-Mart had been receiving? If so, how could Wal-Mart avoid such an impression?

4. Many businesses and corporations have become involved in environmental initiatives. How can a business make its involvement distinctive, credible and noteworthy when many others are also becoming actively involved?

Information for this case was drawn from the following: Wal-Mart Web sites and from Bartels, C. (13 January 2005), "Wal-Mart launches drive to rebut criticism on worker pay, community impact of stores," Associated Press; Barbaro, M. (20 April 2006), "Chief's tone reflects change at Wal-Mart in the last year," New York Times, p. C3; Bartels, C. (13 January 2005), "Wal-Mart launches PR campaign, wants to remove sting of criticism," The Associated Press State & Local Wire; Bergman, A. (19 September 2006), "Wal-Mart sets example for Ark. School and state agency buildings," Associated Press State & Local Wire; Fetterman, M. (6 November 2006), "Q: What are the biggest PR challenges the company faces?" USA Today, www.usatoday.com; (22 December 2007), "5 brands that soared," PRWeek, www.prweekus.com/5-brands-that-saored/PrintArticle/100160/; Hays, C.L. (9 September 2004), "At Wal-Mart, the new word is compromise," The New York Times, www.nytimes. com; Kabel, M. (13 July 2006), "Gore praises Wal-Mart for sustainability plans," Associated Press; Kabel, M. (18 April 2007), "Wal-Mart launches national ads touting green products," Associated Press Financial Wire; Mui, Y.Q. (24 November 2007), "Wal-Mart reaches out in self-defense; retailer embraces political activism," Washington Post, p. A1; Todé, C. (7 April 2008), "Wal-Mart launches month-long green campaign," PRWeek, www.prweekus.com; Wal-Mart Stores, Inc. (21 April 2008), "Wal-Mart consumer behavior shows buying green is going mainstream; nation's leading retailer reveals 66 percent increase in 'Live Better Index' that tracks eco-friendly shopping habits," PR Newswire, www.prnewswire.com; Wal-Mart Stores, Inc. (31 March 2008), "Wal-Mart Earth Month campaign takes 'going green' mainstream; retailer's product selection, advertising and stores show it can be easy being 'green,'" PR Newswire, www.prnewswire.com;

CASE 16. WARNER BROS. (AND OTHERS) ARE WILD ABOUT "HARRY"

The Harry Potter series of books and films has produced magic, not only for its characters, a brown-haired, glasses-wearing young boy and his pals at Hogwarts School of Witchcraft and Wizardry, but for those companies involved in promoting the sales of the books, films, and related Potter merchandise. The seven books in the series have sold more than 350 million copies worldwide in 65 languages, and sales of the final volume, *Harry Potter and the Deathly Hallows*, sold 8.3 million copies in the United States during its first 24 hours on sale. Warner Bros. and its parent company, Time Warner Inc., grossed an estimated $1.5 billion in revenue from worldwide box office receipts and DVD, television, and merchandising sales of *Harry Potter and the Sorcerer's Stone*, the first film in the series.

On November 15, 2002, the film release of *Harry Potter and the Chamber of Secrets* continued the magic, setting box office records everywhere it opened, and surpassing $100 million at both the domestic and international box offices in just 10 days after its initial release. With international box office receipts in excess of $800 million, *Harry Potter and the Chamber of Secrets* soon joined the lists of the highest-grossing films of all time. The 2007 debut of the *Harry Potter and the Order of the Phoenix* film took in $330.3 million during the first week of its worldwide release. In all, the first four Harry Potter films grossed more than $3.5 billion worldwide.

Promoting the Films

The film studio got involved in the Potter phenomenon early and inexpensively. Just before the first book, *Harry Potter and the Sorcerer's Stone*, became an international sensation, Warner Bros. reportedly paid Rowling $50,000 for film rights to the book. The following year, the studio paid an additional $500,000, this time to exercise its option to make a movie.

AOL Time Warner/Warner Bros. offered a variety of ways to promote the films and merchandise. AOL Moviefone offered advance ticket sales for the *Harry Potter and the Chamber of Secrets* three weeks before its U.S. premiere. Moviegoers in most major markets were able to buy tickets either by visiting Moviefone.com, AOL Keyword: Harry Potter, or by calling the AOL Moviefone telephone service, known by familiar local numbers such as 777-FILM. In addition, AOL 8.0's Sneak Peek Sweeps of *Harry Potter and the Chamber of Secrets* offered chances to win passes to one of 20 exclusive sneak preview screenings taking place across the country on November 14, one day before the film's U.S. release. Entrants were also given the chance to win *Harry Potter and the Chamber of Secrets* gift packs, a $1,000 holiday shopping spree, or a year of AOL membership. More than 1 million advance tickets were sold.

A two-minute promotion for *Harry Potter and the Chamber of Secrets* was aired on the WB network in September 2002, the first time such a long clip was used to promote the movie. The clip aired during a premiere of a new WB program, "Family Affair." *Entertainment Weekly* featured a cover story on the release of *Sorcerer's Stone*, and an advance review ran in *Time*. The June 23, 2003 *Time* contained a seven-page article with sidebars titled "The Real Magic of Harry Potter."

Warner Bros. developed a Web site (http://harrypotter.warnerbros.com) that features information on the characters, cast, and crew of the films, Hogwarts-inspired games, merchandise, activities, music from the soundtrack, deleted scenes from the films, and a chat room. Visitors may order DVDs or videos of the films online at the site. Reuters reported that in the weeks prior to the November 2001 release of *Harry Potter and the Sorcerer's Stone*, the Web site drew some 573,000 unique visitors, and more than 3.8 million unique visitors visited the site when the film opened. In November 2002, when the second movie was released, more than 3 million visitors again came to the site. The Warner Bros. *Order of the Phoenix* Web site had more than 446,000 different visitors in May 2007 alone.

Magical Merchandising

EastWest Creative designed a four-week promotion to support the release of *The Sorcerer's Stone* video and DVD that involved a Web-based trivia competition. As players answered questions correctly, they were sent to one of 90 worldwide partner sites to search for the messenger owls. Those who found them earned rewards such as a screensaver or bookmark, and some 17,000 "instant pop-up" winners received posters, coloring books, postcard books, and T-shirts. Ten grand-prize winners were flown to London for the release of the *Harry Potter and the Chamber of Secrets* film, and one bonus winner got a walk-on role in the film. The game, launched in 12 countries and in seven languages, was promoted in the United States by print ads in AOL Time Warner's *People*, AOL banners, and on-air live "owl sightings" during national broadcast of the Atlanta Braves games.

Coca-Cola invested an estimated $150 million to participate in the Potter film promotion in 43 countries. The investment included usage rights to advertising campaigns to contests. In October and November, Coca-Cola offered a "Catch the Golden Snitch and Win" promotion in which game cards were enclosed in multipacks of Coca-Cola Classic and caffeine-free Coca-Cola. Those who found the Golden Snitch card were then eligible to win a trip to London and receive $5 movie certificates. The 925 game winners were rewarded with visits to castles such as Herstmonceaux Castle, Great Fosters, and Windsor Castle in which Potter themes were developed through costuming and special events. The closing banquet in the Natural History Museum featured appetizers and drinks named after Potter characters or objects.

Special codes on the eight cards also allowed consumers to find behind-the-scenes images of the film when they visited Livethemagic.com. Similar prizes were available through Coca-Cola's Minute Maid juices. The soft-drink corporation also used its Potter promotion to tie in with a national literacy-promotion program in which it donated 1 million books to schoolchildren.

To avoid oversaturation, Warner Bros. offered licenses to fewer than 90 U.S. licensing partners, and only a few hundred products were released. But that left room for the development of Harry Potter party napkins, figurines, snow-domes, stuffed animals, candy, bookends, lamps, candy, tattoos, wrapping paper, lunchboxes, picture frames, calendars, ornaments, sweatshirts, backpacks, key chains, CD wallets, stationery, and rubber stamps. Retailers such as Toys R Us and Kmart featured merchandise tied to the *Sorcerer's Stone* film, and sales were strong. Mattel Inc. was the master licensee for the games, puzzles, trading cards, and other items. Lego Systems Inc. offered a Hogwarts Express train and Hogwarts Castle kits. Electronic Arts offered video games and computer-based ancillaries. The release of the fifth book, *Harry Potter and the Order of the Phoenix*, brought with it new merchandise, such as a robe with fiber-optic lights, a magic wand, and fake forehead scars.

The promotions were apparently effective. The NPD Group, a firm that provided marketing information online, began offering a "Harry Potter Prophet" in March 2001, a series of seven reports to track popularity of the Harry Potter products and attitudes and behaviors of children and adults relating to the books and films. According to their first report based on a March 2001 survey of 1,511 adults and children, 95% of children and 90% of adults surveyed had heard of Harry Potter, more than half of the children had read at least one of the books, and of those who read at least one book, almost two-thirds of children planned to see the movies. The Prophet also reported that 40% of children and adults who had read at least one of the books had already purchased a Harry Potter-related product.

Celebrating the Books

As each book in the series was released, the book publisher and bookstore owners held special events and promotions to tout the new novels. For example, to celebrate the publication of the final Potter book, the U.S. publisher of the series, Scholastic, Inc., created a street celebration in New York City it called "Harry Potter Place," which opened one day before the book release. It featured a giant Muggle Board, a 20-foot high moving Whomping Willow, and various entertainments such as wand-making, fire-eaters, and magicians. A replica of the triple-decker bus from the Potter books, the Deathly Hallows Knight Bus, was parked for children; inside, children could film a 20-second video featuring their views about the books.

Scholastic also sponsored a sweepstakes that would give seven fans a prize of joining author J.K. Rowling in London for the midnight launch of the *Deathly Hallows* book.

Earlier, Scholastic spent more than $3 million to promote the June 2003 release of *Harry Potter and the Order of the Phoenix*. Readers could reserve copies of the book during the five months prior to its release. More than 1.3 million copies of the book were ordered through Amazon's Web sites; Barnes & Noble.com reported it sold 896,000 copies the first day, and the Barnes & Noble bookstores sold 286,000 copies in just 60 minutes. The book's release at 12:01 a.m. on June 21 was touted through parties, advertising, and promotions. A countdown in New York's Times Square and a billboard on Sunset Strip announced the release. Wal-Mart supercenters held special midnight events featuring cupcakes with Harry Potter themes. Many bookstores across the globe featured theme parties with employees dressed as characters.

A national billboard campaign supported the book's release. The Seattle Mariners, Baltimore Orioles, Oakland Athletics, and Houston Astros held "Harry Potter" days with costume contests and scoreboard promotions. Scholastic distributed more than 15,000 "event kits" to bookstores and other retailers that planned release parties. The kits included stickers, buttons, a trivia quiz, and suggestions for handling long lines of prospective buyers. Scholastic distributed 3 million bumper stickers, 50,000 window displays, 9,500 countertop cutouts, 24,000 stand-up posters with countdown clocks, and 400,000 buttons to promote the *Phoenix* release. Scholastic also held an essay contest with the top prize of a trip to London to hear J.K. Rowling read from the book and participate in an interview at the Royal Albert Hall.

Rowling donated the only signed copy of the *Order of the Phoenix* to the New York Public Library, with an inscription that read "To the People of New York with Love and Admiration from J.K. Rowling."

Scholastic Inc. planned a first printing of 6.8 million copies, an all-time U.S. publishing record. When Scholastic released *Harry Potter and the Goblet of Fire* in July 2000, it became the fastest-selling book in history. Within 48 hours, 3 million copies were sold and Scholastic went back to press for an additional 3 million immediately.

Scholastic also used its Web site to promote the Potter books. Readers can use a pronunciation guide and find discussion guides for the five books. There is also a chat room for comments from student readers and a screensaver that can be downloaded. The page also contains recommendations for other "great" children's books.

Scholastic Corporation is the world's largest publisher and distributor of children's books and also provides a variety of other learning resources.

~~

QUESTIONS FOR REFLECTION

1. How may public relations practice augment product promotion? What aspects of this case illustrate traditional public relations practice and which illustrate more integrated-communication efforts?

2. Should the techniques of product promotion be the same for products marketed to children as those marketed to adults?

3. What are the benefits gained by generating such widespread publicity for a product's release? Are there cautions as well?

4. Evaluate the strengths and weaknesses of the cross-merchandising efforts highlighted in this case.

5. What are the public relations challenges and opportunities when a highly successful series or product like the Potter novels comes to an end?

Information for this case was drawn from the following: Web sites cited earlier and www.aoltw. com/companies/warner_bros_index.adp and www.scholastica.com. Other sources included A.C. Nielsen. (10 July 2007), "Harry Potter charms the entertainment industry," *PR Newswire US*, www. prenewswire.com; Blais, J. (5 June 2003), "Creating magic with marketing," *USA Today*, p. D2; Brady, D. (30 June 2003), "Harry Potter and—what else?" *BusinessWeek*, pp. 79-80; Capell, K., et al. (9 August 1999), "Just wild about Harry Potter," *BusinessWeek*, p. 54; D'Innocenzio, A. (29 October 2001), "Harry Potter merchandise is magical," *AP Online*; Germaion, D. (16 July 2007), "'Phoenix' works magic in debut," *Atlanta Journal-Constitution*, D1; Gibbs, N. (23 June 2003), "The real magic of Harry Potter," *Time*, pp. 61-67; (19 June 2003), "Harry Potter fever heats up as 'Phoenix' readies to rise," *Agency France Presse*; Hein, K. (7 October 2002), "Coke puts players in the game to help unveil Potter's secrets," *Brandweek*, p. 6; Hobbs, L. (4 July 2000), "Greet Harry at a Potter party: Stores get mystical for latest book in series," *Palm Beach Post*, p. A1; Italie, H. (5 June 2003), "Publisher revs up promotion for new Harry Potter Book," Associated Press Worldstream; Katz, R. (9 December 2002), "Harry Potter fans get thrills at Coke incentive," *MeetingNews*, p. 11; Kirkpatrick, D.D. (16 June 2003), "Merchandisers try to harness Harry Potter's magic," *International Herald Tribune*; Leith, S. (1 February 2002), "Coke confident of 'Potter' benefits," *Atlanta Journal-Constitution*, pp. C1, 8; Lyman, R. (30 December 2002), "A big fat increase at the box office," *The New York Times*, p. E1; Murphy, D.5; (21 June 2003), "Harry fans count down, raise a butterbeer," *Portland Press Herald*, p. A1; Mnyandu, E. (11 June 2003), "Harry Potter not magic enough for U.S. bookstores," *Reuters Entertainment*; Odell, P. (1 May 2003), "Bird watching," *Promo, 16*(6); Palmeri, C., et al. (3 December 2001), "Boffo at the box office, scarce on the shelves," *BusinessWeek*, p. 53; Reuters (11 September 2002),"'Harry' synergy/The WB plugs 'Potter' movie," *Newsday*, p. A18; (28 March 2001), "NPD introduces new report to track Harry Potter phenomenon," Release, *Business Wire*; Sanger, E. (10 July 2000), "Potter and the toymakers' tale," *Newsday*, p. 18; Scholastic Corp. (2 August 2007), "Scholastic announces record breaking sales of 11.5 million copies of Harry Potter and the Deathly Hallows in first ten days," *PR Newswire*, www.prnewswire.com; Scholastic Corp. (26 June 2007), "Scholastic to host 'Harry Potter Place,'" *PR Newswire U.S.*, www.prnewswire.com; Thorn, P. (11 February 2001), "Potter, Potter everywhere," *Denver Rocky Mountain News*, p. 1E; Thorn, P. (20 June 2003), "Get caught up on all things 'Potter': The future," *Denver Rocky Mountain News*, p. D27; (1 November 2001), "Traffic skyrockets at studio's Harry Potter Web site," *The Toronto Star*.

PROFESSIONAL INSIGHT

PUBLIC RELATIONS IN THE IPOD GENERATION

Richard D. French, president and chief executive officer, French/West/
Vaughan

The other night I sat down with my daughters to watch television and after 10 minutes or so of channel surfing my oldest daughter turned the television off and proclaimed there 'was nothing on.' Six hundred digital cable channels, a library of movies on demand, more than 100 format-specific music channels and still 'nothing on.' The funny thing is many of us probably feel that way from time to time and it has less to do with the quality of programming and more to do with the other information and entertainment options available to us in our daily lives.

This leads to some interesting questions for those of us in the business of shaping opinions and influencing behavior. If the traditional tools we have come to rely on to deliver our messages—the television, newspaper, magazines and radio—can't be counted on to hold the interest of today's youth, and tomorrow's consumer, what message delivery vehicles can, and how do we get those younger consumers who have been conditioned to 'surf' from one thing to another to pay attention to them?

Reaching kids like me who grew up in the '60s and early '70s was relatively easy. You had the daily newspaper—or two if you lived in a larger city—a few broadcast networks and UPN stations, local radio with a relatively weak signal and little in the way of specialized magazine content for teens or kids (with apologies to *Teen Beat*). So we grew up reading the newspaper, watching local news for lack of a wide variety of programming, and listening to radio for the first singles released by our favorite artists on vinyl. These mediums were the way in which we received information and ultimately what influenced our likes and dislikes. So as creatures of habit, those of us who grew up in that era—the Baby Boomer Generation—still tend to read the newspaper, watch the news and listen to radio. But alas, our children aren't and that is why we see newspaper readership continuing to decline year after year, ratings drops for both local and national television news, and radio struggling to hold listeners when tech savvy youth have already downloaded their favorite music to their iPod before a station's programming director can get a new artist's songs into rotation.

So society and the way it chooses to receive its information has changed; so too must those of us in the public relations profession whose job it is to shape beliefs and influence behavior.

So here is my prediction: the practice of public relations over the next decade will evolve from targeting traditional mass media as the primary message delivery vehicle to practitioners spending the majority of their time crafting one-on-one messages for key constituency groups with the hope those messages will be shared among their peer groups. As a result, we will see the disciplines of PR, direct and word-of-mouth marketing converge in a social media landscape where consumers have almost total control over how and when they receive their information and with whom they choose to share it. Which means the time is coming where a blog posting or podcast that can be shared with millions of people and discussed online among interested parties will be more valuable to a company and its brands than a great hit in *USA Today*.

Rick French is president and chief executive officer of French/West/Vaughan, a public relations, public affairs, advertising and emerging media agency with offices in Raleigh, New York City and Tampa. In 2004, the firm was named National Consumer Agency of the Year by the Holmes Report and has been ranked among the nation's 20 largest independently-owned PR agencies.

5

Stakeholders: Media

Media relations is a two-way street where the rules of the road are observed as courtesies rather than enforceable regulations. In one direction, journalists ask practitioners for help in gathering information for news stories or verifying details. In the other, practitioners distribute news announcements to the media or ask journalists to consider story ideas for publication.

This traffic generally moves smoothly at high speed, though collisions occur when drivers don't know the rules or don't care to follow them. For practitioners, the rules include conventions like the use of Associated Press style in news releases, courtesies like returning phone calls promptly, and an absolute rejection of falsehoods and deception.

MEDIA STAKEHOLDERS SERVE INTERVENING PUBLICS

Reporters and editors are seldom the ultimate target of public relations programming. Instead, gatekeepers who work in broadcasting and publishing represent an intervening public, controlling the flow and presentation of information to readers, listeners, and viewers. Ultimately, public relations programs aim to reach consumers, regulators, government officials, activists, and others whose opinions and actions will affect the practitioner's organization.

PURPOSES OF MEDIA RELATIONS

Reaching target publics through news media exposure is a common practice in public relations for at least six reasons:

- *Efficiency*: Mass media, such as Web sites, daily newspapers, and television, reach individuals by the hundreds of thousands or even millions with unsurpassed speed.
- *Credibility*: Individuals often believe that information in reputable media, such as *The New York Times* or CBS-TV's "60 Minutes," is more trustworthy than the same information presented by an organization.

- *Targeting*: Individuals who read or watch certain kinds of media or programming may have predictable interests or habits, enabling the practitioner to tailor messages with greater precision and mutual benefit.
- *Agenda setting*: Media attention often determines which topics come up in general conversation, and a practitioner may want to get people talking about a specific subject.
- *Economy*: Messages that appear in the news media involve comparatively low costs for the practitioner's organization.
- *Time shifting*: Print media, in particular, allow individuals to pick their own best time and place to digest information. The same is true, to a lesser extent, for Web sites, CDs, and DVDs.

THE SELF-INTERESTS OF THE MEDIA

Reporters and editors care little about the reasons that lead practitioners to favor news media for distributing information. Instead, journalists focus on satisfying their audiences' needs for news and their preferences in entertainment. If public relations materials help a news organization do its job well, journalists are happy to use them. Materials that contain no news or useful information are tossed.

In developing strategies and key messages to reach the ultimate target public, practitioners usually give painstaking thought to the target's self-interest and to circumstances that will make it easy for a target public to follow through with whatever action is desired. Yet, practitioners often neglect the self-interests of the intervening public—the editors and reporters—as well as the mission of a news organization.

At a personal level, journalists want many of the same things practitioners want: good income, increasing responsibility, stability with a respected employer. In journalism, these rewards depend on gaining the respect of peers, career advancement, challenging assignments, and recognition.

Reporters rate themselves and others according to the importance of assignments they handle, the number and quality of the stories they get published or broadcast, and the prominence given their stories in the news product (front page, above the fold, top of the newscast, and so on).

TIME PRESSURES IN MEDIA RELATIONS

To do their jobs well on a daily basis, most reporters must focus on choosing a story idea or chasing one down, gathering information efficiently, finding a strong news peg, and writing a vivid and compelling account. They must do it quickly, never falling behind the competition and beating it if possible, and they must meet the deadline of their publication or newscast. Before handing in a news story, a reporter needs time to check it to make sure that it's fair, accurate, and reasonably complete.

Considering these time pressures, no one should be surprised that journalists prefer to deal with a practitioner who has earned their trust by providing information that's never misleading, earned their appreciation by providing it quickly, and earned their respect by packaging it in formats that are easy to digest and use. Accommodating the self-interests of intervening publics serves the self-interest of the practitioner's organization.

ELECTRONIC MEDIA RELATIONS

The Internet gives a media relations practitioner a number of tools to use in helping reporters do their jobs faster and better. Almost all organizations—big and small—maintain Web sites, and on the home page of these Web sites is a hypertext link to what is often called the press center or news bureau. A prominent and easy-to-find link will get more use.

Journalists often visit an organization's Web site, looking for information they need, before placing a phone call to a media relations manager. Because it's available around the clock and throughout the week, reporters can get details they need whenever they want them.

A Web site's news bureau usually contains recent news releases and archives of old ones. An elementary online news bureau also should list the names, phone numbers, and e-mail addresses of the media relations staff.

Better Web sites contain much more. The news bureau page should offer links to:

- Fact sheets.
- Organizational history.
- Executive biographies.
- High-resolution photos of leaders, products, and operations.
- Reproducible charts and graphs.
- Annual and quarterly reports.
- Electronic news kits.
- Executive speeches.
- Significant dates in the organization's past.
- A calendar of major upcoming events.

Some Web sites include audio files for radio actualities, video clips of products in use, PowerPoint presentations, and spreadsheets for financial information.

UP TO DATE AND EASY TO USE

To protect reporters from using out-of-date information, media relations sites need regular attention from practitioners to keep facts, figures, and faces current. Items like biographies and fact sheets should indicate when their most recent update occurred, reassuring journalists that the information is fresh.

Because these pages for the news media should load quickly into an Internet browser, they should look spare, clean and uncomplicated, placing a premium on ease of navigation. A search function can make a Web site easier to use, but it's not a substitute for careful planning in creating and positioning hypertext navigation links.

The news bureau pages should avoid files that load slowly or that are difficult or slow to print through office printers. Some portable-document-format (PDF) files, though preserving the appearance of the original paper document, often are slower in loading, reading, and printing.

The Internet also gives media relations practitioners the opportunity to maintain relationships with reporters through e-mail, but it's a mixed blessing. E-mail has been abused by marketing spammers and lazy public relations practitioners so that reporters may not bother to read your e-mail unless they know you, trust you, and sense news potential in the subject line of your message. The purpose of the subject line is similar to that of a headline: to get attention and convey the essence of a message.

Reporters say that they're unlikely to open an e-mail with attachments because it carries the risk of a computer virus infection.

Research sponsored by the Institute for Public Relations (IPR) found that practitioners and reporters alike said in 2001 that the Internet has led to improvements in news reporting and the practice of media relations.

"Journalists believe the Internet has made their jobs easier and improved the quality of their work," according to IPR's *Magic Communication Machine* report. "Journalists now rate e-mail equal to the telephone as the preferred medium for interviewing news sources. And, journalists report they regularly use the Internet when gathering information for news stories."

NO SUBSTITUTE FOR HUMAN CONTACT

Despite the efficiency offered by the Internet, reporters and practitioners point out that it's no substitute for a trusting relationship. Web sites make facts and figures easily accessible, but tracking down non-routine details still requires human contact. To make stories come alive, journalists need to quote what people—not documents—say, and media relations managers set up the interviews that add depth and humanity to news. Reporters and practitioners need each other.

Bobbie Battista, former host of CNN's *Talk Back* cable program and now a media relations consultant, offered this advice: "Establish a relationship with one reporter at each station or publication. Over time, if you always are honest and straight, rapport will become trust."

The cases in this chapter illustrate the many ways in which organizations interact with media stakeholders, using the controlled media of advertising and publicity materials, focusing on the type of coverage desired, and responding to investigative reporting and documentaries, which may prove uncomfortable and negative. As you probe the cases, seek to identify the public relations problem or opportunity, the methods and tools used to resolve the situation, and how one might evaluate the success or failure of the public relations efforts. Ask yourself these questions: What news values were demonstrated in the stories carried by media outlets? What news values were promoted by the public relations practitioners here? What has been the impact of the shift toward digital, individual media, and what further impacts might be anticipated? What would the practitioners in these cases have wanted their media counterparts to do, or to do differently, and how might they have promoted those alternatives?

ADDITIONAL READINGS

Henderson, David. (2006). *Making news: A straight-shooting guide to media relations.* Bloomington, IN: iUniverse.

Jones, Clarence. (2001). *Winning with the news media.* Tampa, FL: Video Consultants, Inc.

Kent, Michael L., & Maureen Taylor. (Spring 2003). *Maximizing media relations: A Web site checklist.* Rhinebeck, NY: Public Relations Quarterly.

Wade, John. (1992). *Dealing effectively with the media.* Menlo Park, CA: Crisp Publications.

Wright, Donald K. (2001). *The magic communication machine: Examining the Internet's impact on public relations, journalism, and the public.* Gainesville, FL: Institute for Public Relations.

CASE 17. MEDIA INTEREST IN TRANSPLANT DRAMA STOKES ANXIETY IN HEALTH CARE PROFESSIONALS

Jesica Santillan spent most of her childhood in Arroyo Hondo, a sun-baked Mexican village of 400 people surrounded by fields of sugarcane. Located halfway between the Jalisco state capital of Guadalajara and Puerto Vallarta on the Pacific Coast, the village has one paved road and little else in community resources. Arroyo Hondo families have a hard life; many depend on work in cane fields or the local sugar mill, and individuals often earn less than $10 for a 12-hour day.

Jesica's mother, Magdalena, learned early that her daughter suffered from restrictive cardiomyopathy, a condition involving heart muscle stiffness that also affects breathing. No cure for the disease exists, and about 70% of those who develop it die within five years of the onset of symptoms. In most cases, the only satisfactory solution is a heart transplant.

The Santillan family could not arrange transplant surgery for Jesica in Mexico. Desperate and determined, they took their 13-year-old daughter to the United States illegally in 1999 and made their way to North Carolina, where relatives were living.

The family moved into a mobile home in a rural county northeast of Raleigh and began investigating what they would have to do to get Jesica's life-threatening condition corrected. Knowing medical care for Jesica would be far beyond their means (some estimates put the figure at a half-million dollars), the family solicited donations from friends and neighbors, while churches and civic groups put containers in local shops to collect contributions.

Now Near Duke

The Santillans' new Carolina home was only an hour's drive from the Durham campus of Duke University Medical Center, one of the preeminent health care organizations in the United States.

Year after year, *U.S. News & World Report* had ranked Duke among the nation's top hospitals. Separately, Duke specialties such as heart, pulmonary, and pediatrics also earned high rankings on the *U.S. News* lists. The Discovery Channel ran a documentary series, called "Hospital," on the lives of patients and caregivers at Duke Hospital, and *Time* magazine published a cover story on a day in the life of Duke. CBS-TV's "60 Minutes" program profiled a Duke oncologist in 2002. By most accounts, the institution's public relations efforts were highly successful.

The medical center is proud of its reputation—justifiably so. Describing its approach to medicine, Duke says that "patients can count on receiving high-quality healthcare that is delivered with empathy and compassion. The medical leadership that has earned Duke such renown is the result of an innovative approach that stresses multidisciplinary collaboration and a close 'bench-to-

Figure 5.1 During the 2002 holidays, Jesica Santillan posed with her mother, younger sister and brother for a family photo (Photo by Mack Mahoney)

bedside' relationship between clinical care and research that gives our patients access to the very latest treatments."

For Jesica, her family, and friends in North Carolina and Arroyo Hondo, Duke Hospital represented her best chance at life. They were full of hope.

Mack Mahoney Aids Santillan Family

One of Jesica's new friends was Mack Mahoney, a Carolina homebuilder who'd seen her story in a local newspaper. Inspired by her struggle for survival, he organized efforts to raise funds for a transplant operation. Fluent in Spanish, Mr. Mahoney also assisted Jesica's family, whose conversational English was limited, in their discussions with the health care professionals at Duke. Subsequently, he received medical power of attorney to participate in the Santillans' health care decisions.

As Jesica's case attracted the attention of major news outlets in Raleigh and Durham, Mr. Mahoney persuaded one of North Carolina's U.S. senators to help shield the family from deportation while they waited for organs that would be suitable for transplant. The operation, surgeons had decided, would require a set of lungs as well as a heart.

Finding compatible organs for a heart-lung transplant is a long shot. To match an organ donor and recipient, health agencies consider their physical size, blood type, the expected time in transit for the organs, and the recipient's position on the national waiting list. At any time, the national list of individuals awaiting this combination may include 200 names, but the number of heart-lung transplant operations performed in the United States in a single year might not exceed 30.

The United Network for Organ Sharing administers the nation's organ procurement and transplantation network, collecting and sharing information on organ need and availability. The network includes regional organizations that enlist donors and monitor availability.

Transplant Surgery Scheduled

On Friday, February 7, 2003, a Duke surgeon learned from the network that a heart and lungs were available from the New England Organ Bank. He reserved them for Jesica, now 17, who was expected to live only six more months with her own heart. A Duke surgical team flew to Boston to remove the organs and hurry them back to Durham. (Heart and lungs ordinarily must be implanted no more than eight hours after removal.)

Meanwhile, Jesica's surgeon timed his procedures so that he would complete the removal of her organs at about the same time that the donor's heart and lungs arrived at Duke. The coordination itself was successful, but routine tests performed near the end of the surgery disclosed a tragic error. Although the transplant network and Duke both had procedures to ensure blood group compatibility between donor and recipient even before surgery could be scheduled, the safeguards had failed somehow.

The donor's blood group was A, and Jesica's was O. People with blood group O, the most common group in the U.S. population, are universal donors; they can give blood to other groups. However, people in blood group O can safely receive blood or organs only from people in group O.

The operating team finished its work, and the surgeon went immediately to Jesica's parents to tell them of the mistake and its implications. Her body's immune response would attack the incompatible organs as it would an infection, and her only hope of survival would be a second heart-lung transplant using organs from a group O donor. Duke notified the United Network for Organ Sharing that Jesica urgently needed another set of organs.

Figure 5.2 The vision statement of Duke University Hospital is "To be the leading academic health services provider by delivering high quality, innovative responses to society's changing health care needs"

Media Kept in the Dark

Meanwhile, the family, physicians, and the hospital's public relations staff agreed privately that, until more was known about what went wrong, the media would be given only basic reports on her condition. The organ mismatch would remain confidential as the search for a new donor was pressed.

In the days immediately after the operation, the director of the medical center's news office told reporters: "She is rejecting the organs that were transplanted into her." Nothing was said about the error.

Hour by hour, the Santillans and Mr. Mahoney grew more fearful that the girl would die before the transplant network could find a donor in blood group O, and they apparently came to believe that a directed donation—where the family of a dying patient would choose Jesica to receive the organs—was the quickest and best solution. To reach as many potential donor families as possible, a broad public appeal in the media would be needed.

While impatience was agitating those closest to Jesica, Duke's reticence stirred suspicion in news reporters from Raleigh and Durham. Five days after the surgery, some reporters heard privately from Mack Mahoney that the transplanted organs came from a donor with a different blood type, but the media held back those details, apparently unable to verify them.

The director of the medical center's news office told the media: "It's far too early to have definitive answers regarding this case. Any comments now would be speculative. Nevertheless, this patient's sequence of care is under careful review."

News of Error Breaks

Then, Mr. Mahoney openly discussed the organ mismatch on Friday, February 14, after waiting a week for Duke to get results using the transplant network. The first media report of the error appeared the same day. A day later, Duke dodged the truth when reporters asked if the family's version of events was true.

The associate director of the medical center's news office told reporters: "Duke Hospital is continuing a careful review of the sequence of care that she received. That's the only information I have for you. This is all I can say. At this point, our priority is to help Jesica and her family through this difficult situation. We hope a suitable donor can be found."

While Duke remained tight-lipped, the family's account of the surgery gained the attention of national news organizations and received heavy coverage in North Carolina.

Late on Monday, February 17, 10 days after the surgery, Duke acknowledged the mismatch in a public statement given to the media and posted on the medical center's Web site under the headline "Duke University Hospital Implements Additional Transplantation Safeguards." Quoting the hospital chief executive officer, the statement said, "This was a tragic error, and we accept responsibility for our part."

The New England Organ Bank said its records showed Duke was told the donor's blood group at several points in the procurement process, and the information also accompanied the organs on the trip to Durham. Duke did not dispute the statement.

On Tuesday, the organ mismatch story got coverage throughout the day on CNN Headline News and Fox News Channel, as well as on cable's news/talk programs. *The New York Times* was preparing a front-page article for the following day. The Associated Press, Reuters, BBC, and other worldwide news organizations carried reports.

A Second Donor Is Found

Despite the long odds against finding a compatible set of organs for a second operation, the transplant network told Duke near midnight Wednesday that a donor had been identified. Surgery began at 6 a.m. Thursday and finished at 10:15 a.m. At first, Jesica appeared to tolerate the second operation well, but the initial outlook dimmed quickly. She was pronounced dead on Saturday, February 22.

Seventeen days after Jesica's death, the chief executive officer of the Duke University Health System sent a memo to the health care staff offering his perspective on the tragic error and suggesting what the institution might learn from the following events and the attention they received in the media. The CEO, a physician named Ralph Snyderman who also served as Duke's chancellor for health affairs, said the case involved three central issues:

- Medical questions about mistakes and how to prevent them.
- Ethical questions about transplants and end-of-life decisions.
- Communications questions about a patient's privacy rights, needs of the patient's family, and the public's right to know.

"Some have asked, why didn't Duke announce the blood-typing mistake immediately after the first transplant and launch a public appeal for compatible organs?" he wrote on March 11. "One reason is that Jesica's family initially asked us not to. Another reason is that it would not have been appropriate for us to initiate publicity. The organ procurement system used by all hospitals was designed to allocate organs on a fair and equitable basis while considering the degree of need."

A "60 Minutes" Interview

As Duke employees were digesting the memo, Dr. Snyderman and Jesica's surgeon, Dr. James Jaggers, were sitting for videotaped interviews with CBS-TV's "60 Minutes." In a segment that aired March 16, the two physicians and others at Duke recounted the fateful steps that led to the failed transplant.

When journalists in Durham and Raleigh learned that "60 Minutes" was interviewing Duke's top medical officer, some suggested that the medical center was continuing to stiff-arm them. Durham's *Herald-Sun* noted that Dr. Snyderman "still hasn't responded to repeated requests by *The Herald-Sun* for an on-the-record interview about the tragedy," but the CEO and Jesica's surgeon "have granted interviews to CBS '60 Minutes' reporter Ed Bradley."

On the day after the "60 Minutes" broadcast, the medical center's Web site offered this explanation for Duke's decision to welcome the CBS crew: "Because of the widespread publicity regarding this patient, Duke University Hospital felt it important to address some of the complex issues in a nationwide forum. We agreed to participate in a '60 Minutes' story because they offered to address this event in a fair and comprehensive manner."

Acknowledging Mistakes

Dr. Snyderman wrote a reflective op-ed column, published under the headline "Owning Up to Mistakes in Medicine," that appeared April 26, 2003, in *The News & Observer* of Raleigh.

"In order to prevent mistakes, one needs a culture of safety and an openness to identify risks freely," he wrote. "If mistakes or near misses occur, healthcare workers must own up to them promptly and honestly so they can be addressed and corrected. But doing this is extremely difficult because the current environment for litigation encourages professionals to do otherwise."

He mentioned, approvingly, proposed federal legislation that would create a system for voluntary, confidential, nonpunitive error reporting to encourage analysis of mistakes and improvement of patient safety.

"We believe that disclosure of errors in an atmosphere that focuses on solutions, not blame, will make healthcare safer for everyone," he wrote.

QUESTIONS FOR REFLECTION

1. What's meant by a "bench-to-bedside" relationship?
2. What reasons might explain Duke University Hospital's initial decision to provide the news media with reports only on Jesica's condition?
3. The Santillan family and friends decided to pursue a broad public appeal for a second set of organs for transplant. What strategy and tactics would you have recommended?
4. Duke's chancellor for health affairs said the case involved questions concerning a patient's privacy rights, needs of the patient's family, and the public's right to know. How would you rank or balance these three?

Information for this case was drawn from the following: the Duke University Medical Center Web sites at http://news.mc.duke.edu/mediakits/detail.php?id=6498 and www.dukehealth.org/news/default.asp; Avery, S., & Martinez, A. (25 February 2003), "Duke caught in PR quagmire," *The News & Observer*, p. A1; Cheng, V. (19 February 2003), "Duke's image takes a blow," *The News & Observer*, p. A9; Draper, M. (13 February 2003), "Girl's miracle fleeting," *The News & Observer*, p. A1; (30 May 2003), "Duke's amazing PR coup continues," *The Herald-Sun*, p. B1; Eisley, M. (16 February 2003), "Mistake alleged in blood match," *The News & Observer*, p. B1; Fass, A. (9 June 2003), "Duking it out," *Forbes*, p. 134; Grady, D. (19 February 2003), "Donor mix-up leaves girl, 17, fighting for life," *The New York Times*, p. A1; Kirkpatrick, C. (18 June 2003), "Duke Hospital admits to botching transplant," *The Herald-Sun*, p. A1; Snyderman, R. (26 April 2003), "Owning up to mistakes in medicine," *The News & Observer*, p. A19; Weissert, W. (7 March 2003), "Mexican village was ready, but Jesica's funeral not to be," *The Herald-Sun*, p. A10.

CASE 18. FAKE NEWS RELEASE LEADS TO ARREST

The evening shift at Internet Wire in Los Angeles gave routine handling to a request from Porter and Smith PR for distribution of an Emulex Corporation news release. The e-mail message from Ross Porter, with release attached, asked for distribution the following day, Friday, August 25, 2000, at 9:30 a.m. EDT.

Porter's e-mail message used jargon, such as "please bill me as the first release out of the 10 pack," that was familiar to Internet Wire staffers and led them to accept its authenticity. Accordingly, they prepared the release for transmission to the thousands of news organizations and financial analysts reached by Internet Wire.

Teed Up for Trouble

Although the distribution request itself appeared routine, the content of the news release was anything but. It announced that:

- Emulex was revising downward the earnings figures issued earlier in the month.
- The SEC was investigating the company's accounting practices.
- Paul Folino, the Emulex chief executive officer, was leaving.

As predetermined, Internet Wire dispatched the release as stock markets in New York City were opening Friday, and it was soon picked up and passed along by reputable financial news outlets such as Bloomberg News and the CNBC television channel. The price of Emulex common shares, which had closed the previous day at $113.06 on the Nasdaq Stock Market, began slipping, slowly at first and then with gathering speed after Bloomberg published its first headline at 10:13 a.m. EDT. Soon, the news was mentioned on CNBC, Dow Jones News Service, the CBS Marketwatch Web site, and others.

Back at Emulex headquarters in Costa Mesa, California, executives had begun arriving for work about 7 a.m. PDT and were stunned by the plunging share price. The company's recent financial results had been exceptional, and its outlook was promising. Emulex described itself in 2000 as "the world's largest supplier of fibre channel host adapters," devices used by equipment makers such as Hewlett-Packard and IBM in networking applications. In an earnings news release issued August 3, Emulex had trumpeted record levels of revenues and earnings for the company's most recent quarter and reported revenues of $140 million and net income of $33 million for fiscal year 2000, which ended July 2. Emulex CEO Paul Folino indicated that Emulex was well-positioned to benefit from growth.

Trading Halted

Like others at the company, Mr. Folino was shocked to hear about the stock's nosedive when he walked into his office shortly after 7 a.m. Friday and began trying to figure out what could account for it. He soon heard about the news release on Internet Wire and realized that the company was the victim of a cruel hoax. Promptly, he asked authorities at Nasdaq to halt trading in Emulex and protect investors from further effects of the fraud.

In the 16 minutes before Nasdaq suspended Emulex trades at 10:29 a.m. EDT, the price of a common share had plunged from $103.94 to a bottom of $43. Investors who sold shares that morning lost almost $110 million and had little hope of recovering it.

Once trading was suspended, Mr. Folino and others went to work on a news release explaining what had happened and refuting the claims contained in the false release. The rebuttal circulated widely across the Internet and financial news wires, and Nasdaq reopened trading at 1:30 p.m. EDT. By the end of the day, the stock had climbed to $105.75 a share.

Although the stock snapped back quickly, questions lingered about the performance of financial news organizations and their rush to publish without independent verification. At Bloomberg News, an editor said that standard practice calls for a reporter to check with a company before writing a story, but the protocol was skipped in this instance. A Dow Jones News Service editor said that his organization trusts the verification process of electronic-release distribution services, such as Business Wire and PR Newswire, and had received assurances that Internet Wire used a similar procedure.

From the moment the fraud was discovered, Emulex management had wondered who the culprit was and why he or she had done it. Authorities quickly determined that Ross Porter, author of the e-mail that conveyed the false release to Internet Wire, was fictitious, as was the Porter and Smith PR firm. They suspected that someone with inside knowledge of Internet Wire had concocted the hoax to drive down the price of Emulex shares. A drop in price could benefit an investor who had sold Emulex short.

Short Sellers Expect Bad News to Be Good

In investing, most people expect to benefit when good news causes a company's stock price to rise. However, some investors—short sellers—benefit when bad news causes a stock to drop in price. Here's how:

A short seller anticipates, presumably for good reasons, that the price of a certain stock is too high and will fall below current levels. Using a brokerage firm's services, he or she borrows shares from a stockowner and sells them to other investors at the current price. The short seller expects to purchase shares after the price has fallen, replace the borrowed shares, and pocket the difference between the current and future (presumably lower) price.

The practice involves the risk of losing money—potentially a lot of money—if the share price goes up instead of down and the short seller must purchase pricier shares to replace the ones that he or she borrowed and sold.

Investigators Get a Lead

To solve the Emulex mystery, law enforcement authorities began looking for someone who knew Internet Wire's operating procedures and also had been involved in trading Emulex shares. They asked if any employees had recently quit the public relations wire service and were told that Mark Simeon Jakob, a 23-year-old man from El Segundo, California, had left on good terms about a week earlier. From separate sources, they learned that Mr. Jakob had been involved in short selling 3,000 Emulex shares on August 17 and 18, expecting the price to drop below $81 a share.

Mr. Jakob had studied during the summer at El Camino College in Torrance, a two-year institution not far from his home. Soon after classes ended, he quit his Internet Wire job and went on vacation, registering Wednesday, August 23, at the Luxor Resort & Casino in Las Vegas for a three-day stay.

The Luxor is a gambling palace that envelops guests in opulence and fantasy. A 10-story sphinx, taller than Egypt's original, towers above the entrance. The hotel itself, a 350-foot-high pyramid encased in glass the color of onyx, shoots the brightest beam of light on the planet skyward from its pinnacle, and the casino floor below covers almost three acres.

While Mr. Jakob was enjoying what the hotel describes as "accommodations and amenities worthy of Queen Nefertiti herself," Emulex began trading above $100 per share, far more than the $81 price that prevailed when Mr. Jakob borrowed 3,000 shares. On Thursday, the young man's brokerage firm issued a $20,000 margin call, requiring him to place that amount of cash into his account to partially cover the increased value of the shares he had borrowed and sold but had not yet replaced. With Emulex trading above $113 per share, Mr. Jakob faced a potential loss of $97,000 on his short sale if the stock did not come down.

After receiving the margin call, he flew back to Los Angeles and drove to the Library Media Technology Center at El Camino College, though he was no longer a student there. He used the library's computers to draft the fake Emulex news release and open a Yahoo! e-mail account under the name of the fictitious Porter and Smith PR agency. As Ross Porter, he sent the damaging release to Internet Wire, climbed into his car, and drove back to Las Vegas.

Timing Is Everything

At Internet Wire, the staff accepted "Porter's" apparent authority and assumed the release had been verified. Using normal procedures, they readied it for distribution.

Internet Wire was incorporated in 1999, evolving from a similar service started five years earlier. It has emphasized its pricing advantage in competing with the established giants of the electronic-release distribution business, PR Newswire and Business Wire. All three services offer publicly held companies a convenient and dependable mechanism for providing timely and fair disclosure of important news, as required by the SEC.

When a company plans to announce news that might affect an investor's decision on buying or selling its stock, it often provides the release to a service such as Internet Wire a few hours in advance, with instructions to distribute it when notified or, alternatively, at a specific time. Companies often prefer to issue major news outside regular trading hours of the major stock exchanges to give investors time to digest it before acting, sending it either after the market closes for the day or well before it opens in the morning. The Nasdaq Stock Market and New York Stock Exchange, for example, both are open from 9:30 a.m. to 4 p.m. on weekdays.

On Friday morning after the fake Emulex release went out, Mr. Jakob checked financial news sites on the Internet and saw that his plot was succeeding. His release had been used by major news services like CNBC, and the price of Emulex stock was slipping. Using his online brokerage account, he covered his short sales by purchasing 3,000 shares at about $62 per share to replace those he borrowed when the price was around $81. Far from facing a $97,000 loss, he made a profit of about $54,000.

When the price continued downward, Mr. Jakob purchased another 3,500 shares of Emulex for an average near $52, expecting the price would climb again when the hoax was discovered, as it did. He sold these additional shares on Monday at a profit exceeding $186,000.

An Arrest Is Made

An investigation by the FBI, SEC, and U.S. Attorney's office identified Mr. Jakob in a matter of days, and he was arrested on Thursday, August 31. He pleaded guilty four months later to two counts of securities fraud and one count of wire fraud and was sentenced in August 2001 to 44 months in federal prison.

The day before Mr. Jakob's arrest, *The New York Times* scolded Internet Wire, the financial news media, Emulex, and the Nasdaq in an editorial headlined "Caveat Investors."

"Internet Wire has called the perpetrator a 'very sophisticated criminal.' But in truth, the low-cost service and several reputable media organizations dropped the ball; this criminal could have been thwarted with a single phone call. Emulex and the Nasdaq can also be faulted for not reacting more quickly to events. Surely in this day and age investors should not lose billions to fraud simply because California is in a different time zone."

In 2003, Internet Wire changed its name to Market Wire.

Mistaken Story Causes Value Loss Again

In September 2008, a six-year-old *Chicago Tribune* article was posted on the Web site of another newspaper. A securities research firm assumed it was a new story and mistakenly posted a link to it on Bloomberg News, triggering a news alert headline. The out-of-date article noted that United Airlines had filed for bankruptcy. Within one hour, United Airlines shares fell from more than $12 to about $3, causing a loss of more than $1 billion in value. When the false headline was found, United asked Nasdaq to halt trading in its stocks. A correction to the stories was sent out, and trading in the shares resumed about one and one-half hours later. Shares recovered some value by the end of the day but were still down 11.2%.

QUESTIONS FOR REFLECTION

1. Internet Wire faced the challenge of restoring customer trust in its distribution services. What steps would you recommend to rebuild confidence?
2. Though Emulex was an innocent victim of this fraud, were there any precautions that the company might have adopted to prevent or minimize this situation?
3. The Dow Jones News Service said that it has relied on the verification procedures of distribution companies like PR Newswire and Internet Wire to confirm the authenticity of new releases. Do you agree that news organizations have no obligation to check further?
4. What changes would you make in Internet Wire's operations?
5. A six-year-old news article about a United Airlines bankruptcy filing accidentally reappeared as a new news story on September 9, 2008. In less than an hour after the "news" was posted by Bloomberg, the value of United's stock dropped by more than $1 billion. Trading in United shares was quickly suspended, and a correction was issued. What can companies do to protect their integrity from the carelessness of others?

Information for this case was drawn from the following: the Emulex Web site atwww.emulex.com/ corp/index.html; Market Wire Web site at www.marketwire.com/mw/corp_co_overview; (30 August 2000), "Caveat investors," *The New York Times*, p. A22; (8 August 2001), "Defendant in Emulex hoax sentenced," U.S. Securities and Exchange Commission news release; (11 September 2000), "Emulex's swift IR limits bogus release damage," *Investor Relations Business*, p. 1; Ewing, T., Rose,

M., Rundle, R., & Fields, G. (1 September 2000), "E-mail trail leads to Emulex hoax suspect," *The Wall Street Journal*, p. C1; Ewing, T., Waldman, P., & Rose, M. (28 August 2000), "Bogus report sends Emulex on a wild ride," *The Wall Street Journal*, p. C1; Gentile, G. (1 September 2000), "Portrait of a criminal," *The Associated Press*; Glassman, J. (30 August 2000), "Stock hoax should affirm faith in markets," *The Wall Street Journal*, p. A26; (1 August 2001), "Hoaxer is sentenced to 44 months in jail in Emulex Corp. case," *The Wall Street Journal*, p. A4; Maynard, M. (9 September 2008). "A mistaken news report hurts United," *The New York Times*, www.nytimes.com, Mrozek, T. (6 August 2001), "Man who perpetrated $110 million fraud against Emulex stockholders sentenced to nearly four years in prison," U.S. Department of Justice news release; (31 August 2000), "Stock hoax suspect had motive," Wired News, www.wired.com.

CASE 19. BISHOPS, PRIESTS, AND REPORTERS: THE CATHOLIC CHURCH AND MEDIA COVERAGE OF SEX ABUSE SCANDALS

The scandals involving how the Catholic hierarchy dealt with priests accused or suspected of improper sexual behaviors became national news after *The Boston Globe*'s Pulitzer Prize-winning January 2002 series reported that Catholic priest John Geoghan, accused of molesting children in his parishes, had for more than three decades been shuffled from parish to parish rather than being turned over to authorities for prosecution.

Although there had been some coverage of the issue in 1985 when the U.S. Conference of Catholic Bishops adopted policies that were to address how the Church would deal with such troubled priests, renewed media coverage of the issue captured the attention of other reporters, attorneys, Catholic laity, government officials, and self-reported victims across the nation and across the world.

After the series began, similar revelations came from across the country; bishops in Palm Beach, Lexington, Milwaukee, and New York resigned after it became known that priests in their dioceses had also been reassigned rather than turned over to civilian authorities for prosecution. Investigative articles appeared in Dallas and in other Boston newspapers, as well as on ABC and NBC News, and then appeared in newspapers and broadcast stations across the country as self-reported victims came forward, pressing suits and seeking to tell their stories. To help journalists understand developments across the country, The Poynter Institute for Media Studies hosted an Abuse Tracker on its Web site where published stories could be posted for referrals.

Since the scandal became public, more than 225 clergy (of the more than 46,000 U.S. priests) have been taken off duty or have resigned, according to the Associated Press. Six U.S. bishops have resigned in connection with the scandal, and priests and bishops from Australia, Hong Kong, South Africa, Ireland, Poland, and Canada were implicated in either the scandal or cover-ups of sex-abuse cases. *PRWeek* reported in April 2002 that since 1985, the church had paid an estimated $1 billion to resolve molestation charges against its priests.

Church's Response to Stories Varies

The Catholic leadership responded to the media stories and lawsuits in numerous ways, ranging from negotiations to denials to acts of penance. Andrew Walsh, writing in the fall 2002 *Religion in the News*, said, "The American bishops are caught between a Vatican that resists structural change, and a laity and media that want more accountability."

In an April 2002 article in *PRWeek*, James Burnett detailed some of the problems with the church's reaction to the crisis. The church did not use a single spokesperson, but used a variety of local leaders. Different parishes developed and instituted different plans for dealing with past and existing abuse crimes. Church leaders were often too slow to respond when the allegations became public, thereby allowing time for media coverage to set the public agenda.

Some dioceses did make some effort to counter media coverage. The Los Angeles Archdiocese hired crisis communication specialists Sitrick & Co. to help it communicate newly adopted policies dealing with sexual offenders. In the summer of 1997, the Diocese of Dallas, Texas, had hired a public relations counselor to help it respond when it was ordered to pay damages totaling nearly $120 million for harboring a priest who had molested children. The Diocese of Oakland established its Ministry for Victims of Clergy Sexual Abuse; the chancellor of the diocese, Sister Barbara Flannery, acted as spokesperson for the diocese during the crisis.

One example of the church's delayed reactions to intense media coverage: A 76-page report compiled by the Massachusetts attorney general released in July 2003 reported that at least 789 children and perhaps more than 1,000 were abused by 250 priests and other church workers since 1940; the report was based on a 16-month investigation that involved the review of 30,000 pages of church documents and 100 hours of grand-jury testimony. A church spokesperson issued a written statement the afternoon the report was released saying the archdiocese would review the findings over the next few days "before making any further public response."

Anvil Publishing reported that Donna Morrisey, spokesperson for the Archdiocese of Boston, told a March 20, 2003, meeting of the Boston PRSA that she believed she had not been kept fully informed about the clergy scandal in Boston. She said she was only able to admit there had been problems after thousands of documents became public following a court order to open them. The documents detailed the abuses and the church's knowledge of them. She and only one administrative assistant worked to field up to 300 media calls a day during the crisis.

Lay Catholics reported they felt the church had mishandled the crisis, according to results of a New York Times-CBS poll cited in the June 2002 edition of *Baptists Today*. Only 27% of the Catholics interviewed said the leaders had done a good job of handling the issue, although some 63% approved of their parish priest. The poll of 1,172 adults reported that 88% said church leaders should be held responsible for the way they deal with the problem. A group of laypersons within the Catholic Church formed an activist group, Voice of the Faithful, to seek reform.

The Leadership Contemplates Changes

The U.S. Conference of Catholic Bishops did attempt to forge a response to the crisis. The conference assembled in Dallas in June 2002, but *PRWeek* called what ensued nothing less than a "communications circus." More than 700 U.S. and international journalists and numerous activists arrived to cover the meeting. For the first time at such a meeting, laypersons were invited to address the bishops. The bishops released the Charter for the Protection of Children and Young People, which called for local dioceses to form oversight committees to be staffed by laity. Accused priests were to be treated with "zero tolerance."

Kathleen McChesney, a former FBI official, was selected to run the office that would audit U.S. dioceses to determine if they were following the guidelines to prevent abuses. However, the Vatican did not approve the U.S. plan for intervention. Pope John Paul II argued that the "zero tolerance" policy did not demonstrate a belief in repentance or forgiveness, and thus he told the U.S. cardinals to reconsider procedures for dealing with priests.

Catholic bishops met in Washington in November 2002 to consider how they would adapt their plans to the Vatican's orders. This time the conference was more private; Bishop Wilton Gregory, president of the U.S. Conference of Catholic Bishops, would not agree to media interviews until after the discussion and vote. (The group did revise its guidelines to comply with the Vatican's orders.)

Following the U.S. crisis, the Catholic Church of England and Wales released a set of public relations guidelines. The approach called for openness and the creation of a new oversight group, the Church Office for the Protection of Children and Vulnerable Adults.

A U.S. oversight committee was also formed. It was initially headed by former Oklahoma Gov. Frank Keating, president of the American Council of Life Insurers. The committee of laypeople included businesspeople, attorneys, a psychiatrist and psychologist, and former White House chief of staff Leon E. Panetta. The group was asked to issue an annual report.

However, before such a report could be issued, the group became involved in its own public controversy. In May, Los Angeles Cardinal Roger M. Mahony had led the California bishops to pass a resolution saying they would not respond to the committee's surveys that had been designed to assess the extent of the abuse problem in the church. New York Cardinal Edward M. Egan told a council of priests that he would not reveal names of accused priests nor how the cases had been resolved. Keating then gave an interview to the *Los Angeles Times* in which he said the bishops were somewhat like "La Cosa Nostra" in their willingness to cover up wrongdoing. Following that interview, a majority of the 13-person board of laypeople said the comments were inappropriate and that Keating should resign. In June 2003, he did so, which prompted a renewed concentration of media attention on the church.

After resigning, Keating wrote a June 19 *New York Times* op-ed piece in which he outlined his views about the church's future. Acknowledging that he was resigning in order to resume working full time and from frustration over the lack of cooperation from what he called a "small minority of church leaders," he went on to say that he was optimistic that the board's work would be successful. He wrote a "few opponents of the board have said we went too far, engaging in what one resistant diocesan newspaper termed a "witch hunt.'" Keating said a few leaders "turned to their lawyers when they should have looked in their hearts." However, he wrote, the responsibility of the board, church leaders, and laity is to restore "trust in our church. That work continues. With God's help, it will succeed in cleansing the church of a vast stain."

Coverage Continues

Public disclosures about the crisis continued throughout the summer of 2003, as bishops in New Hampshire and Arizona revealed they had signed government agreements indicating there had been some diocese involvement with reassigning accused priests. On a more positive note, in August 2003, following the resignation of Boston Archbishop Bernard Law, Sean O'Malley was appointed as archbishop to provide leadership in Boston where the media crisis had begun. According to *The New York Times*, one of his first actions was to dismiss the attorneys who had been negotiating settlements and to hire an attorney he had worked with earlier to reach settlements with abuse victims in his former parish. Within days, he announced the first concrete settlement of $55 million for 542 victims. The actions were greeted with positive media coverage across the country.

⌒〜
QUESTIONS FOR REFLECTION

1. The scandal offers an ongoing example of the powerful interaction of media, opinion leaders, government, and sources. Identify the priority publics for the U.S. Catholic Church in this crisis. What would have characterized effective communication interactions with each?

2. Journalists covering this story often reflected publicly about their struggles with the ethical and moral ways to report stories involving an organization to which they and/or many readers were deeply committed. What principles should guide such coverage?

3. This crisis involved privacy issues involving priests, victims, and settlements. What principles should guide public communications about such sensitive issues?

4. The Roman Catholic Church is a highly diverse, international organization. What does this crisis imply about the need for crisis planning for such organizations?

Information for this case was drawn from numerous press stories about the crisis, including: Associated Press (13 August 2003), "Files show archdiocese paid $21 million in abuse cases," *The New York Times*; Barnett, D. (18 October 2002), "Vatican rejects U.S. bishops' sex abuse guidelines," Agence France Presse; Burnett, J. (22 April 2002), "Crisis and the cross," *PRWeek*, p. 17; Butterfield, F. (24 July 2003), "789 children abused by priests since 1940, Massachusetts says," *The New York Times*;

Chabria, A. (17 June 2002), "Comms circus ensues as Catholic bishops convene," *PRWeek*, p. 3; Chabria, A. (1 July 2002), "Church starts long journey to PR redemption in Dallas," *PRWeek*, p. 9; Chabria, A. (10 June 2002), "LA archdiocese accused of generating a 'PR snafu,'" *PRWeek*, p. 2; Chabria, A. (2 September 2002), "New cathedral helps rebuild LA archdiocese's reputation," *PRWeek*, p. 2; DePasquale, R. (23 July 2002), "Archdiocese rebuffs reform group," AP Online; Editorial. (12 August 2003), "Boston's exemplary friar," *The New York Times*; Goodstein, L. (13 June 2003), "Bishops uneasy on whom to protect," *The New York Times*; Goodstein, L. (16 June 2003), "Chief of panel on priest abuse will step down," *The New York Times*; Goodstein, L. (11 June 2003), "Louisville archdiocese to pay $25 million abuse settlement," *The New York Times*; Griese, N., ed. (April 2003), "Boston archdiocese spokeswoman: PR was kept in the dark on crisis," Crisis Counselor, www.anvilpub.com/cc_april_2003.htm; Hood, J. (13 May 2002), "Media drawn to church's abuse-prevention program," *PRWeek*, p. 4; Keating, F. (19 June 2003),"Finding hope in my faith," *The New York Times*; Lampman, J. (6 November 2002), "Bishops walk fine line on abuse policy," *The Christian Science Monitor*, p. 3; LeDuff, C. (3 June 2003), "Phoenix bishop admits moving accused priests," *The New York Times*; Lepper, J. (6 May 2002), "US scandal prompts UK church's PR drive," *PRWeek*, p. 4; Nolan, B. (10 November 2002), "U.S. bishops to vote on revised policy,"(New Orleans, LA) *Times-Picayune*, p. 1; Patriot Ledger staff and news services (18 October 2002), "Lawyer: 'It's no surprise': Felt they were sacrificed, priests hail the decision," *The Patriot Ledger* (MA), p. 1; Paulson, M. (27 April 2002), "Law seeks to curb organizing by laity," *The Boston Globe*, p. A1; Paulson, M. (17 December 2002), "Vatican: Final OK given to U.S. bishops; child-protection policy," *The Boston Globe*, p. A39; Pfeiffer, S., & Carroll, M. (23 July 2002), "Law to reject donations from Voice of the Faithful," *The Boston Globe*, p. A1; Religious News Service (June 2002), "Poll shows divide between lay Catholics, church leaders," Baptists Today, p. 16; Rezendes, M., & Robinson, W. V. (23 November 2002), "Church tries to block public access to files," *The Boston Globe*, p. A1; Sims, C. (3 April 2003), "Boston archdiocese is sued by San Bernardino diocese," *The New York Times*; Walsh, A. (Summer 2002), "Bishops up against the wall," *Religion in the News*, 5(2), 8-11; Walsh, A. (Fall 2002), "Scandal without end," and "After the Globe," *Religion in the News*, 5(3), pp. 4-7; White, G. (5 June 2002), "Church may ban future molesters," *The Atlanta Journal-Constitution*, p. A3; and Zezima, K. (21 July 2003), "Massachusetts won't charge church chiefs in sex scandal," *The New York Times*; The Poynter Institute for Media Studies maintained an "Abuse Tracker: A digest of links to media coverage of clergy abuse" on its Web site at www.poynter.org.

CASE 20 *BOWLING FOR COLUMBINE* STRIKES AMMUNITION SALES AT KMART CORP.

Public relations practitioners may have become used to e-mailed questions or phone calls from reporters, and some have faced the glare of video cameras from "60 Minutes" or "Dateline" television reporters. Imagine, however, being called to the lobby of corporate headquarters to respond to a request from documentary filmmaker and social critic Michael Moore to accept the "return" of bullets purchased at a Kmart store that were used in the 1999 Columbine High School shootings in Littleton, Colorado; bullets that were now lodged in the bodies of two students who survived the assaults. Kmart public relations practitioners at the corporation's headquarters in Troy, Michigan, did indeed have to respond to such a request—and used it as an opportunity to announce a change in corporate marketing strategy that turned what could have been a dark and painful media image for the retail chain into a strong statement of corporate social responsibility captured in the documentary *Bowling for Columbine*.

Prize-Winning Documentary Investigates Gun Violence

Bowling for Columbine, which won the 55th Anniversary Prize at the 2002 Cannes Film Festival and the 2003 Oscar for best documentary, was directed by Michael Moore. Moore is well known for his first documentary, the 1989 *Roger & Me*, in which he attempted to question the CEO of General Motors, Roger Smith, about the closing of a GM plant in Flint, Michigan, and for other books and film projects that focus on American corporate and political policies Moore finds unacceptable.

The *Bowling* documentary focuses on gun violence and fear in America. It includes investigations into the shooting of a child by a child in Flint, Michigan, an interview with National Rifle Association (NRA) president Charlton Heston, and gun sales and use in Canada. The emotional climax of the documentary, however, may lie in the two visits Moore makes to Kmart corporate headquarters with the students. The ammunition used by the teenage killers at the high school had been purchased at Kmart.

Film critic Roger Ebert described the documentary's scene this way: "The moment comes at the conclusion of one of the public psychodramas he has become expert in staging, in which he dramatizes evildoing (as defined by Moore) in the way calculated to maximize the embarrassment of the evildoer."

The first visit to the headquarters was brief. A public relations official met with the three. Then, Moore and the young students are shown shopping in a Kmart store where the teens purchase many rounds of ammunition to remove them from the store.

The second visit to headquarters was quite different. That time, a corporate spokesperson announced that Kmart will phase out the sale of ammunition over the next 90 days. The cancellation of ammunition sales was to be completed within three months as stocks were depleted. Company officials made the announcement in June 2001 at a press conference following a four-hour meeting of executives, Moore, and the students. Moore said, "I'm totally, totally stunned by the response from Kmart today."

Company spokesperson Julie Fracker told the Associated Press that the abolition of sale of guns and ammunition was based on marketing concerns and had been under review prior to the filmmaker's visit. "Obviously, we consider ourselves a socially conscious business, but this was a business decision made in the best interests of the company," she said.

Moore said he got the surprise of his life when Kmart officials announced they would quit selling handgun ammunition. Moore told The Sacramento Bee: "It stunned me. You can see it in the film. I'm so used to rejection."

The president and CEO of the National Shooting Sports Foundation commented on the decision for the Associated Press, saying: "It is both unfortunate and inappropriate that Mr. Moore has used media scare tactics to strong arm Kmart into making this decision. All Americans are deeply concerned about the issue of school violence, but to blame a retailer who sells ammunition for causing these tragedies is intellectually lazy and dishonest."

(The documentary came at a time of economic crisis for the chain. Kmart Corp. became the largest U.S. retailer ever to seek bankruptcy protection in January 2002 when it filed for Chapter 11 reorganization. The reorganization strategy included closing more than 320 stores and one distribution center. The corporation emerged from bankruptcy in spring 2003.)

Previous Lawsuits Targeted Gun Sales at Kmart

Moore was not the first celebrity to focus attention on Kmart's gun and ammunition sales. Before the filming of the documentary, celebrity spokesperson Rosie O'Donnell had resigned from her representation of Kmart in protest of its gun and ammunition sales. Activist groups had protested sales at Kmart and other large retailers.

Kmart had faced increasing costs for insurance against liabilities for workers' compensation plans and for gun sales. In 2001, Kmart was ordered to pay $1.5 million in compensation and another $1.5 million in punitive damages to the parents of a Park City, Utah, man who had purchased a 12-gauge shotgun, which he used the next day to commit suicide. The gun was sold by a 17-year-old salesperson who the store's ex-security officer testified had never signed a gun-sales training manual indicating he had read it. In 1993 Kmart had been ordered to pay $12.5 million in damages to a woman left a quadriplegic after being shot by her former boyfriend with a .22-caliber rifle he bought at a Kmart in West Palm Beach, Florida. The ex-boyfriend was reportedly so intoxicated when he purchased the rifle that he could not legibly complete the federal firearms form required by law, and the Kmart clerk completed the form for him, *Business Week* reported. The corporation appealed the ruling.

~

QUESTIONS FOR REFLECTION

1. How may an organization or individual prepare for hostile media inquiries or "ambush" interviews? Conversely, how may an organization or individual benefit from speaking out on issues brought onto the public's agenda by news coverage?

2. Documentaries and films offer a depth of coverage unlike that found in most media. Are there special practices that should be used in this type of media relations?

3. How should corporations respond when faced with liability lawsuits? What responsibilities do organizations assume when they manufacture or sell products that require due care in use?

Information for this case was drawn from the following: Associated Press (2 July 2001),"Kmart pulls handgun ammo from shelves," ESPN.com; Ebert, R. (7 September 2002), "Moore hits corporate target in 'Columbine,'" *Chicago Sun-Times*, p. 22; Hunt, S. (14 September 2001), "Federal jury tells Kmart to pay another $1.5 million," *The Salt Lake Tribune*, www.sltrib.com; Merrick, A. (22 January 2002), "Kmart lays out plans to trim its size, boost efficiency, in bankruptcy filing," *The Wall Street Journal*, WSJ.com; Kmart Corp.(14 January 2003), "Kmart received commitment for $2 billion in exit financing as company prepares to emerge from Chapter 11," PR Newswire; Reid, D. (25 October 2002), "'I'm trying to connect the dots between the local violence and the global violence,' says director Michael Moore of his new film, 'Bowling for Columbine.'" *The Sacramento Bee*. Accessed at www.bowlingforcolumbine.com/reviews/2002-10-25-sacra.php. More information about the documentary is also available at that Web site.

CASE 21. CREATING AND CONTROLLING—A DIALOGUE ON ENERGY: CHEVRON LAUNCHES WORLDWIDE ADVERTISING CAMPAIGN

American drivers of 2004 expressed concern when the average price per gallon for regular gasoline rose above $2 for the first time. Some activists tried to stir up anger against Big Oil by declaring that May 19 would be 'Stick it to them' day—a day when no one would buy a single drop of gasoline.

The energy corporations and various trade associations sought to calm public opinion and present their perspective on energy issues by taking charge of media coverage through controlled issue advertising.

New Chevron Advertising Targets Dialogue about Global Energy Issues

Chevron, with energy operations in almost 180 countries, chose to engage in a long-term information and persuasion campaign using multiple media venues. This July 5, 2005, corporate release explained the energy company's multimedia engagement strategy and tactics:

Campaign Integrates Print, Broadcast and Web; Engages Wide Range of Stakeholders.

SAN RAMON, Calif., July 5, 2005 — Chevron Corporation today launched a new global advertising campaign to raise awareness and encourage discussion about important issues facing the energy industry, including supply and demand, the role of alternative and renewable energy sources and the promise of technology.

"Energy – how we find it, produce it and use it – is one of the critical issues of the 21st century," said Chevron Chairman and CEO Dave O'Reilly. "Energy affects everyone. And we think everyone should be involved in the dialogue about the future of energy."

The campaign will include print and broadcast in major media, and an innovative website, willyoujoinus.com, that will provide a forum for discussion among a wide range of stakeholders. The site currently offers viewpoints on energy by John Elkington, the Chair of SustainAbility and Jerry Taylor, Director of Natural Resource Studies, The Cato Institute.

Vice President of Policy, Government and Public Affairs Patricia Yarrington said, "We developed a campaign that is rooted in the real issues facing our industry. They are issues that affect everyone who has a stake in energy – consumers, businesses, policymakers, environmentalists, educators and political leaders. We think it's a very compelling campaign about a very compelling subject."

The campaign is breaking in major print media on July 5 with advertising focusing on the challenge of maximizing the world's supply of oil and gas. Broadcast spots will focus on key facts highlighting the dynamic balance between supply and demand.

Yarrington added, "Chevron is not attempting to solve the world's energy problems alone, but rather use human energy to bring people together to discuss real issues and to think about developing real world solutions. We are hoping to encourage people to see and understand others' points of view with a goal of moving the debate from entrenched rhetoric to pragmatic solutions. Chevron is optimistic about the future and believes that by asking the tough questions now we can help determine how we will best meet the energy needs of the world in decades to come."

Chevron encourages people to visit http://www.willyoujoinus.com to join in the debate. The website will periodically explore a new energy issue and visitors can voice their opinion and join in the discussion on a message board, managed and monitored by a third party.

The campaign will launch in print, outdoor, online and TV teaser ads in global media targeted at influentials who are involved with leading the energy debate. The ads will appear in publications such as the Economist, Wall Street Journal and Financial Times, on U.S. and pan regional TV such as CNN, BBC Africa, Asia, Middle East and Latin America and in airport locations such as Beijing, Moscow and Washington, DC.

Chevron Corporation is one of the world's leading energy companies. With more than 47,000 employees, Chevron subsidiaries conduct business in approximately 180 countries around the world, producing and transporting crude oil and natural gas, and refining, marketing and distributing fuels and other energy products. Chevron is based in San Ramon, California, USA. More information on Chevron is available at http://www.chevron.com.

Chevron continued using ads to explain its position on energy markets and in January 2007, a two-page advertisement ran in *The New York Times*. The ad showed an executive desk, covered with notes about oil issues and a checklist of corporate philanthropic deeds. Text on the ad indicated that oil prices are due to "a world of rising demand, supply disruption, natural disasters and unstable regimes."

The Foundation For Taxpayer and Consumer Rights, a California-based public-interest group, responded by complaining the ad was deceptive by omission. In a release on PR Newswire, the research director of the foundation said, "Chevron, aside from trying to shift the discussion away from its own behavior in the gasoline market, appears to be intent on quelling any trade regulation that might restrict its dealings with abusive regimes."

"Power of Human Energy" Launches

In September 2007, Chevron launched an expansion of the global integrated marketing campaign with a new focus on the steps Chevron was taking to provide more energy supplies. The campaign, called the "Power of Human Energy," was launched with a new 2:30 minute advertisement on the September 30 broadcast of "60 Minutes." The new ad, titled "Untapped Energy," was created by McGarry Bowen agency and was directed by Lance Acord, the cinematographer from *Lost in Translation, Being John Malkovich* and *Marie Antoinette*. Music for the ad was written by the British composer Paul Leonard-Morgan, and the voice-over was recorded by actor Campbell Scott. Scenes were shot in 22 locations in 13 countries over three months, with real Chevron employees and some actors.

The commercial begins with photos of rainfall, glaciers, and a lighted skyscraper. When the narration begins, other images such as an oil derrick, oil wells and a mass protest are shown. The ad then talks about the employees of Chevron who are working on new options for energy and shows more inspiring images.

Gordon Bowen, creative director and partner of McGarry Bowen, told the *Washington Post*: "You're always looking for a core idea, and the power of human energy was a huge idea for Chevron. We felt strongly that there had to be a message that was not just factual but emotional, that was optimistic about what could be done by human beings."

The launch advertisement was followed by 60-second and 30-second spots titled "The Impossible," "New Frontiers," and "Renewable Energy" that would appear on other U.S. and international programs. The spots would be shown not only on U.S. television, but also in Latin America, Europe, Africa, Asia, and the Middle East.

The Chevron Web site was also revised, with interactive news stories and a global issues section. An interactive game, "Energyville," that allowed people to see the trade-offs from different energy sources used in the game's city was available, drawing more than 150,000 hits in its first three weeks on the website. Chevron says it is designed to help visitors explore the environmental, security and economic impact of energy choices. The blog site, www.willyoujoinus.com, was continued. Chevron reported nearly two million visitors to the site since its 2005 launch.

Reactions to the Campaign

The Foundation For Taxpayer and Consumer Rights again criticized the campaign, arguing in a release that it was a "gauzy, Hollywood-slick $15-million ad campaign to improve its public image," just a strategy to support high profits and delay committing to renewable energy.

Business Week reported that according to TNS Media Intelligence, Chevron, BP and ExxonMobil spent a combined $327 million on advertising in 2007.

The multiple media messages seem to be having a positive impact on attitudes toward the large oil companies, however. A Gallup survey in May 2008 showed that only 20% of those surveyed blamed the oil companies for the $4-a-gallon price for gasoline, down from the 34% in the poll a year earlier.

QUESTIONS FOR REFLECTION

1. What advantages does the use of controlled media such as advertisements and proprietary Web sites offer organizations? What are the drawbacks to such use?

2. Chevron invested in the quality of its broadcast advertising. Again, what are the advantages of producing high-quality advertising? Are there disadvantages to this strategy?

3. The Foundation for Taxpayer and Consumer Rights sought to counter the effectiveness of the ads through publicity releases. What other tactics might they or other groups use to counter the industry ads?

4. What do the choices of advertising placement and content and Web site content tell you about the stakeholders Chevron considers critical?

Information for this case was drawn from the following: the Chevron Web site at www.chevron.com; and Dugan, J. (28 September 2007), "Chevron's $15 million ads, $15 billion stock buyback are PR greenwashing, stockholder appeasement, says watchdog group," Foundation for Taxpayer and Consumer Rights Release, www.prnewswire.com; (23 January 2007), "Group says Chevron's costly, double-page ad deceptive," US Fed News, accessed from PR Newswire, www.prnewswire.com; Halliday, J. (1 October 2007), "Chevron says: Yes, we have humanity; petroleum giant unleashes $15 million push to win over public," *Advertising Age*, p. 8; Mufson, S. (28 September 2007), "Recasting Big Oil's battered image; ads by Chevron and others aim to send positive messages," *Washington Post*, D1; Palmeri, C. (16 June 2008), "Now this really is an oil shock; a new poll says fewer Americans blame the industry for $4-a-gallon gas," *Business Week*, p. 34; Price, S. (28 September 2007), "Chevron announces new global 'human energy' advertising campaign; new campaign to launch with 2:30-minute spot on CBS's '60 Minutes,'" Chevron Release, www.chevron.com; (2 October 2007), "Consumer group blast's Chevron's new ad campaign," CSNews Online, www.csnews.com; (18 May 2004), "Gasoline jumps above $2 a gallon," CNN/Money, accessed at http://money.cnn.com/2004/05/18/pf/autos/gas_prices/index.htm

PROFESSIONAL INSIGHT

MAKING NEWS IN A NEW MEDIA WORLD

David Henderson, author, "Making News: A Straight-shooting Guide to Media Relations" and "The Media Savvy Leader"

We live in a fiercely competitive world where many people and organizations clamber for attention before media that are fractured by the rapid impact of the digital revolution, audience desires, and changing revenue streams.

These are times of national discontent and tremendous change—in the political arena, among demographics, and within our society.

The media, too, are struggling to reinvent themselves, connect with audiences and give their audiences what they want and expect to hear. Today's news business is increasingly opinionated, polarized and salacious, with the driving forces of news leaders locked in competitive struggles to attract audiences and money. The only constant about the news media today is change.

While the practice of media relations in today's environment is challenging, the value of favorable media coverage is often more influential, powerful and lasting than any other tool in an organization's marketing strategy.

Success can be within your grasp when you understand four elements of making news in a New Media world:

- Craft messages that are clear, compelling and honest. Make your messages timely, relevant, and free of jargon and ensure they connect and resonate with audiences on emotional, logical, and factual levels.
- Get to know journalists. Establish trust and working relationships with a handful of influential reporters who are interested in what you have to say. Learn what they need and the difference between a legitimate news story and PR fluff.
- Understand that the old-fashioned practice of relying on press releases to get coverage is folly in today's world, and the least effective way of getting the media's attention.
- Use the diversity of emerging online technology wisely and avoid fads. Only use new tools for communications if they underscore credibility and importance of what you have to say.

Media coverage can boost brand awareness for an organization, prominently position a product or service, provide clear and accurate information in a crisis, and help to right a wrong, among other desired results.

Here's a tip: If you want to control the news angle of a story you are taking to the media, write it first. Draft a story of about 300 to 400 words in length and really work to make it read like a legitimate and timely news story, exactly like something you might want to read in tomorrow's newspaper or an online news resource. Then, when you pitch the story to a reporter, you will have a better focus on how the story elements—the interviews, facts, background information, opposing viewpoints—should come together for the reporter you have approached.

I bet you will find that parts of your own version just may appear in the reporter's final story.

David Henderson is a communications strategist, author and award-winning journalist in Washington, D.C. More information is available at www. davidhenderson.com.

6
Stakeholders: Investors

One of the hottest investment stories of 2004 involved speculation about Google's plan for an initial public offering (IPO) of common stock. Created in 1998 by two Stanford University graduate students, Google quickly replaced Yahoo! as the world's leading Web search site and was handling more than 200 million queries daily when rumors about an IPO began circulating.

Web users knew that Google was technologically successful, but hard information about its performance as a business—its operating and financial results—was unavailable. As a privately owned company, Google was not obligated to share the details with anyone. It did not publish an annual report and did not release news about quarterly earnings.

The Wall Street Journal said that people familiar with the numbers estimated 2003 revenues at $800 million and net income between $100 million and $200 million. Google generated revenues by selling advertising space on its Web pages and by licensing its search technology to companies like Time Warner's America Online.

AN ATTRACTIVE INVESTMENT

If the estimates were correct, the company represented an appealing investment opportunity: its net profit margin exceeded 12% (at least a third higher than the margin of public technology companies at the time), and its usage growth rate was the best in its business segment.

The people who built Google into a valuable property had few avenues to get access to the wealth they had created. Venture capital firms had provided funds for Google's growth. The founders and other employees had devoted their human capital—ingenuity, talent, time, faith—to make the enterprise successful. People had risked cash and careers to start the company, manage it effectively, and earn its top ranking. Now, gaining a financial reward beyond a paycheck would require changing the company from a privately held organization to a public stock corporation with shares trading on an exchange.

The Wall Street Journal and other business media said that investment bankers estimated Google's value at $15 billion to $25 billion. The value, or market capitalization, would be the product of the number of Google shares sold multiplied by the price per share.

INVESTMENT BANKING ADVISORS

Generally, companies had used investment bankers, such as Morgan Stanley or Goldman Sachs, for help in issuing new securities, including IPOs of common stocks. The 2008 whirl of mergers, bankruptcies and bailouts thinned the ranks of these investment advisors and changed the nature of their structures, but public companies will continue to need assistance from surviving advisors who offer expertise in:

- Setting the price at which new stocks will start trading.
- Lining up likely investors in advance.
- Using networks of stockbrokers to market the new securities once they are available.

Investment advisors also help companies prepare the documents they are required to file with the SEC in advance of an IPO. For weeks before a public offering of stock and for weeks afterward, companies face SEC restrictions on what they may say publicly about their operations, their outlook, or their results. This interval is called the quiet period, and its purpose is to restrain exuberant promotion of stocks. It applies to all newly registered securities, not just IPOs. Companies generally avoid publicity during the quiet period and use their Web sites to fully disclose relevant information in dispassionate terms. In investor relations, the quiet period is a sensitive time. Fearful of risking SEC sanctions, practitioners often avoid public statements altogether because the SEC has provided little guidance. The same restraint applies to other functions in public relations, such as media relations and employee communication.

QUIET PERIOD NOT DEFINED

According to the SEC:

The federal securities laws do not define the term "quiet period," which is also referred to as the "waiting period." However, historically, a quiet period extended from the time a company files a registration statement with the SEC until SEC staff declared the registration statement "effective." During that period, the federal securities laws limited what information a company and related parties can release to the public.

Despite the restrictions, the SEC encouraged companies to continue making normal corporate announcements in the ordinary course of business during the quiet period. In 2005, the rules were relaxed somewhat, recognizing the role of Internet communications and the general value of sharing, rather than restricting, information.

When the quiet period is over, companies are free to provide investors and potential investors with as much information as they might need to make a sound decision on whether to buy, sell, or hold securities. Additionally, the commission watches companies closely to ensure that investor information does not frame the facts to emphasize the good news and obscure the bad news. Regulations also govern the minimum amount of information that companies must disclose.

SEC GOALS

The SEC describes its role like this:

> The laws and rules that govern the securities industry in the United States derive from a simple and straightforward concept: all investors, whether large institutions or private individuals, should have access to certain basic facts about an investment prior to buying it, and so long as they hold it. To achieve this, the SEC requires public companies to disclose meaningful financial and other information to the public. This provides a common pool of knowledge for all investors to use to judge for themselves whether to buy, sell, or hold a particular security. Only through the steady flow of timely, comprehensive, and accurate information can people make sound investment decisions.

The commission enforces rules to prevent an inequitable distribution of information that might benefit large or well-connected investors at the expense of smaller investors or those who are less sophisticated. The fair disclosure rule, known as Regulation FD, aims to give everyone an equal chance to gain from stock market opportunities and avoid losses in market declines. According to the SEC, "Regulation FD provides that when an issuer discloses material nonpublic information to certain individuals or entities—generally, securities market professionals, such as stock analysts, or holders of the issuer's securities who may well trade on the basis of the information—the issuer must make public disclosure of that information. In this way, the new rule aims to promote the full and fair disclosure."

INSTITUTIONAL AND INDIVIDUAL INVESTORS

In the United States and many other nations that rely on free-market capitalism to drive the economy, the ownership of stock equities, either directly or through mutual funds, is common. In 2005, Standard & Poor's said an estimate from investment-industry research indicated that more than half of all U.S. households owned shares in companies or mutual funds. The report said that nearly 57 million households owned shares in 2005, up from 40 million in 1995 and

16 million in 1983. Many individuals and families have built up investment portfolios in stocks and mutual funds through 401(k) plans offered by employers. Usually, an employer contributes a certain amount for each dollar that an employee puts into the plan. Some companies offer employee stock ownership programs, using a system similar to a 401(k) plan, that enable employees to buy stock in the employer at a discount.

Investor relations professionals agree that companies now must do a better job of informing individual investors about business plans, performance, and prospects. Many practitioners have been accustomed to focusing their communications efforts on institutional investors. Compared with individual investors, institutional investors are small in number but huge in the volume of shares they own and trade. Institutional investors include pension funds, such as CalPERS (California Public Employees' Retirement System); mutual funds, such as the Vanguard Group; insurance companies, such as Prudential; and similar large financial organizations.

The value of institutional holdings is immense. For example, CalPERs alone owned almost $150 billion worth of stocks in September 2008.

PAYING ATTENTION TO INDIVIDUALS

A report issued by The Conference Board in 2008 said that institutional investors owned more than 76% of the shares of the 1,000 largest U.S. corporations, and pensions funds that manage workers' retirement savings accounted for more ownership than any other group. *Investor Relations Business*, a twice monthly magazine for investor relations and public relations professionals, has said that companies should use their Web sites more effectively to build relationships with their individual investors. "Although individual investors prefer to get information directly from the web site of the company they want to invest in, in many cases the IR section is not up to date," the magazine said.

As you approach these cases, explore these questions: What motivates individuals and investment groups to invest capital in these corporations? What information do investor stakeholders want and need from businesses, and what are the most effective ways for such information to be provided? How can corporations maintain credible relationships with key investors, even during times of crisis or transition? What are some ethical principles that should underlie investor communication?

ADDITIONAL READINGS

Droms, William G. (1997). *Finance and accounting for non-financial managers*. Reading, MA: Addison-Wesley.

Hermann, Keith R. (2001). *Visualizing your business: Let graphics tell the story*. New York: Wiley.

Kurtz, Howard. (2000). *The fortune tellers: Inside Wall Street's game of money, media and manipulation*. New York: The Free Press.

Walton, Wesley S., & Joseph M. Lesko. (2002). *Corporate communications handbook: A guide to press releases and other informal disclosure for public corporations.* New York: Clark Boardman Callaghan.

CASE 22. THE COMMUNICATIONS COMPANY THAT DIDN'T COMMUNICATE: WORLDCOM

In the 1980s and 1990s, under the leadership of CEO Bernie Ebbers, WorldCom grew into the second-largest telecommunications company in America. Then, in 2002, the corporation filed the largest bankruptcy in history after losing more than $120 billion of equity in three years. Ebbers himself was named as part of a $4 billion fraud case.

The story of the company may in essence be the story of its CEO and his interactions with board members and employees. Pai Sarkar, writing in the December 27, 2002, *San Francisco Chronicle*, concluded: "It was just one man, one company, one downfall. But in the grander scheme of men and companies and downfalls, Bernie Ebbers of WorldCom stuck out as a glaring example of what went wrong with corporate America in a year defined by greed and deceit—and the loss of public trust." As such, it illustrates the need for truthful, timely communication with board members, shareholders, employees, creditors, analysts, and regulators.

Bernie Ebbers Builds a Network

Ebbers was a charismatic CEO, known for his personal Christian faith and charity work. Born in Edmonton, Alberta, he was raised in New Mexico where his father was a business manager for a Christian mission. Reports say Ebbers flunked out of the University of Alberta and Calvin College before enrolling at Mississippi College, where Ebbers said his life changed. He graduated in 1967 and went to work as a teacher and coach in a small town south of Mississippi's capital, Jackson. He then founded a small chain of hotels, working with two friends who later sat on the WorldCom board.

In 1983, he and several other businessmen took advantage of the AT&T telephone breakup and started a company that would resell bandwidth, the data-carrying capacity of telephone lines, to small businesses. Sensing an opportunity, he bought 75 companies in the next 15 years. He took his company, Long Distance Discount Service, public in 1989. It was reported that Ebbers boasted that LDDS never grew at less than 16%. He encouraged employees to buy stock options, a practice that would continue throughout his career. His practice of offering large personal loans to key employees for them to buy stock was well known. He also became known as not being involved in the actual operations of the telecommunication industry, but intensely interested in the possibilities for mergers and acquisitions within it.

In the early 1990s, Ebbers began to buy companies that owned fiber-optic lines so that he could move data on his own lines. In August 1994, he bought Wiltel, a Tulsa, Oklahoma, company that owned the fourth-largest fiber network in the United States, and renamed it WorldCom. That enabled him to take advantage of the burst of interest in the Internet during the mid-1990s. By 1997, WorldCom owned 20% of the Internet fiber network, and the corporation grew rapidly. The stock value attracted investors who put all their funds in the one stock. On June 21, 1999, WorldCom stock reached a high of $64.50 per share, and Ebbers was listed by *Forbes* as among the richest men in the world, ranking his personal fortune at some $1.4 billion. Ebbers reportedly enjoyed his wealth. He paid $47 million to buy the largest working ranch in Canada, a half-million acre spread with cattle, a fishing village, and a heavy-equipment dealership.

In 1997, Ebbers made his boldest move, buying MCI's residential and long-distance telephone service for $37 billion. Yet, he sold off its Internet network when faced with federal regulators' protests about fears of limiting fiber-optic competition. A 1999 attempt to merge with Sprint was blocked by American and European regulators. At the same time, growth in the Internet dropped by 90%. Stock values dropped. Ebbers' fortune also dropped; he was forced to sell three million shares of his WorldCom stock in October 2000 to raise $84 million to pay off investment debts.

Ebbers prepared to sell more shares in January 2002. The WorldCom board, afraid that such a sale would drop the stock value even further below the $9.80 it was then valued at, loaned Ebbers more than $400 million at 2.2% interest.

Reaction to this arrangement created outrage among other investors who had seen their share values drop precipitously. In March, the SEC requested information related to WorldCom accounting procedures and loans to officers. Ebbers resigned in April, taking with him an annual pension of $1.5 million.

Investigation Reveals a Tangled Network of Accounting

That might have ended the story, had not an investigation revealed other problems. Reports in June 2002 documented that the company had designated $3.8 billion as assets instead of expenses to cover a net loss for 2001 and the first quarter of 2002, and chief financial officer (CFO) Scott Sullivan was fired. Following an internal audit, WorldCom admitted inflating earnings over a period dating back to 1999. For example, it claimed that the costs of leasing telephone lines from other companies were capital investments. It would later argue in court that its internal accounting records were so confused that it was impossible to verify or balance them. (Subsequently, the SEC asserted the improper bookkeeping had totaled more than $9 billion.) The corporation began laying off thousands of employees in June 2002.

The new CEO, John Sidgmore, held a press conference in Washington to apologize for the accounting scandal. He said the company hoped to avoid bankruptcy. However, WorldCom filed for Chapter 11 bankruptcy on July 21, 2002, listing $103.9 billion in assets. The corporation owed $67 billion to its creditors. Shares traded at less than $1 by the end of that year. Sidgmore resigned as CEO in September.

Two corporate officers, including CFO Scott Sullivan, were charged in August 2002 by federal officials with securities fraud and filing false statements with the SEC. In September, the corporation's former controller pleaded guilty to three counts of conspiracy, securities fraud, and making false statements to the SEC. The next month, the former accounting director pleaded guilty to two counts of securities fraud and conspiracy.

Rebuilding a Network for Leadership

In November, WorldCom reached a settlement with the SEC. In December, federal judges approved the hiring of new CEO Michael Cappellas, former Hewlett-Packard president. The board of directors was also reformed after six directors resigned. The board had included the former head of the National Association of Securities Dealers, the chairman of Moody's Investors Service, and the dean of the Georgetown University Law Center, along with several company chief executives. A report compiled by a committee of new directors said the previous board had been given information that "was both false and plausible." The board had met infrequently, sometimes only three to five hours a year.

Its operations changed dramatically after the reorganization. New CEO Capellas told the *Washington Post*, "The company has already implemented many of the proposed corporate reforms, but we know we have to do even more to regain public trust." *The Washington Post* described how the new board considered buying remaining shares of Digex Inc. It had been given a detailed report from its investment bankers and a presentation from the corporate development team, and the Digex chairman was available to answer questions. The directors then met privately to discuss the $18 million purchase. The *Post* said the last time WorldCom had considered a deal to buy the corporate "parent" of Digex, Intermedia Communications, the board approved the $6 billion acquisition after only 35 minutes of discussion. Board members had been given no written material to review, and some were not told that such an acquisition was due for a vote until two hours before a convened conference call.

The federal monitor, Richard C. Breedon, a former SEC chairman, required the new board to meet at least 10 times a year and to replace at least one member every 12 months. No director would be allowed to remain on the board more than 10 years. With the exception of the CEO, directors were required to have no outside ties to the company. Pay for directors was boosted to $150,000 a year, but they were required to take at least 25% of the salary in stock. Stock options would not be granted to employees and board members. Instead, they would be granted restricted company shares with rules limiting when they could be sold. The cost of the stock grants would be included in profit-and-loss statements.

The reformed corporation took out a full-page advertisement in leading U.S. newspapers in December 2002 to offer what it called a "Summary of Progress." The ad's headline proclaimed, "WorldCom Wants You To Know: From governance to finances, quality of service to customer commitment, we've made significant progress. And we're just beginning." It touted the hiring of a new CEO and new independent board members, the generation of more than $1 billion in cash and available financing, the meeting of service benchmarks, and its ability to retain customers and to attract new ones. More information, the ad said, would be available on the corporate Web site at www.worldcom.com/update.

By April 2003, WorldCom announced a reorganization plan to erase most of its debt and to rename itself after its long-distance unit, MCI. Headquarters for the corporation would be moved to Ashburn, Virginia. The corporation agreed to pay investors $500 million to settle civil fraud charges and a $750 million settlement with federal regulators. According to the *Washington Post*, the corporation emerged from bankruptcy with $4.6 billion in cash. MCI was acquired by Verizon in 2005.

In August 2003, Ebbers was arraigned and charged by the state of Oklahoma on 15 fraud counts. He pleaded innocent to the charges. Four other executives were charged by the state. In March 2004, Sullivan pleaded guilty to criminal charges. On March 15, 2005, Ebbers was found guilty of conspiracy, securities fraud and seven counts of making false filings to the SEC and was sentenced in July to 25 years in prison. He appealed the decision, but a federal appeals court upheld his fraud conviction in July 2006.

QUESTIONS FOR REFLECTION

1. Working with a powerful CEO can pose challenges for public relations practitioners and others responsible for communicating truthfully within and outside a corporation. What practices might have addressed some of these challenges successfully?

2. How much knowledge of sound business practices is required for the effective practice of investor relations by public relations professionals?

3. How do corporations faced with such scandals regain public trust?

Sources for this case include: Catan, T., Kirchgaessner, S., Ratner, J., & Larsen, P.T. (19 December 2002), "Before the fall: How, from the outset, Bernie Ebbers' character and business methods sowed the seeds of disaster," *The Financial Times*, p. 17; Cohn, D., & Herera, S. (28 August 2003), "Former WorldCom CEO Bernie Ebbers to turn himself over to Oklahoma authorities next week to face charges of fraud," CNBC Business Center; (4 September 2003), "Former WorldCom CEO pleads not guilty," *Washington Post*, p. E2; Glovin, D. (29 July 2006), "WorldCom founder on brink of prison as conviction upheld," *The Atlanta Journal-Constitution*, p. F3; Hilzenrath, D.S. (16 June 2003), "How a distinguished roster of board members failed to detect company's problems," *Washington Post*, p. E1; Reuters and washingtonpost.com (5 August 2003), Timeline of history of WorldCom, www.washingtonpost.com; Rovella, D. (13 August 2003), "Enron, WorldCom chiefs may never be charged," *The Sun* (New York), p. 9; Sarker, P. (27 December 2003), "Year in Review: People in crisis: WorldCom Unravels; Ex-CEO Bernie Ebbers flew high, fell hard and took the telecom giant with him," *San Francisco Chronicle*, p. B1; Staples, D. (1 August 2002), "God, markets, mergers and money: Part I: Edmonton's Bernie Ebbers rose from milkman to herald of the new economy," *Ottawa Citizen*, p. F2; Stark, B. (28 June 2002), "WorldCom begins laying off employees," ABC News "World News

Tonight"; Stern, C. (8 September 2003), "Hoping to shed a scandal," *Washington Post*, p. E1; Stern, C. (6 November 2002), "SEC case against WorldCom grows," *Washington Post*, p. E1; Stern, C. (16 September 2003), "WorldCom tells of snarled records," *Washington Post*, p. E1; and (16 December 2002), "Summary of Progress," WorldCom Advertisement, *The Atlanta Journal-Constitution*, p. C5.

CASE 23. APPEARANCES OR SUBSTANCE: WHICH IS MORE IMPORTANT?

Martha Stewart built a successful international business on the canons of style. Through her books, magazines and television programs, she taught a mostly middle-aged, middle-income audience how to prepare foods that look as great as they taste, how to color-coordinate bath accessories for highest appeal to eye and touch, and how to furnish the family room so that it unites functionality and fashion.

Her focus on perfecting domestic details and controlling each element of graceful living invited parody and lampooning on late-night television, but it also made her popular with millions and made millions of dollars for her, as well. Just when she reached the pinnacle of success, she seemed to forget how much appearances count or, perhaps, how easily appearances are misinterpreted.

Raised in a New Jersey family of six children, Martha began her business career as a stockbroker after graduating from Barnard College. Later, she set up her own catering business and won a reputation for staging parties of insuperable taste. From this experience, she wrote *Entertaining*, a book that has sold more than a half-million copies since its first printing in 1982.

Buying Her Own Magazine

Working with Time Warner, she launched *Martha Stewart Living* magazine in 1991 and built up its circulation as editor. In 1997, she bought out her corporate partner's interest and gained control of the publication. At about the same time, Kmart began selling a wide selection of Martha Stewart-brand merchandise that ranged from bath towels to garden trowels. By then, the Martha Stewart media empire had grown to include a syndicated newspaper column, regular

Figure 6.1 Newsweek magazine put Martha Stewart on its cover when a federal investigation of insider trading began

appearances on CBS-TV's "Early Show," her own cable television programs, and more.

The business grew around her personal interests, her talents, her public personality, a winning smile, and dogged determination. She worked extraordinarily hard and received a queen's reward when her company went public in 1999. The IPO of common stock in Martha Stewart Living Omnimedia Inc. began trading at $18 a share on October 19 and raised $149 million in equity capital. On the day of the IPO, Ms. Stewart was present at the New York Stock Exchange to see her company's stock symbol, MSO, appear on the Big Board for the first time. The stock soon rose to $36 in the euphoric securities market of 1999 before settling into the $20s.

Here's how the company has described itself:

> Martha Stewart Living Omnimedia Inc. is a leading provider of original how-to content and products for the home. We leverage the well-known "Martha Stewart" brand name across four business segments—publishing, television, merchandising and internet/direct commerce—and provide consumers with the how-to ideas, products and other resources they need to raise the quality of living in and around their homes. Our two primary strategic objectives are to provide our original how-to content and information to as many consumers as possible and to turn dreamers into "doers" by offering our consumers the information and products they need for do-it-yourself ingenuity—the "Martha Stewart" way.

The Company Martha Keeps

Three months after the IPO, *Business Week* published a cover story on Stewart and her triumphs. The magazine pointed out that the company, though known by its famous founder's name, was led by a management team of broad experience and deep talent. The president was a former McKinsey & Company consultant and Cablevision Systems Corporation executive. The editor-in-chief had worked for *The New York Times Travel & Leisure* magazine. The creative director had been a publishing executive before joining Stewart in 1990. The chief financial officer had led an IPO at a recording company. Altogether, the staff consisted of more than 400 people with bright ideas about cooking, crafts, holidays, weddings, babies, and other essentials of the domestic arts.

Yet, Martha was the face, voice, and inspiration known best by customers, investors, and the media. The brand was Martha Stewart, and she was the brand. The two were truly inseparable. Conveniently, the linked identity offered a ready platform for expansion into new media ventures and markets. In 2000, *Business Week* pointed out that it also represented a risk.

"While the company is now playing up other talent—and taking out massive insurance policies on its ubiquitous chief—Stewart remains the walking, talking personification of her brand," the business weekly said. "No wonder investors are worried about the fate of their stock if Stewart should, say, choke on a bad batch of butter cream."

A Promising Financial Performance

Investors may have worried about overreliance on Martha Stewart's image, but MSO shareowners certainly relished the company's early financial performance. For the company's first full year of operation as a publicly traded entity, the 2000 annual report listed revenues of $285.8 million dollars and $37.3 million in income before income taxes. Revenues were 23% higher than the preceding year's, and income before income taxes was up 63.3%. Overall, prospects looked delicious.

A stock analysis posted on The Motley Fool Web site (www.fool.com) in May 2001 echoed the upbeat rhythm for the company, but it, too, noted the risk of hitching your future to a single star. "What happens to the company when there's no Martha?" the author asked. "This is a risk investors should weigh heavily, but I feel her spirit will live on years after her departure."

Like *Business Week*, The Motley Fool pinpointed the source of the risk, but neither divined its true nature. It wasn't Martha's inevitable exit that presented the problem but rather her imminent entanglement in a prolonged stock scandal and her method of dealing with it. To some, she appeared arrogant in avoiding questions about the problems, contradicting her axiom that appearances count.

The public first became familiar with the issue when news broke on June 6, 2002, that federal investigators were looking into her sale of ImClone common shares on December 27 of the preceding year.

ImClone Systems Inc. was a small biotechnology company with a promising new cancer drug under review at the Food and Drug Administration (FDA). On December 26, the ImClone chief executive, Samuel Waksal, learned that the FDA was likely to reject the drug, an action sure to hurt the value of his company's stock. In violation of federal securities regulations, Dr. Waksal attempted to sell his shares before news of the rejection became public and, according to the SEC, warned his daughter and father to do the same.

Martha Stewart, who owned about 4,000 shares of ImClone, was a good friend of Dr. Waksal. She sold out her investment at $58 a share on the same day that the Waksals sold large blocks of shares. After the stock market closed the following day, news about the FDA rejection was released to the public for the first time. The stock dropped to $46.46 when trading resumed. By selling ahead of the news, Ms. Stewart received about $43,000 more than she might have a few days later—a year's income for many families but not a large sum for such a wealthy businesswoman.

An Insistence of Innocence

A congressional subcommittee began investigating suspicious trading in ImClone stock and learned about Martha Stewart's sale of shares from the drug company's attorneys. Phone records of Ms. Stewart, her broker, and Dr. Waksal were examined for evidence that information might have been passed along illegally. The records showed that Ms. Stewart had returned a call from her broker, sold her stock, and then placed a call to Dr. Waksal's office and left a message asking him to call her back, which he did not do.

Ms. Stewart told her company's staff, board members, and large shareholders that she had done nothing wrong, and she answered questions about the transaction. She issued a statement on June 12 to say that she had no inside information on ImClone and sold the stock under conditions prearranged with her broker. She said they had agreed to sell if the price dropped to $60. In fact, *The Wall Street Journal* acknowledged that she cooperated—up to a point.

"Although early on, Ms. Stewart provided a detailed explanation of her stock trade, she hasn't elaborated publicly since investigators started questioning her story," the newspaper said. The questions stemmed from inconsistencies between Martha's version of events and those of others involved. The *WSJ* article's headline read, "Martha Stewart: Project for July Is Image Repair." Other publications also focused on her public relations dilemma. A *New York Times* headline said, "Stewart's Image Woes Hurt Shares of Company," and the *PR Reporter* newsletter devoted its front page to her on July 15, 2002, under this headline: "Martha Stewart—Another Casualty of Plummeting Public Trust in Business."

Bad Company in Business Headlines

As the newsletter headline suggested, disclosures about her timely stock sale first appeared in a season where headlines about big-business misbehavior had become commonplace. Senior executives at Enron, Arthur Andersen, WorldCom, Adelphi, Global Crossing, and other companies had gained media attention for the use of misleading, and in some cases illegal, financial devices. Reports suggested that Stewart might be another business bigwig with something to hide.

As the news media pressed harder for answers, Stewart grew firmer in resisting them. She dodged reporters by using a private entrance and service elevator when they staked out a building where she was scheduled to appear. During her regular culinary appearance on "The Early Show," Martha kept chopping vegetables when the show's anchor posed questions about the ImClone trade. Her reply was, "I want to focus on my salad."

Martha Stewart Living Omnimedia hired a strategic public relations firm at the end of June to help with the new distractions caused by the media attention, and Stewart got a lot of unsolicited public relations advice in the news columns, as well. Some of the kibitzers told her to go public and fight back. Others said a public fight would simply cause more damage. Some suggested that she tell everything and hold back nothing. A few said no one could know the best course to take.

In the month after Martha Stewart's name was linked to the ImClone scandal, MSO shares lost 39% of their value, dropping to $11.67 on July 3.

A Bad Situation Gets Worse

One year after Martha Stewart was first linked to the ImClone investigation, a federal grand jury indicted her on five criminal counts of securities fraud, conspiracy, and making false statements. In a separate civil case, the SEC charged her with insider trading.

Ms. Stewart relinquished her posts as chairman and chief executive officer at her company but remained a member of the board of directors and assumed the title of chief creative officer. The day following the indictments, she took out a full-page ad in *USA Today* asserting her innocence and launched a personal Web site, www.marthatalks.com, on which she offered an open letter responding to the charges. It said:

To My Friends and Loyal Supporters,

> After more than a year, the government has decided to bring charges against me for matters that are personal and entirely unrelated to the business of Martha Stewart Living Omnimedia.
>
> I want you to know that I am innocent—and that I will fight to clear my name. I simply returned a call from my stockbroker. Based in large part on prior discussions with my broker about price, I authorized a sale of my remaining shares in a biotech company called ImClone.
>
> I later denied any wrongdoing in public statements and in voluntary interviews with prosecutors. The government's attempt to criminalize these actions makes no sense to me. I am confident I will be exonerated of these baseless charges, but a trial unfortunately won't take place for months.
>
> I want to thank you for your extraordinary support for the past year—I appreciate it more than you will ever know.

The Web site turned out to be quite popular. It got two million hits on the day it appeared and logged nearly 13 million within its first six weeks of existence. In the same period, more than 60,000 visitors used its interactive features to offer messages of support.

Yet the ongoing investigation and media attention hurt the financial performance of Martha Stewart Living Omnimedia. In the first half of 2003, the company lost $3.58 million, compared with a profit of $6.51 million in the first six months of 2002. In a statement accompanying the earnings figures, the company suggested a gloomy prospect. "We believe that the Martha Stewart

Living core brand will continue to be under pressure until resolution of Martha Stewart's personal legal situation," the statement said.

Suspicions Engendered

From the day that Martha Stewart's name first appeared in news accounts of the ImClone episode, some people, friend and foe alike, suspected that Stewart's gender was partially responsible for attracting the attention of federal prosecutors. They pointed out that she had competed aggressively in an arena usually dominated by men, that she had acquired a reputation as a demanding and successful leader, and that she fought back defiantly rather than retreating demurely. Perhaps to neutralize such claims, the U.S. Attorney responsible for the case appointed a woman as lead prosecutor, and the federal prosecution succeeded. On Friday, March 5, 2004, a jury of eight women and four men found the business executive guilty of obstructing justice and making false statements to government investigators about the sale of ImClone stock. Ten days later, she resigned from her positions as chief creative officer and a director of the company and assumed a new title as founding editorial director.

Ms. Stewart served her short prison term and then returned to work with Martha Stewart Living Omnimedia. In August 2006, she reached a settlement with the SEC on the insider-trading accusations and paid a fine of $195,000, although she neither admitted nor denied wrongdoing. Within a year, the company's share price recovered and its financial results improved.

QUESTIONS FOR REFLECTION

1. Some public relations practitioners said that Martha Stewart should have apologized for bad judgment, even if she did nothing illegal, as soon as insinuations of inside trading surfaced. Would such a course have saved her reputation?

2. How can a company that seems inseparable from its founder—such as Martha Stewart, Oprah Winfrey, Bill Gates or, in an earlier time, Walt Disney—protect itself from a catastrophe that might befall the human symbol of the company?

3. Martha Stewart mostly avoided the media for more than a year after federal investigators took an interest in her affairs. What would you have advised her to do during this period?

4. Some people said that interest in Martha Stewart's problems was an example of schadenfreude, a German word meaning malicious satisfaction in the misfortune of others. Do you agree?

Information for this case was drawn from the following: the Martha Stewart Living Omnimedia Web site at www.marthastewart.com; Martha Stewart's personal Web site www.marthatalks.com; Brady, D. (17 January 2000), "Martha Inc.: Inside the growing empire of America's lifestyle queen," *Business Week*, p. 62; Cohen, L. (7 July 2003), "U.S. wants 'gender card' out of Stewart case," *The Wall Street Journal*, p. C1. Hays, C., & Pollack, A. (4 July 2002), "Stewart's image woes hurt shares of company," *The New York Times*, p. C1; (15 July 2002), "Martha Stewart—Another casualty of plummeting public trust in business," *PR Reporter*, p. 1; Rose, M. (2 July 2002), "Martha Stewart: Project for July is image repair," *The Wall Street Journal*, p. B1; Thomas, L. (8 august 2006), "Stewart deal resolves stock case," *The New York Times*, www.nytimes.com; and Trigg, M. (8 May 2001), "Martha Stewart Living Omnimedia; A stock for Mom," The Motley Fool, www.fool.com

CASE 24. A HABIT OF ACTIVISM

Sister Patricia Daly, a member of the Sisters of St. Dominic of Caldwell, New Jersey, is in the habit of using the power of stock ownership to lobby U.S. corporations. She and her colleagues at the Tri-State Coalition for Responsible Investment characterize an emerging and powerful type of investor who seeks to affect corporate actions through investor resolutions and shareholder voting.

Sister Daly committed to the convent right after graduating from college in 1976. She taught at a Catholic high school in New Jersey but soon became interested in corporate management practices.

She told the *Chicago Tribune* that a labor dispute at J.P. Stevens & Co. textile mills, the story eventually portrayed in the film *Norma Rae*, drew her to her first stockholder activities. The nuns in her convent owned some Stevens shares in their retirement portfolio, which entitled them to attend the shareholder annual meetings. At these meetings, Daly says she met others who were interested in pressuring the companies in which they owned stock to address critical social issues. She became her order's representative on the Tri-State Coalition for Responsible Investment; she later also worked with the Christian Brothers Investment services.

Daly explained to *The New York Times* that she did not select the investments for the convent's retirement accounts, but that she was responsible for noting those who could be encouraged to improve. Describing her work, she said: "The Dominicans are an order of preachers. I do it in boardrooms, and those kind of inner arenas. It's not always public preaching. But preaching is really the mission."

Interfaith Center for Corporate Responsibility

As her interest and energies began to focus more and more on responsible investing, she became executive director of the Tri-State Coalition and, later, its representative on the Interfaith Center for Corporate Responsibility (ICCR), a group of almost 300 faith-based institutional investors with a portfolio of more than $100 billion in value. The ICCR uses the power of that portfolio to gain the attention of corporations through involvement in shareholder meetings, resolutions and lobbying.

The ICCR states on its Web site that it "seeks to offer a moral voice—grounded in faith-based beliefs—to corporations and religion institutions. Building upon more than thirty years of experience, ICCR members combine the approach of organized engagement and dialogue as we partner with others working in socially responsible investing in order to affect a more just economic order and a more peaceful world." It identifies issues ranging from the environment to sweatshops to violence and the militarization of society to diversity as areas of ICCR involvement.

Activist Shareholders

Such shareholder involvement is becoming more common. Under current SEC policy, one who has owned stock in a corporation for at least a year can submit a shareholder resolution. More than 1,100 proxy resolutions were filed in 2007, and almost one-third of those related to social issues.

However, proxy resolutions are usually not binding on the corporate board of directors, so their influence may not be direct. But they may make it possible for dissident shareholders to express their views through the language chosen for the resolutions. Their introduction may also present opportunities for proponents to make argumentative presentations to the board of directors who attend shareholder meetings.

Not all activist investors have religious or social-justice motivations. Some, like legendary investor Carl Icahn, are eager for increased profitability or for different leadership. The June 11, 2007, *Business Week* noted that companies as diverse as Home Depot, Blockbuster and Aflac have responded to shareholder initiatives on some critical management issues. Yet a growing number of investors, in formal groups or through dedicated money-management accounts, want their faith or ethical commitments to determine how they invest.

Describing her personal approach, Sister Daly told the June 12, 2005, *Chicago Tribune*: "I don't use the God card. I'm not saying I'm speaking for Jesus here. But if people see the Dominicans and the Jesuits on a shareholder resolution, they're going to say, 'These are people with some credibility.'"

GE's Reaction

Such involvement from the religiously motivated shareholders has not always been welcomed. In one example, the *Chicago Tribune* reproduced part of an exchange between Sister Daly and then General Electric CEO Jack Welch during the 1998 GE shareholders' meeting originally published in *Harper's*. For years, Sister Daly and her colleagues had lobbied for GE to clean up the PCB contamination it had caused in the Hudson River and other plant locations.

According to the *Tribune's* recounting, Daly compared GE's denials of the harms caused by PCB to those of the CEOs of tobacco companies who had testified that cigarettes were not harmful.

Mr. Welch replied: "That is an outrageous comparison…"

Daly: "Mr. Welch, I am sorry, but we need to have the independent scientific community decide this, not the GE scientific community."

Welch replied: "Twenty-seven studies, 21 of them independent, have concluded there is not correlation…You have to stop this conversation. You owe it to God to be on the side of truth here."

Daly: "I am on the side of truth…"

Yet in 2006, after 10 years of shareholder resolutions introduced by the Tri-State Coalition, General Electric did disclose the $800 million it had spent on PCB-related matters from 1990-2005 cleaning up three sites, some $122 million spent on public relations and lobbying, $2.1 million on governmental relations, and $86.6 million in legal costs. An ICCR release quoted New York Attorney General Elliot Spitzer: "I applaud Sister Pat Daly and the Tri-State Coalition for Responsible Investment for their efforts to obtain full disclosure from GE."

Other Results

Some other examples of Sister Daly and her group's successes:

- In December 2006, a group of auto industry companies including Ford, General Motors, Johnson Controls, DaimlerChrysler, Exel, Honda North America and Yazaki announced they would collaborate to improve the working conditions for those employed by their suppliers. ICCR had promoted this for more than five years.
- In May 2008, Ford announced that it would become the first U.S. auto company to reduce by at least 30% the greenhouse gas emissions from its vehicle feet. The Sisters of St. Dominic and 14 other members of the Interfaith Center had filed the shareholder resolution. In a May 27, 2008, ICCR release, Sister Daly said: "Ford has set the bar at a high level for the auto industry. It has done the hard work of scenario planning and developing models to insure future profitability and reduced emissions." She called on General Motors to follow suit. Her group and other supporters filed a similar resolution to be considered by shareholders at the 2008 GM annual meeting.

During a May 2, 2006, presentation on environmental stewardship for the Center for American Progress, Sister Daly acknowledged that many within corporations share her group's priorities and concerns:

Some of the work over the years, I think it appears that some of the faith communities have attempted to demonize some of the corporations. I think especially on this issue, and in many others…once we get beyond and actually get in the door, all right, it's truly an honor to work with people who come at these concerns not just for the business health of that company, but are really driven by many, many other values and are committed to working within the corporation to bring about a really new day that this company will be responsible and will contribute to a sustainability as we look at development in the future.

And Sister Daly, her coalition and many others will continue to press for that type of investor-management partnership.

QUESTIONS FOR REFLECTION

1. Why would corporations encourage all shareholders to be actively involved? Why might they discourage such involvement?
2. What communication tools and practices would help activist shareholders be effective? How might they attract media coverage?
3. Evaluate the practice of the coalitions described in this case. What advantages and risks are present when an individual or group joins with others of similar interests?
4. Do shareholders bear ethical or moral responsibility for the actions of corporations in which they own stock?

Information for this case was drawn from the following: the Web sites of the Tri-State Coalition for Responsible Investment at www.tricri.org, and The Interfaith Center on Corporate Responsibility at www.incr.com; and The Center for American Progress (2 May 2006), "Climate and culture: religious perspectives on environmental stewardship," www.americanprogress.org/events/2006/5/b593305ct2249681.html; Dougherty, G. (12 June 2005), "Face of faith-based investors a nun CEOs are recognizing." *Chicago Tribune, Business* p. 1; ICCR (28 May 2008), "After Ford takes historic step, GM faces shareholder vote next week seeking a comparable plan for a major cut in greenhouse gas emissions," Release, www.iccr.org/news/press_releases/2008/pr_gm05.27.08.htm; ICCR (4 December 2006), "Faith-based investors applaud the automotive industry's collaborative project to advance workplace human rights," Release, PR Newswire, www.prnewswire.com; Investrend (11 January 2006), "Religious shareholders force GE to disclose millions spent to delay PCB cleanups," M2 FinancialWire, www.m2.com; McGregor, J. (11 June 2007), "Activist investors get more respect," *Business Week*, www.businessweek.com; Slater, D. (12 August 2007), "Resolved: public corporations shall take us seriously," *The New York Times*, www.nytimes.com; Wray, R. (5 February 2007), "God and mammon on her side," *The Guardian*, www.guardian.co.uk/business.

CASE 25. HEWLETT-PACKARD SEEKS TO PLUG LEAKS WITH A SECRET INVESTIGATION

Leaks from Hewlett-Packard's board of directors' meetings led to a 2006 investigation of the private phone records of board members, two employees—including its corporate spokesman—and nine journalists, including at least one reporter from *The New York Times*, three from CNET, two at *The Wall Street Journal* and three at *Business Week*. The investigation also resulted in the resignation of two members of the board of directors and its chair.

HP Investigates Press Leaks

The HP investigation was prompted when an article posted on CNET, a technology news Web site, offered information about an HP board meeting that could only have come from someone at the meeting. The Associated Press said the offensive information was the quote, "By the time the lectures were done at 10 p.m., we were pooped and went to bed," describing a meeting of HP directors at a spa in California.

HP had experienced some difficult issues that had garnered a great deal of media scrutiny. In 2002, a merger with Compaq Computer had involved eight months of contentious shareholder debate, and the 2005 resignation of chairman and CEO Carly Fiorina, who acknowledged differences with the board had influenced her decision, suggested continuing problems.

Perhaps that is why the chair of the HP board, Patricia C. Dunn, then ordered an investigation. She hired an outside firm to look into where the leaks were coming from—and to whom the information was being leaked. The firm she hired employed outside investigators who apparently engaged in a practice known as "pretexting" to get access to private phone records as part of the search.

"Pretexting" occurs when someone finds personal information online or by other means and then uses it to pretend to be the person to access other personal accounts. For example, someone might use Social Security numbers to access phone or bank records. It is against federal law to "pretext" to obtain financial information, and the Federal Trade Commission and the Justice Department say it is illegal to use "pretexting" to obtain phone records.

The investigation pointed to board member George A. Keyworth II, who was the longest-serving board member. Results of the investigation were revealed at a board meeting; Keyworth was then asked to resign and would not. Another board member, Thomas J. Perkins, did resign immediately because he objected to the way the investigation had been conducted and his fellow board members had been treated.

Perkins then conducted his own investigation with AT&T, which confirmed that his phone records had been disclosed to a third party who had used the last four digits of his Social Security number in January. Perkins then requested that the FTC, FCC, and Justice Department investigate the surveillance of the directors. He insisted the corporation reveal to the SEC that he had resigned in disagreement, which is required by law, which eventually led to the public disclosure of the investigation and its methods. Keyworth resigned from the board in September.

The Investigation is Investigated

On September 6, HP did disclose to the SEC that it had hired an outside consultant who had used "pretexting" as part of the probe and that the California Attorney General was investigating the techniques used.

On September 12, *Business Week* reported that HP issued a statement explaining that it did believe that director Keyworth's discussions with the CNET reporter had been intended to further HP's interests, as Keyworth had maintained. Keyworth had apparently often been asked by the public relations staff to meet with reporters on behalf of the corporation.

The next day, responding to the controversy, board chair Dunn sent a message to all HP employees. According to AP reports, she told them: "I extend my sincere apologies to those individuals who have been affected. What happened here is contrary to HP's values and business practices. And for that I will always be deeply sorry."

The House Energy and Commerce Committee held hearings about the matter in September 2007. The 10 witnesses from HP who were asked to appear didn't testify, citing a Fifth Amendment right against self-incrimination. According to *The Philadelphia Inquirer*, the committee did release documents that indicated the investigation cost HP about $325,000, with more than $51,000 used to have personal phone records checked. Background checks on HP's media-relations department cost $6,435.

Media Respond to the Investigation

The New York Times responded to news of the investigation in a statement from attorney David McCraw. In the September 8, 2006, edition of the paper, he stated: "We are deeply concerned by reports that the rights of one of our reporters were violated…We expect as an initial step that H.P. will make a prompt and full disclosure of what took place in regards to our reporter."

In the same *Times* story, CNET spokesperson Susan Cain stated, "These actions not only violated the privacy rights of our employee, but also the rights of all reporters to protect their confidential sources."

Hewlett-Packard spokesperson Michael Moeller told *The New York Times*, "H.P. is dismayed that the phone records of journalists were accessed without their knowledge."

At a news conference held September 22, CEO Mark Hurd said, "I extend my sincerest apologies to those journalists who were investigated and to everyone who was impacted."

Consequences of the Investigation

Dunn resigned as chair of the board of directors and was replaced by CEO Hurd. Felony indictments were filed in October 2006 by California's Attorney General against Dunn, a former senior lawyer at HP, and three consultant investigators who had worked on the case for HP. Four charges were included: identity theft; unauthorized access to computer data; using of false or fraudulent pretenses to obtain confidential information from a public utility; and conspiracy to commit each of these. The charges against Dunn were dismissed in March 2007, and the judge in the case ruled that charges against the others would be dismissed if they completed community service and made any restitution required by September 12.

A civil suit filed by the state was settled, and Hewlett-Packard paid $14.5 million in fines and agreed to other changes in practice.

In February 2008, *The New York Times* and three *Business Week* journalists agreed to a financial settlement with HP. Terms were not disclosed. *The New York Times* donated money from the settlement to several journalism groups, including the Center for Investigative Reporting and the Investigative Journalism Program at the University of California, Berkeley.

~

QUESTIONS FOR REFLECTION

1. Relationships between directors and corporate executives should ideally be based on mutual trust and respect. How would you advise CEO Hurd to improve the communication and trust among these groups at HP?

2. This case illustrates the sometime contentious relationships between reporters and the businesses they cover. How would you suggest Hewlett-Packard seek to repair relationships with the media in the aftermath of this incident?

3. HP also chose to investigate two of its public-relations employees to see if they were the source of the leaks. What impact do you think such an investigation might have on internal relations at the corporation?

4. Media leaks can become problematic for corporations and other organizations. To what length should businesses go to uncover leaks within their organizations? What legal and ethical tactics and strategies might be taken within organizations to prevent such leaks from occurring?

Information for this case was drawn from: Associated Press (6 September 2006), "Hewlett-Packard says California attorney general investigating board leak probe," Associated Press Worldstream; Darlin, D. (5 October 2006), "Ex-head of HP is charged in spying case," International Herald Tribune, p. 1; Darlin, D. (8 September 2006), "Hewlett-Packard spied on writers in leaks," *The New York Times*, www.nytimes.com; Darlin, D. (7 September 2006), "Leak, inquiry and resignation rock a boardroom," *The New York Times*, www.nytimes.com; Guglielmo, C. (4 October 2006), "HP paid $325,000 to spy on its directors," *The Philadelphia Inquirer*, p. C3; Kaplan, D.A. (15 October 2007), "HP may face civil charges," *Newsweek*, www.newsweek.com/id/45239; Kaplan, D.A. (21 August 2007), "Intrigue in high places," *Newsweek*, www.newsweek.com/id/37886; Kaplan, D.A. (21 August 2007), "A playbook for the HP hearings," *Newsweek*, www.newsweek.com/id/37880; Konrad, R. (6 September 2006), "HP probing directors' phone records to investigate leaky source," Associated Press Financial Wire; LaMonica, M. (9 February 2005), "Fiorina steps down at HP," CNET News, http://news.cnet.com; Lawton, C., Searcey, D., & Young, S. (7 September 2006), "H-P faces probe over handling of board leaks," *The Wall Street Journal*, pp. A1, A18; Richtel, M. (14 February 2008), "Hewlett-Packard settles spying case," *The New York Times*, www.nytimes.com; Robertson, J. (22 September 2006), "CEO expected to address leak probe as HP stock falters," Associated Press Worldstream; Robertson, J. (22 September 2006), "HP chair resigns amid fallout from boardroom leak probe, succeeded by CEO Hurd," Associated Press Worldstream; Sandovel, G. (9 October 2006), "Dunn, Fiorina lash out at HP board," CNET News, http://news.cnet.com; Woellert, L. (25 September 2006), "HP's most trustworthy man; e-mails obtained by *Business Week* show that George Keyworth was considered a key part of Hewlett-Packard's media relations team," Business Week Online, www.businessweek.com/technology/content/sep2006/tc20060926_264939.htm.

PROFESSIONAL INSIGHT

INTEGRATED COMMUNICATION AND SHAREHOLDER WEALTH

Linda Kelleher, executive vice president, National Investor Relations Institute

Public companies exist to increase their shareholders' wealth. From this simple premise flows a complex web of activities and interactions within a public company that are designed to achieve the stated goal. The human resources (HR) department recruits the most qualified employees; product development designs a superior product; marketing produces highly targeted promotional campaigns; sales signs on new customers; accounting prepares the financial statements; revenues and earnings increase, and the company's stock price rises, right?

Missing from this simplistic view are many of the company's communications activities. In the traditional model of the well-oiled public company profit machine, HR communicates with employees, marketing and sales advertise and pitch products and services to prospects, a public relations (PR) department communicates with the media, and an investor relations (IR) department communicates with the investment community. These separate departments tend to operate as individual silos, not necessarily coordinating or even communicating with each other.

The clear danger in this traditional approach is that the messages may be out of sync: the HR message to employees differs from that conveyed in marketing ads, which vary from the PR and IR messages, and so on. Today, employees tend also to be customers and investors. Customers are often investors, and investors do copious due diligence into companies in which they invest. Mixed or conflicting messages to any or all of these stakeholders damage a company's credibility and reputation, the well-oiled profit machine sputters, and the stock price suffers.

More and more of today's public company executives recognize that reputation is a strategic asset that takes years to build, but can be lost overnight. They recognize, too, that despite the disparity of their audiences, their message must be unified—that through *integrated communication* they gain strategic advantage over their traditional-minded competitors. They know this because of recent studies that have, for example, shown that a quarter or more of a company's stock market value is attributable to intangibles like reputation.

What is integrated communication? It is the convergence of internal and external corporate communication functions—investor and public relations, as well as employee, marketing and corporate communications. Intentionally designing the corporate communications function to incorporate all communication enables a company to realize benefits. Message unity contributes to management credibility, the keystone for corporate success. An integrated approach facilitates cross-marketing opportunities. Message consistency ensures all audiences form appropriate expectations, which is especially critical in the investor community when a mistaken perception can lead to the loss of billions of dollars of market value in an instant.

While still a relatively new concept, more of today's top executives are turning to integrated communication to set expectations, burnish corporate reputations, improve credibility and enhance sales. Efficient capital markets, through which corporate executives and employees monetize stock options and shareholders increasingly rely on for retirement wealth, depend on access to timely and accurate information. And so, with information at the nexus of corporate performance and shareholder wealth, corporate executives looking for success either embrace the significant benefits of integrated communication, or ignore them at their peril.

Linda Y. Kelleher was named executive vice president of the National Investor Relations Institute in 2007. NIRI is a professional association of corporate officers and investor relations consultants responsible for communication among corporate management, the investing public and the financial community.

7

Stakeholders: Members and Volunteers

Of all stakeholder relationships, those that nonprofit organizations have with members or volunteers may be at the same time the most tenuous and the most necessary. Stakeholders who enter into a relationship with a nonprofit group, whether it is an alumni association, a professional group, or a social service agency, usually have some need or goal that motivates their joining, donating, serving, or attending. Yet that need or goal is usually self-directed, meaning that if it is not satisfied or supported, the individual will find another source for satisfaction or motivation. Similarly, most, if not all, membership- or volunteer-based organizations have needs or goals as well. To address their missions, most often the need is financial, with the organization heavily dependent on donations to maintain activities or services. The need may also be for staffing, where, in essence, the volunteers are functioning as quasi-employees of the organization. Such great pressures may tempt organizations to exploit donors, volunteers, or clients or to forego truthful disclosure when puffery or evasion may bring quicker returns.

MUTUAL TRUST, MUTUAL NEEDS AND INTERESTS

The relationships between such organizations and their stakeholders are best maintained when they are founded on mutual trust, built and maintained through meeting mutually recognized needs and interests. Organizations with a clear sense of their mission and an articulation of how the stakeholders are aligned with that mission are the most likely to succeed in building those types of relationships. However, no matter how lofty the expressed mission and purpose statement of an organization may be, the most pertinent factor in determining an ongoing relationship is found in satisfying the donor's, volunteer's, or member's multiple motivations, as well as the overall objectives of the group. For example, donors may be highly sympathetic to the mission an organization has to offer, say, support services for cancer patients in their area. An altruistic desire to help those in need may drive donors to offer financial support.

Yet, donors may also be highly motivated by the need to obtain documentation of their giving so they may use it to reduce income tax liabilities, or they may be motivated by the desire to gain recognition for their donations as when a building or center is named in their honor. Such multiple motivations are to be expected—and indeed encouraged. Individuals are far more likely to continue a costly relationship such as this when they are given multiple incentives or rewards. The public relations pay-off for "catching someone doing good" may also serve as incentive for recruiting others to awareness or activity.

Practitioners may face the challenge of balancing their interactions with members or volunteers who have offered different levels of support to the organization. On a practical note, practitioners will need to develop ways of expressing appreciation for large and small levels of support so that neither group feels slighted, while also maintaining ways for both groups to offer input and feedback. Organizations also are dependent on increased involvement. Donors who may have offered initial small gifts or pledges, for example, may later become major donors or may become active volunteers. Volunteers may become so committed to the service or mission of the organization that they invest not only their time and talents, but also their financial resources. Individuals who find their own involvement to be rewarding will also become great ambassadors for the involvement of their friends or associates. Everyone in such an organization will benefit if the expressed and unexpressed motivations of donors, members, and volunteers are recognized, acknowledged, and authenticated by leadership within the organization.

COMMUNICATING WITH VOLUNTEERS AND MEMBERS

Practitioners are often charged with the details of developing and deepening relationships between members and volunteers and organizations. This may entail the detailed work of maintaining data files with names, addresses, and personal histories. The tracking may also involve recognition, matching levels of involvement with appropriate rewards: receipts, thank-you letters, certificates, plaques, T-shirts, pins, invitations, and even planning annual special celebrations.

The task of informing these stakeholders may also fall to the practitioner. Print and digital newsletters, direct mail, magazines, Web sites, personal visits, telephone calls, meetings, and special events may all be used by practitioners to ensure that members and volunteers are kept up to date about the activities and accomplishments of the organization. If the relationship is to deepen, such regular and personal contact is vital.

However, it is also critical for the practitioner to devise means for soliciting input from the stakeholders so that it does not appear that they are exploited for the resources they can bring with them to the organization. Such methods may be informal: debriefings after a special project or event, or occasional visits by a representative board. For example, many colleges and universities maintain alumni councils that gather once or twice a year to plan alumni events but also to respond to questions or to ask questions of administrative leaders. The growing popularity of e-mail and social networking has made it easier for organizations to design links from a Web site for questions or comments to be directed to public relations or management personnel, or for those who are committed to similar causes to link together in an electronic community. A Facebook group of volunteers may provide a great opportunity for personal networking but also for practitioners to gain new perspectives on the opinions, beliefs, and attitudes of those actively participating.

More formal methods for stimulating input and feedback may also be used. Surveys or focus groups may yield important results. In-depth interviews are also helpful in obtaining the opinions and attitudes of stakeholders. Members or volunteers who are empowered to affect change by offering their insights will be far more likely to continue the relationship than those who are not allowed to become part of the strategic enterprise of the organization. However the feedback and/or input is generated, sharing some of that with other members or volunteers underscores the seriousness with which the practitioners and management are considering it. Having a "letter to the editor" section in the organization's magazine or a question-and-answer period at monthly or quarterly meetings with responses stressed and demonstrated are just some ways that management may demonstrate its commitment to the two-way communication flow.

SPECIAL CONCERNS

The relationships are not always positive or easy. Some membership groups become so closely knit that they are not open to newcomers or to input from newcomers. Balancing organizational commitment, which is a positive attribute of these relationships, with a need to maintain openness may demand action from the practitioner. For example, what orientation is offered to newcomers? Involving veterans in that process may help demonstrate the need for inclusion.

Occasionally, some gifts of involvement, time, or money come with implicit or explicit conditions. Practitioners may need to lead management to establish and then should publicize policies concerning such gifts and the like before sensitive situations develop.

Policies for recruiting and involving members and volunteers need to be developed to help manage other issues as well. Will volunteers be required to complete specialized training or have a formal background check? The organization may need to establish standards for dependability and performance; even though the volunteer is not an official employee, some method may be needed to ensure that each individual meets the requirements of the various tasks. Legal issues involving liability and privacy should also be addressed. Using the image of a volunteer or member in a publication may require signed consent, for example, and certainly using the image of a nonprofit's client might require such. Membership organizations may need very detailed descriptions as to who qualifies. If there are educational or geographic or accomplishment requirements, for example, they need to be publicized clearly.

Practitioners and their organizations should also have policies that address the ethical and legal concerns of clients or volunteers. For example, how may the service accomplishments of a health care organization be publicized without invading the privacy of clients or patients or their families? In a litigious culture, volunteers or the organization may require specialized education about the legal issues involved in their activities. Agencies that solicit donations for children or other protected groups may need policies regarding volunteer access to knowing the identities or other private information about those in the groups. One temptation in fund raising may be to overly emotionalize those who benefit from the donations. In a nonprofit environment filled with organizations that may all have equally worthy missions and yet must vie against each other for the available time, money, and effort of volunteers and members, practitioners may find the competition so tough that it may be easy to argue that the end justifies the means. However, whether the practitioner is one within a nonprofit organization or one within an agency contemplating charitable pro bono work, ethical practice would be characterized by a commitment to contextually truthful presentation of information that treats donors and the recipients of services with the same levels of dignity and respect.

The cases in this chapter explore the relationships of donors, volunteers and the nonprofits that depend on their support. Several cases raise issues of law, ethics and responsibility, others provide examples of public/private partnerships. As you research these cases, ask yourself: What motivates lead members of the public to become involved? Are the nonprofits' relationships with their key stakeholders consistent with their missions? How can these stakeholders work together even more effectively to accomplish their common purposes?

ADDITIONAL READINGS

Austin, Erica W., & Pinkleton, Bruce E. (2001). *Strategic public relations management. Planning and managing effective communication programs.* Mahwah, NJ: Lawrence Erlbaum Associates.

Bonk, Kathy, Henry Griggs, & Emily Tunes. (1999). *The Jossey-Bass guide to strategic communications for nonprofits.* New York: Jossey-Bass.

Kelly, Kathleen S. (1996). *Effective fund-raising management.* Mahwah, NJ: Lawrence Erlbaum Associates.

Radtke, Janel. (1998). *Strategic communications for nonprofit organizations: Seven steps to creating a successful plan.* New York: Wiley.

CASE 26. DESIGNATED DONATIONS? THE AMERICAN RED CROSS AND THE LIBERTY FUND

September 11, 2001: Virtually every household in the United States and millions across the globe shared in the fear, the anger, the disbelief, and the sorrow resulting from the terrorist attacks on New York City and Washington, D.C. Many wanted to do something to reach out to the thousands of victims and their families and to offer assistance to those who were actively giving support.

Creation of the Liberty Fund

The American Red Cross quickly responded to the disaster and perhaps just as quickly created the Liberty Fund, a special opportunity for donations that would go to support the aid and recovery efforts. The creation of a special fund was unexpected. Traditionally, when soliciting funds, the Red Cross had asked donors to give to its Disaster Relief Fund where money raised could be used in connection with whatever disasters arose. By the end of October, the Liberty Fund had received $547 million in pledges.

The Associated Press (AP) reported that the Red Cross had spent more than $140 million on terrorism-related efforts. Nearly $44 million was used through the Family Gift Program to help cover the costs of housing, food, child care, and other expenses for more than 2,200 affected families in New York and Washington. *The Toronto Star* reported on November 7 that victims' families had received an average of $25,000 for three-months' living expenses from the fund, meaning that only about one-third of the amount raised in the Liberty Fund had gone directly to victims and their families. The AP said about $67 million was spent on immediate disaster-relief needs such as shelter, on-site food, on-site counseling, and other support for victims' families and rescue workers. More than $11.5 million went to blood-donor programs, $14.7 million to nationwide community outreach, and another $2.5 million to indirect support costs.

Too Much Support?

There was just one problem. The Red Cross said it did not require all the money in the Liberty Fund to address the needs. Red Cross CEO Bernadine Healy reported that $200 million of the fund would be used to support other Red Cross efforts, an announcement that spawned a negative uproar and prompted two congressional hearings. When donors found out that up to half of the Liberty Fund was going to be used to support other projects, national reaction was swift. Some people felt they had been misled. They had given money believing it would be used to support the victims or the survivors of the disasters, and they wanted the funds to be used in that way.

The uproar led to changes at the Red Cross. Dr. Healy resigned as CEO on October 26, citing differences with the governing board. She was allowed to keep the title of president until the end of 2001.

Harold Decker, who had served as the organization's deputy general counsel since February 2001 and general counsel since September 2001, was named interim CEO in October. One of his first actions was to announce that as of October 31, the Red Cross would cease soliciting donations for the Liberty Fund. Contributions received from that point on would be added to the group's Disaster Relief Fund unless donors specifically targeted the Liberty Fund for their donations. Accounting firm KPMG was hired to audit the Liberty Fund.

In the November 14, 2001, release announcing the change, Decker said:

> Americans have spoken loudly and clearly that they want our relief efforts directed at the people affected by the September 11 tragedies. We deeply regret that our activities over the past eight weeks have not been as sharply focused as America wants, nor as focused as the victims of this tragedy deserve. The people affected by this terrible tragedy have been our first priority, and beginning today, they will be the only priority of the Liberty Fund.

David T. McLaughlin, chair of the Red Cross Board of Governors, said in the release:

> The people of this country have given the Red Cross their hard-earned dollars, their trust and very clear direction for our September 11 relief efforts. Regrettably, it took us too long to hear their message. Now we must change course to restore the faith of our donors and the trust of Americans and, most importantly, to devote 100 percent of our energy and resources in helping the victims of the terrorist attacks.

Former Senate Majority Leader George Mitchell was named as the "independent overseer" of the fund in January 2002. The former senator had become known for his leadership in the negotiations to foster peace in Ireland and in the Middle East. He was charged with helping to develop a plan for use of the Liberty Fund monies. Mitchell led the group to declare that 90% of the $360 million dedicated for victims would be spent by the first anniversary of the attacks, with the remainder to be earmarked for long-term aid.

The Red Cross also created a "Celebrity Cabinet" in February 2002 to promote its work. Celebrities such as actors Jennifer Love Hewitt and Jane Seymour and Mets catcher Mike Piazza were included in the first group.

New guidelines for the Liberty Fund were developed. Families who had members killed or seriously injured in the attacks were to receive financial support through the Family Gift program for one year, an extension of the initial three-month funding period. The remaining needs of the families would be studied, the Red Cross said in a November 2001 release; it may be that financial support would be needed even longer. The names of the 25,000 families it had supported would be shared in a database with other relief agencies in an effort to help coordinate relief.

In addition to its decision to extend longer-term help to victims' families, the Red Cross said it would charge operating costs for the Liberty Fund and services, such as the toll-free information lines, to the interest earned on the fund balance, rather than directly to the fund itself. An additional 200 caseworkers were being hired, and more full-time staff members were moved to the Long-Time Disaster Recovery Unit.

The Red Cross said it expected to spend about $300 million in 2003 to further these efforts, and the remaining $200 million-plus would be held in trust for later help to victims. The Red Cross said it was also contacting the victims of the postal-anthrax attacks and that it had already given money to the families of three anthrax victims.

The Changes Prompt Praise and Criticism

According to a Red Cross news release on November 14, 2001, the Oversight and Investigations Subcommittee of the U.S. House Energy and Commerce Committee endorsed the Red Cross's decision to use all the Liberty Fund donations to support the needs of people affected by the terrorist attacks. Appearing with the Red Cross officials, committee chair Rep. James C. Greenwood (R-Pa.) was quoted on National Public Radio's (NPR) "All Things Considered" endorsing the changes. He said this was a "first-rate response" from the group.

Other members of the Oversight Committee promised continuing scrutiny. Rep. Bart Stupak (D-Mich.) said the news conference alone was not enough. He told "All Things Considered" on NPR: "This is really just the beginning of it. We will continue our oversight of the American Red Cross. We'll continue to make sure that donors' intents and wishes are followed through."

Reacting to the controversy, Daniel Borochoff, president of the American Institute of Philanthropy, a charity watchdog group, told Knight Ridder Washington Bureau reporter Kevin Murphy, on November 15, 2001, that when the Red Cross set up the Liberty Fund, "The message in most people's minds was that 100 percent would go to victims' families and relief work." The earlier decision to use the fund to help support other Red Cross efforts may offer a lesson, however. "People understand the important role the Red Cross plays in disaster relief, but I think it will lead to some healthy skepticism. It won't be enough for them to say, 'give us some money for this disaster.' People will want to know how much do you really have, how much do you need, what are you doing with it?"

Paul Clolery, editor-in-chief of the *NonProfit Times*, a bimonthly trade paper, told Knight Ridder, "It is the first time I know of that they set up a separate fund, and therein was their huge mistake." Before when they responded to disasters with appeals, "They always couched it in phrases like 'for this and other disasters,' which is the correct way because you never know how much money you are going to need."

Lasting Changes at the Red Cross

Following this controversy, the Red Cross said it would remove references to a specific crisis from its advertising, and that it would make a public announcement at the point when it had received enough money to cover a relief effort. A system for double-checking to ensure that designated gifts are used where the donor intended would also be instituted, NPR reported in June 2002. According to a June story in *The Atlanta Journal-Constitution*, all disaster-related appeals would contain this statement: "You can help the victims of (this disaster) and thousands of other disasters across the country each year by making a financial gift to the American Red Cross Disaster Relief Fund, which enables the Red Cross to provide shelter, food, counseling and other assistance to those in need."

Donations to the general Disaster Relief Fund also dropped in the months following the terrorist attacks. Chief financial officer Jack Campbell told the AP in October 2001 that the disaster fund held only about $26 million as of September 30, whereas its target goal had been about $57 million. In March 2002, *The Dallas Morning News* reported that the Wise Giving Alliance of the Better Business Bureau had removed its seal of approval for the Red Cross, saying it would not be restored until the charity demonstrated it was meeting all standards for good management.

However, Alliance president Art Taylor commended the changes in fund-raising announced in June by the Red Cross. He was quoted in *The Atlanta Journal-Constitution* in June, saying, "We believe that donors, beneficiaries and the charity itself all benefit when there is a clear understanding of how donations will be used."

Giving to chapters across the country was affected by the controversy. "There are 1,100 chapters across the U.S., and we're all suffering to some degree from the national negative publicity about the organization," Greg Hill, director of communications and marketing at the Dallas chapter told Todd Gillman of *The Dallas Morning News*, "and whether it's justified or not doesn't matter." The St. Louis chapter cut 14 jobs and closed two offices after a drop in donations, and chapters from North Carolina to Maine reported troubles in fund raising. At the national headquarters, some 30 communication and marketing department employees were expected to be laid off by summer 2002, according to *PRWeek*, and a hiring freeze was in place while an internal reorganization was being led by interim CEO Decker.

Yet by March 2002, Red Cross national spokeswoman Devorah Goldberg told *The Dallas Morning News*: "It's obviously settled down quite a bit…Controversies come and go. We respond to more than 67,000 disasters every year. We're still there, we're still serving communities nationwide."

In August 2002, the Red Cross named Rear Admiral Marsha Evans as CEO. Evans had been heading the Girl Scouts of the USA. Darren Irby, the Red Cross director of external communications, told *PRWeek* in August 2002: "Some people criticized us for not being as up front as we could be about where their donation was going, so we took a real hard look, and our commitment now is to be the leader in transparency and accountability." Irby said future tactics included clearer and simpler statements about how donations will be used because most Americans don't understand the work of charities.

He also said recruiting more third parties to speak for the organization and better cross-training of volunteers would help. "All we can do is be a leader in responding to the lessons we learned, and hope that other nonprofits will learn from that," Irby told *PRWeek*.

Yet, controversy arose again in spring 2003 when tax documents released by the Red Cross showed that during her last six months of employment as CEO and president of the Red Cross from July through December 2001, Healey had received some $1.3 million in deferred compensation, almost $300,000 in salary, an additional $228,929 in severance pay, $50,000 in expense allowances, and $5,622 in benefits. The documents showed that her chief of staff, Catharine "Kate" Berry, who was fired 11 days after Healy's resignation, received $73,602 in salary and benefits, $132,509 in severance pay, and $403,473 in deferred compensation during that time period. The compensation Healy received during the last six months of 2001 was more than twice what she had received during her first 22 months at the Red Cross and exceeded the highest salary of $690,000 listed by *The Chronicle of Philanthropy*'s October 2002 report, which said 34 of 282 large nonprofits paid their CEOs more than $500,000.

Other September 11-Related Charities Also Come Under Criticism

The Red Cross was not the only charity to be questioned about its disbursement of terrorism-related donations. According to a report in the June 23, 2002, *New York Times*, the September 11 Fund, a joint project of the New York City United Way and the New York Community Trust, had distributed less than half of the $456 million it had received. The Robin Hood Relief Fund in Manhattan had $23 million in undistributed donations, the World Trade Center Relief Fund had $29 million of its $65 million remaining, and the Uniformed Firefighters Association was reported to be negotiating about how to distribute its $60 million. Many of the charities' leaders reported that the immediate needs of victims had been met, and they were dealing with how to finance longer-term needs such as mental-health counseling and job training.

~

QUESTIONS FOR REFLECTION

1. What characterizes a mutually beneficial relationship between a charitable organization and its donors or members? What duties or responsibilities do nonprofits or charities owe to their donors and their clients?

2. What responsibility do governments and regulators have in overseeing the operations of nonprofit, fund-raising organizations?

3. Identify some of the ethical and managerial responsibilities of the leaders of nonprofits or charities.

4. What environmental factors may have contributed to this crisis for the American Red Cross?

Information for this case came from the following: Blaul, B. (30 October 2001), "American Red Cross names Harold Decker interim CEO," American Red Cross Release, PR Newswire; Irby, D. (14 November 2001), "Members of Congress praise Red Cross for policy changes with Liberty disaster fund," American Red Cross Release, PR Newswire; Flaherty, M. P., & Gaul, G. M. (19 November 2001), "Red Cross has pattern of diverting donations," *Washington Post*, p. A1; Gillman, T.J. (11 March 2002), "Red Cross faces continuing queries about Sept. 11 funds," *The Dallas Morning News*; Irby, D. (14 November 2001), "Red Cross announces major changes in Liberty Fund," American Red Cross News Release, US Newswire; Mollison, A. (6 June 2002), "Red Cross changes the way it solicits funds," *The Atlanta Journal-Constitution*, p. A14; Mollison, A. (19 April 2003), "Red Cross chief got $1.9 million gold parachute," *The Atlanta Journal-Constitution*, pp. A1, A13; Murphy, K. (15 November 2001), "Charity watchdog agency wants Red Cross to be more candid about donations," Knight Ridder Washington Bureau; Quenqua, D. (25 August 2002), "Cross purpose," *PRWeek*, p. 19; Rabin, P. (6 May 2002), "Red Cross reorganization results in comms cutback," *PRWeek*, p. 2; (15 November 2001), "Red Cross' correction' redirects reserve funds," *The Washington Times*; Seabrook, A. (5 June 2002), "American Red Cross makes changes in money solicitation," NPR "All Things Considered"; Seabrook, A. (14 November 2001), "Red Cross announces all donations to its Liberty Fund will be used for victims of Sept. 11," NPR All Things Considered; Strom, S. (21 June 2002), "Charitable contributions in 2001 reached $212 billion," *The New York Times*, www.nytimes. com; Strom, S. (23 June 2002), "Families fret as charities hold a billion dollars in 9/11 aid," *The New York Times*, www/nytimes.com; Strom, S. (2 February 2003), "With a lawsuit pending, charities are divided over disclosure," *The New York Times*, www.nytimes.com; Superville, D. (30 October 2001), "Red Cross to cease solicitations for Sept. 11 disaster relief fund, introduces interim CEO," Associated Press; (27 December 2001), "Mitchell heads WTC Red Cross fund," United Press International; Walker, W. (7 November 2001), "U.S. Red Cross may double victims' payout," *The Toronto Star*, p. A8; and Zepeda, P. (3 February 2003), "Senator Mitchell praises Red Cross for its 'excellent service to America,'" American Red Cross Release, www.redcross.org/press.

CASE 27. OFFERING "1-888-995-HOPE" TO HOMEOWNERS

The sub-prime mortgage crisis that developed in 2007 did not surprise everyone. During the height of what some have called the "real estate bubble," home sales were booming and buyers were signing onto mortgages that put them at risk for too much debt. However, some began to recognize the risks as early as 2006, and a coalition of nonprofit organizations then worked together to develop a pilot public-education campaign to educate homeowners in an attempt to reduce home foreclosures in the metro Atlanta, Georgia, area.

Research and Planning

The organizations, Consumer Credit Counseling Service of Atlanta (CCCS), Fannie Mae Foundation, Homeownership Preservation Foundation, NeighborWorks America and the United Way, called on the Jackson Spalding agency to develop the campaign. Working with agency partners PRecise Communications and ignition, Inc., the creative team at Jackson Spalding Communications began by reviewing research of the homeownership and economic conditions in the Atlanta metropolitan area. One study conducted in December 2005 indicated that about one-third of those who lose their homes through foreclosure had never contacted their mortgage companies. Georgia had one of the country's highest foreclosure rates in 2006, and the Atlanta area ranked second among the top 100 metropolitan areas. The research enabled the partners to target specific communities that were most at risk and in need of information.

The agency had to decide how to break through the complacency about risk and, indeed, excitement about opportunity that were present in the real-estate market at that time. In 2008, account team member Victoria Lelash said that one of the most significant challenges faced in planning the campaign was "waving the red flag on foreclosures before most people really understood the crisis that was about to hit and the massive ripple effect it would have on the economy."

The goals of the campaign were simple:

- Publicize a trademarked telephone number, 1-888-995-HOPE hotline, to Georgia residents as the easy source of information for homeowners in mortgage difficulties or those who were facing foreclosure.
- Generate a minimum of 5,000 calls to the hotline.
- Convert 2,000 hotline calls into face-to-face counseling sessions through local NeighborWorks organizations such as the Reynoldstown Revitalization Corporation, or into telephone counseling sessions with one of four counseling groups such as the Consumer Credit Counseling Service of Greater Atlanta.

Communication Tactics

Media relations and print and radio advertising therefore were critical to the information campaign. Direct mail was also implemented, with postcards mailed to more than 300,000 metro homes. The City of Atlanta helped support the direct-mail effort by including information on water bills that went to every resident. The tactics worked. More than 13 million media impressions resulted from the print, radio, television and online coverage of the campaign.

Key partnerships helped generate coverage. On January 31, 2007, Atlanta Mayor Shirley Franklin and the chief executives of two major metro Atlanta counties formally endorsed the campaign. In a campaign release, Mayor Franklin stated: "Hope is not lost for homeowners in financial crisis. The city is committed to identifying ways to prevent foreclosure, and it begins with making sure homeowners know about the 888-995-HOPE hotline and options that can save their homes." U.S. Treasurer Anna Escobedo Cabral went to Atlanta in November to offer a speech about the ways homeowners could get help if they needed it. The speech was hosted by NeighborWorks America and CCCS of Greater Atlanta.

Nontraditional methods were also used. The businesses in targeted neighborhoods were canvassed by street teams with fliers; information about the impact foreclosures in the community would have locally was shared. Special events were held by community groups in salons to provide an informal setting for homeowners to ask questions and get information. Information, including posters and bookmarks, was sent to area churches for distribution

Evaluation and Impact

Like the media tactics, these nontraditional tactics worked, too. Goals were exceeded within three months. By June, the hotline had received 8,205 calls, and 2,206 homeowners had participated in counseling sessions. By July 2008, more than 30,000 Atlantans had sought counseling from the CCCS of Greater Atlanta.

QUESTIONS FOR REFLECTION

1. This campaign relied on both traditional and nontraditional means of informing area residents. Critique the methods used. Can you identify others that may have been equally or more effective?
2. Discussing sensitive topics such as personal finance may be difficult for some members of the public. How did this coalition seek to ease such fears?
3. What are the advantages and disadvantages of a public/private partnership?
4. If you had been in the public relations department of a bank or other mortgage lender, how would you have reacted to this campaign?

Information drawn from this case came from the following: Jackson Spalding Communications and from CCCS (17 July 2008), "2008 housing counseling demand soars 184 percent at Consumer Credit Counseling Service of Atlanta," PR Newswire, www.prnewswire.com; CCCS (31 January 2007), "Metro-Atlanta leaders announce HOPE for Atlanta residents in danger of foreclosure," PR Newswire US, www.prnewswire.com; States News Service (27 November 2007), "U.S. Treasurer to Visit Atlanta to Offer Mortgage Financing Advice," Treasury Department.

CASE 28. COLOSSAL FOSSIL DOMINATES
CHICAGO'S FIELD MUSEUM

Museums face powerful rivals—sports, movies, theme parks, and others—in the competition for family leisure time. To grab families' attention, museums need irresistible attractions and the showmanship to spotlight them. The Field Museum of Chicago showed how to provide both in planning its permanent exhibit of Sue, the World's largest and best-preserved *Tyrannosaurus rex* fossil. In the first hours after Sue was unveiled on May 17, 2000, more than 10,000 visitors filed past the fossil.

The first day's success rewarded years of hard work. The bones were discovered by Sue Hendrickson, a self-taught paleontologist for whom the fossil was named, in the Black Hills of South Dakota in August 1990. A six-member team of fossil hunters spent 17 days extracting the remains from the hillside where they'd rested since Sue the Dinosaur took her last breath 67 million years ago. The skeleton included 90% of a complete set of 250 bones. Adult humans have 206.

Eventually, the unassembled skeleton was scheduled for sale at Sotheby's auction house in New York in October 1997. Nine serious competitors entered the bidding, including the Field Museum. The Field was established in 1893 as the Columbian Museum of Chicago and was renamed in 1905 to honor its first major benefactor, retailing icon, Marshall Field. Its threefold mission focuses on public education in natural science and natural history, collections in those same areas, and basic research in biology and anthropology.

Enlisting Partners

Realizing that a successful bid could exceed the museum's resources, Field president John McCarter enlisted the support of two major corporate sponsors, McDonald's and Disney, in July 1997. The three organizations were natural partners for the effort because all three focus their public relations programs on families with young children. In return for financial help, the two companies would receive exclusive rights to full-size replica casts of the skeleton.

At Sotheby's, the bidding started at $500,000 and ended eight minutes later when the Field group won with an offer of $7.6 million. Including Sotheby's commission, the total cost was $8.4 million.

Once the Field acquired the bones and moved them to Chicago, a team of 10 experts began the two-year process of cleaning, inspecting, repairing, and preserving them. The two years gave the museum and Sue's corporate sponsors time to develop public relations plans that would build anticipation ahead of the unveiling ceremony and gain maximum visibility in the days following it.

In June 1998, the museum opened the McDonald's Fossil Preparation Laboratory where visitors could watch experts preparing the bones for mounting.

In Florida, a second preparation lab was opened at DinoLand U.S.A. in the Walt Disney World Resort's Animal Kingdom Park.

Nine months later, the museum's Web site introduced an interactive Web camera, the SueCam, that Web users worldwide could use to follow the progress of the restoration. Although visitors could monitor the preparation of individual bones, the skeleton itself was assembled in secrecy to save the surprise of the exhibit's final appearance for the unveiling ceremony on May 17.

Preparing the Media for the Unveiling

Six months before the unveiling, a press kit provided reporters with the background they would need for opening-day news stories as well as for features in advance of the exhibit's formal introduction. The kit included:

- A main news release briefly describing the fossil's discovery, the ceremony and Sue herself, supplemental exhibits, the scientific study of dinosaurs, and the sponsors' participation.
- A second release on McDonald's plans for two identical traveling exhibits that would take Sue replicas on a nationwide tour.
- A science backgrounder on what paleontologists already had learned from analysis of Sue and what more they hoped to learn from the study of fossils.
- A schedule with details on the unveiling and additional special events that would take place on the weekend immediately following the opening-day ceremonies.
- A fact sheet on the exhibition (e.g. subject, location, hours, museum admission fee).
- A second fact sheet on Sue the Dinosaur (e.g. 41 to 45 feet long, seven-ton estimated live weight, one-quart brain cavity, gender undetermined).
- A timeline tracing Sue from birth to death in the Cretaceous Age to her debut in 21st-century Chicago.

In advance of the unveiling, the museum also provided the media with a full-color image of Sue alive and in the flesh, showing sculptor Brian Cooley's recreation of the dinosaur's hungry face based on educated speculation concerning her musculature and hide.

Disney timed the theatrical release of *Dinosaur*, its computer-animated/live-action movie, to coincide with the opening events. A special screening was sponsored by the museum on the first Friday following the unveiling. Advertising and promotion of the movie in the weeks leading up to the museum ceremony also raised public anticipation of the new exhibit.

Waking Up With Sue

The unveiling ceremony itself was scheduled for 6 a.m. CDT on Wednesday, May 17—early for family attendance but ideal for television networks' morning shows, which reach millions of potential visitors. Despite the hour, the sunrise ceremony attracted big crowds. Dinosaur fans also watched the ceremony from home via the SueCam on the Field Museum Web site.

Describing the opening event, CNN said, "The 41-foot-long *T. rex* inspired instant awe from thousands who packed the Chicago museum for the unveiling of 'Sue,' one of the most talked about and debated dinosaur finds in history."

Noting the build-up for the debut, CBS News said: "With Hollywood-style razzle-dazzle, the reassembled skeleton went on display Wednesday for the first time. In advance of the opening at Chicago's Field Museum, dinosaur logos were plastered on T-shirts and city buses."

McDonald's public relations agency, Burson-Marsteller, estimated that media coverage of the event resulted in 750 million impressions worldwide.

From 10 a.m. to 3 p.m. on opening day, the museum offered a variety of interactive programs for visitors, from preschoolers on up, to engage them in learning more about paleontology and to turn the day into something more than a brief or long look at Sue. On the following Saturday and Sunday, the schedule included more events supporting the new exhibit, including a lecture by the paleontologist who was lead researcher on Sue, a performance of "Tyrannosaurus Sue: A Cretaceous Concerto" by the Chicago Chamber Musicians, a puppet theater showing the evolution of dinosaurs, and more.

The following month, Disney erected its full-size replica of Sue at DinoLand U.S.A. in Orlando, Florida, and McDonald's opened the first of its two traveling Sue exhibits in Boston at the Museum of Science.

McDonald's Sends Sue on the Road

For McDonald's, participation in the Sue project had a national objective of strengthening existing links to kids, families, and educators, and it had local objectives of boosting restaurant traffic during tour promotions and making "deposits" in "community trust" banks. Analysis of news reports indicated that McDonald's got the credit it had wanted—a generous company willing to give back to the community.

The traveling exhibition was a complete show. It included a 45-foot-long replica of Sue as well as interactive anatomical models that enabled visitors to manipulate the jaw, neck, tail, and forelimbs of a *T. rex*. Dinosaur fans could touch casts of bones and models of Sue's 12-inch-long teeth, see videos explaining the fossil's restoration, and more. The tour schedule included major metropolitan areas and smaller cities, such as Atlanta; Hays, Kansas; Honolulu; Los Angeles; Muncie, Indiana; and Seattle. McDonald's arranged for fossil hunter Sue Hendrickson to visit some of the cities on the tour, starting with Boston.

To take Sue's story into classrooms, McDonald's distributed the Colossal Fossil Education Program to more than 60,000 elementary schools in the United States. It included a 10-minute video, in-school lessons, and take-home activities exploring the science that led to Sue's discovery and that guided the skeleton's restoration. Burson-Marsteller said that 95% of the teachers they surveyed rated the overall program good or excellent.

Some Reservations Registered

In some news reports on Sue, journalists described two related issues that concerned natural scientists and others:

- The commercialization of museum exhibits through corporate sponsorships.
- The sale of fossil trophies to the highest bidder.

One paleontologist expressed concern to CBS that consumerism could put unhealthy short-term pressures on scientific decision making that could have long-term consequences for the accumulation of knowledge. Another pointed out that the auction of fossils could put highly important finds into the hands of private collectors and make them unavailable for scientific examination.

However, some curators countered that corporate sponsorship enables museums to purchase geological specimens that they could not afford otherwise, and corporate objectives would invariably involve public display. Companies participate primarily to earn the goodwill of customers and other important publics. Often, the sponsors not only provide the money to acquire new exhibits but also promote them to raise awareness, encourage attendance, and win community respect.

For the Field Museum, a spike in attendance was one measure of success of the Sue exhibit. For all of 2000, the museum welcomed 2.3 million visitors, up 50% from the preceding year. The Field's director of exhibitions and education programs estimated half of the increase was attributable to Sue, the world's most complete *T. rex* and Chicago's most attractive museum exhibit of the year.

Museum Continues to Celebrate Sue

The Field Museum continues to focus attention on Sue. Visitors to the Web site, www.fieldmuseum.org/sue/index.html, find extensive information about the fossil. Children may build flip booklets from pictures on line, send Sue e-cards, and order Sue-focused products. Information about where the sponsored traveling exhibit will be showing is available.

To commemorate the fifth anniversary of the exhibit's opening, the museum held a Birthday Party for Sue in 2006, with free admission to the museum and a party complete with a chocolate Sue creation decorated by noted chef Wolfgang Puck and a musical "Happy Birthday" sung by performer Al Jarreau. Giant dinosaur puppets, theater performances and a variety of hands-on activities kept the party family-friendly.

~

QUESTIONS FOR REFLECTION

1. Why would McDonald's and Disney agree to help finance a bid of almost $8 million for a dinosaur fossil? How would they expect to benefit?

2. The unveiling of Sue was held at 6 a.m. CDT to lure coverage by the TV networks' morning shows. Would you have scheduled a more family-friendly time?

3. Families with membership in the Field Museum ($100 per year in 2009) receive special benefits, such as free general admission and free or discounted admission to special exhibits. How might the Field have involved member families in the Sue celebration?

4. Why are dinosaurs and fossils a natural draw for McDonald's target publics?

5. Some critics saw dangers in corporate sponsorship of museum exhibits. What are the risks?

6. How might the museum continue to keep the exhibit exciting for new or returning guests? How might it continue to generate media coverage?

Information for this case was drawn from the following: The Field Museum Web site at www. fieldmuseum.org; Conklin, M. (4 December 2000), "Building momentum from the bones up," *Los Angeles Times*, p. F8; Kinzer, S. (5 November 2002), "Museum's goal: Save the world's wild places," *The New York Times*, p. E1; (16 May 2000), "Massive T. rex invades Chi-town," CBS News, www. cbsnews.com; (accessed 27 June 2002), "McDonald's Sue T-rex sponsorship," The Holmes Report, www.holmesreport.com; (18 May 2000). "Monstrous T. rex is unveiled in Chicago," *Los Angeles Times*, p. 16; Randolph, E., & Goldman, J. (5 October 1997), "Museum snaps up T. rex in historic sale," *Los Angeles Times*, p. A1; (17 May 2000), "Sue, the biggest T. rex, makes her public debut," CNN, www.cnn.com/2000/NATURE/; (3 May 2005), "T.Rex birthday party with Al Jarreau and Wolfgang Puck at Chicago's Field Museum," Field Museum Public Relations Release, www.fieldmuseum.org.

CASE 29: QUEEN LATIFAH INTRODUCES NATIONAL WOMEN'S CONFIDENCE DAY

"Celebrate your strengths; put them into action."
"Speak your mind; don't be afraid to ask for what you want and need."
"Keep self-criticism in check; let constructive criticism motivate you."
—ProjectConfidence bookmarks

These confident assertions epitomize the theme of a jointly sponsored Project Confidence campaign championed by singer/actress Queen Latifah in 2006. The first Wednesday in June was announced as "National Women's Confidence Day" in June 2006 through an Extension of Remarks in the Congressional Record of the House of Representatives sponsored by Rep. Carolyn Maloney (D-NY) and will be commemorated in subsequent years.

Partners Address Women's Esteem Issues

The proclamation helped focus attention on a multi-tiered campaign that seeks to help develop the self-esteem of women, cosponsored by Curvation, which sells underwear for what it calls "curvaceous" women, and the YWCA. The goal of the campaign was to raise awareness of the importance of women's self-confidence, and its success was measured by the number of media placements achieved. The campaign was developed by a team from the Lippe Taylor agency.

The campaign focused on four initiatives:

- National Women's Confidence Day.
- Curvation Project Confidence awards that would be presented to women recognized as personifying confidence.
- Curvation Nation, an online community for women.
- Curvation Project Confidence YWCA Educational Outreach Program.

Celebrity Spokeswoman Adds Support

The campaign was launched with a Queen Latifah concert in Secaucus, N.J., that drew almost 100,000 fans and marked the beginning of Confidence Days with Wal-Mart and Kmart; national in-store promotions at the retailers offered women professional fittings and "Confidence" bracelets.

Queen Latifah, who, along with her acting and recording career, serves as a spokesperson and creative advisor for the Curvation brand, explained her involvement in a 2007 release:

Growing up, I was fortunate enough to have strong women around me—like my mother and grandmother—who encouraged me to believe in myself and let me know that I had the ability to achieve whatever I set my mind to. But I know that not everyone has that support. That's why the Curvation brand, the YWCA and I wanted to address this issue by encouraging women to stand up for themselves and know that any goal is within reach if they believe in themselves. The Project Confidence Outreach Program is the perfect way to share this message and hopefully influence the lives of countless women.

Confidence Awards

The Curvation Project Confidence Awards campaign solicited nominations of women from across the country. Five finalists were selected, each of whom received a $2,000 grant to be used to promote the cause or project with which they were affiliated. Each year, one of the five finalists was selected as the grand prize winner and received an additional $10,000 grant.

The first National Project Confidence Award grand-prize recipient was the founder of a women's self-help group and a "Girl Power" program that helps female inmates strengthen their self-esteem, founded after her 14-year-old daughter was murdered. The 2006 grand-prize recipient was the founder of the nonprofit InnerBeauty Foundation that hosts "Day of Beauty" events for women in homeless shelters.

Outreach Program

The materials for the Project Confidence Outreach Program were developed in stages. First, the YWCA held focus groups in five cities and conducted a national survey of women in 2006. Then, the YWCA developed a curriculum aimed at providing women with information and tools to help them achieve personal goals and develop confidence. Beginning in June 2007, pilot workshops of the Project Confidence Outreach Program using the curriculum were held at YWCA sites in six cities, including Houston; Los Angeles; Brooklyn; Malden, Massachusetts; Marietta, Georgia; and Aurora, Illinois. The nine-month curriculum and "How-To" kit will be given to the 16,000 volunteers and employees who work with the country's nearly 300 YWCAs. Training for local and regional representatives will also be provided.

A Web site supporting the campaign was also developed. It provided "Project Confidence Tips," information and links to Web-based aids in areas such as:

- "Confident Style" that offered information about the importance of dressing well, with a link to Dress for Success, and wearing a correctly sized bra and a link to the Curvation Web site.
- "Career Confidence" that offered information about networking, business language and salary negotiation, with links to other Web sites.

- "Financial Confidence" that offered information on budgeting, with a link to Consumer Credit Services, saving, and understanding credit reports.
- "Confidence for Community Change" that urges women to use their voices to champion change, to plan ways to address racial and gender stereotypes, and to get involved in the community, with links to the YWCA and the Step Up Women's Network.
- "Healthy Body, Confident Body" that provides information about critical medical tests for women of various ages and tips about healthy eating and about feeling confident about one's body.

The site also provided bookmarks with "confident" quotes that could be downloaded for printing.

Queen Latifah told ABC News that she hoped the commemoration of Women's Confidence Day would remind women to reach for their goals. "Today we're not encouraging women to go out and conquer the world. We're encouraging them to begin to conquer their own small world. This day is yours."

QUESTIONS FOR REFLECTION

1. Why would the YWCA partner with a women's apparel company to produce a multi-year program? Why would Curvation be interested in such a partnership?
2. Queen Latifah brings a number of strengths to the role of spokeswoman for this campaign. What qualifications would you recommend a nonprofit look for when selecting a celebrity spokesperson for a campaign?
3. Can you identify other evaluation techniques that might be used to measure the effectiveness of the Educational Outreach Program? Other goals?

Information for this case was drawn from the following: the YWCA Web site, www.ywca.org, the Curvation Web site at www.curvation.com/pc/nwed/php, and the Lippe Taylor Web site at www.lippetaylor.com; and Curvation (6 March 2007), "Queen Latifah announces national award recipient of the Curvation Project Confidence Awards," Press Release, www.prnewswire.com; Dave, Rap News (8 June 2006), "Hip-hop news: Hip hop Queen announces 'National Women's Confidence Day.'" Rap News Network, www.rapnews.net/0-202-261534-00.html; Johnson, B. (7 June 2006), "Queen Latifah announces Women's Confidence Day," ABC News, http://abcnews.go.com/print?id=2051172; McKenna, T. (9 June 2006), "Queen Latifah plays key role in push to boost women's esteem," PRWeek, p. 3; Rok, C.(15 July 2005), "Queen Latifah Launches Curvation Project Confidence Awards with Free Mini Concert," Release from VF Corporation, www.pfnewswire.com;

CASE 30. A NEW WAY FOR THE UNITED WAY OF THE NATIONAL CAPITAL AREA?

Investigations into administrative practices at the United Way of the National Capital Area affiliate in 2002 led to leadership resignations and a new system for board administration, while reminding affiliates across the country of the need for accountability to their donors.

United Way affiliates are typically administered by a director who acts as the CEO and other paid staff members who work with a board of directors composed of volunteers to form policies, lead fund-raising efforts, and make allocation decisions. The National Capital Area affiliate raises money for some 1,100 social-service agencies in the District of Columbia, as well as in its Maryland and Virginia suburbs. It has received donations through payroll deductions from some 350,000 workers and usually raises more than $90 million annually.

Capital Leadership?

Oral Suer had served as the affiliate's director for 27 years. He led in the creation of the affiliate from a merger of two others and then served as the affiliate's chief executive from 1974 to 2001. After his retirement in 2001, the United Way paid Suer a pension settlement of more than $1 million. He also received a $6,000-a-month consulting contract and was allowed to continue using an American Express Platinum card the affiliate issues its executives. Suer was succeeded by Norman O. Taylor, who resigned on September 6, 2002, amid ongoing investigations into how the United Way affiliate had spent its donations. The investigations centered on practices during Suer's leadership. A federal grand jury and at least two federal agencies, including the Department of Labor, were reportedly investigating the group's financial management practices for possible misbehavior, including discriminatory pricing of services, excessive pension payments, and inflation of donation totals.

Following Taylor's resignation, Charles W. Anderson became the chief executive of the affiliate. His task was to help the organization settle its controversy and focus on revitalizing its fund-raising and service efforts.

Investigations Begin

Investigations into leadership compensation at the United Way first began in 2001 when the charity's general counsel was approached by board member Ross W. Dembling, who had questions about how donations were being spent. Dembling was told a few weeks later that his term on the board would not be renewed. News coverage about the incident raised questions, and an accounting firm was asked to audit the affiliate.

In May 2002, the affiliate reported that the audit found nothing significantly wrong in the way the United Way dealt with its finances. The audit report said it found a $1,800 discrepancy in the credit-card purchases of former affiliate executive Suer, but that he had repaid the affiliate for the amounts. Board member Anthony J. Buzzelli, who had overseen the audit, told *The Washington Times*: "The current management has been put under the microscope. The purpose of the report is to make sure that this management that is in place today is one that the public can trust." The audit also reported that reforms were put in place that mandated a competitive-bid policy for expenditures greater than $10,000 and prohibited sale of organization assets to employees or volunteers.

However, questions about the thoroughness of the audit soon were aired. *The Washington Post* said the auditor never interviewed a key executive, Kenneth Unzicker, who told an ethics panel following the audit that his attempts to report misgivings about ethical and accounting issues were "rebuffed or ignored by Norman Taylor and others in control of the organization." He said that Taylor had known of issues concerning credit-card abuses and the consulting contract for Suer. Critics said the accounting firm had been told to limit the scope of the audit to certain procedures.

The board of directors asked for an expanded audit, which was conducted by PriceWaterhouseCooper LLP. In August 2003, the audit said former affiliate head Suer was accused of having taken more than $1.5 million in payments from the United Way, with the knowledge of a few board members. As far back as 1987, auditors said, Suer had received some $470,000 in advances from the United Way of the National Capital Area, and he had told auditors he was "embarrassed by the situation," according to an October 1987 memo by the auditor reported in *The Washington Post*.

At the time, Suer had said he was taking steps to repay the affiliate through payroll deductions. The auditor's report said a few of the leading members of the board had tried to handle the financial matters privately, and apparently the full board was never informed of the advances or the repayment agreement. The audit said that in 1991 Suer had entered into a formal agreement to repay the more than $323,000 owed at that point by surrendering deferred compensation and having $5,000 a month deducted from his pay. He did not repay all of the money, however, and continued to receive more than his $196,000 annual salary, according to the audit.

According to *The Washington Post*, the auditors said: "We found no footnote disclosure of this significant amount of recurring unpaid advances in UWNCA's financial statements. We also found no discussion of this issue in the Board of Director's [sic] meeting minutes." The affiliate had paid Suer some $1.4 million for unused holiday and sick pay and about $230,000 in retirement benefits, according to Associated Press reports. *The Washington Post* also reported that Suer had charged hundreds of dollars on the corporate credit card at retailers and through mail-order catalogs during the 1999 holiday season without filing supporting paperwork for the purchases. Suer said the purchases were gifts for key executives and volunteers.

Responses to the Second Audit

In response to the second audit report, the board of directors for the affiliate was reorganized. Its 21 members meet monthly, rather than quarterly, and it must offer approval for affiliate activities. Employees are no longer paid for unused sick leave and vacation, and the salary and expenses of the chief executive office will be reviewed by the entire board. The affiliate's attorney said in the August 17, 2003, *Washington Post*: "There's nothing that happens now in this organization that isn't shared by all the board members and the management. The level of transparency is as high as I've ever seen at any organization."

CEO Anderson told *The Chronicle of Philanthropy* in May 2007 that the revised structure continues to work well: "Early on, the new board adopted key components to show the public that we were serious about honesty and integrity. Today we've got separate audit, finance, and governance committees as well as an independent ethics committee. What we've done is build in a lot of checks and balances."

It was also recommended that the United Way affiliate eliminate a third of its workforce, cut its budget by 41%, and select a new auditor. The task force recommended that some 30 staff positions be eliminated; during Taylor's tenure, staffing had grown from 67 to 90. The affiliate filed a lawsuit against Suer, charging that he defrauded it of more than $1.5 million.

Focusing on Fund-Raising

The board then sought to emphasize that the problems had been solved. Donations in the 2002 campaign from the private sector had dropped from $45 million to $18 million, which meant that agencies that had depended on United Way support to serve clients were underfunded. The new leadership of the affiliate moved quickly to communicate that the problems had been identified and the affiliate reorganized. Anderson, the new chief executive, met with corporate executives to try to persuade them to support the United Way of the National Capital Area again. The audit was posted on the organizational Web site to allow open access to its findings.

The United Way of America Chief Executive Brian A. Gallagher told the *Post* on August 13, 2003, that the current leadership has "done everything that you would have hoped the former board and management would have done…and now they've got to communicate effectively if folks are going to come back and trust them."

Other Impact?

Did the investigation in Washington, D.C., affect giving to others of the 1,400 local affiliates? *The New York Times* said in September 2002 that the issue had "cast a shadow over the entire United Way." By April 2003, estimates predicted that the national United Way 2002–2003 campaign would raise as much as 4% less than had been raised during the 2001–2002 campaign. A few affiliates, such as Milwaukee and Birmingham, Alabama, saw increases in giving, but some affiliates in larger cities, such as Atlanta and Chicago, saw double-digit drops in giving.

The New York Times reported that donations to the United Way had declined only once since 1971, in 1992 when William Aramony, then president of the United Way of America, was indicted on charges of embezzlement and fraud. Aramony subsequently was sentenced to serve seven years in federal prison after being convicted of defrauding the charity of more than $1 million.

However, new standards for accounting were adopted for the annual campaign, and some argue that the declines in giving could be attributed to those changes. Affiliate campaigns were no longer allowed to count the value of in-kind contributions. The drop in the stock market and a decline in other revenues may have affected people's abilities to give, although traditionally economic downturns have not been reflected in United Way campaigns. Gary Godsey, president of the United Way of Dallas, told *The New York Times* that he had been assured by Dallas businesspeople that the scandal was not responsible for the downfall in Dallas fund-raising: "This is purely economic, and in Dallas, we've been particularly hard hit."

~~~

QUESTIONS FOR REFLECTION

1. How should a nonprofit, its board, and its staff interact? What are the most important responsibilities of these stakeholder relationships?
2. What are the ethical obligations involved in handling donations to a nonprofit service agency? What are the obligations that result from membership on a corporate or nonprofit board of directors?
3. What is the importance of open access to nonprofit records such as audits and financial reports? How does this correspond to the legal requirement for publicly owned companies to publish annual and quarterly reports?

Information for this case came from the following: coverage in *The Washington Post* by Whoriskey, P., & Salmon, J.L. (17 August 2003), "Dealings of charity executive concealed; United Way audit flagged issue in '87," *The Washington Post*, p. C1; Salmon, J.L., & Whoriskey, P. (13 August 2003), "Problems behind us, charity says; United Way partnership divides area employees," *The Washington Post*, p. B1; Whoriskey, P., & Salmon, J.L. (4 September 2002), "United Way audit omitted dissenter," *The Washington Post*, p. B1; and Whoriskey, P., & Salmon, J.L. (8 May 2002), "United Way credit charges described as holiday gifts; nonprofit to release audit in response to financial questions," *The Washington Post*, p. B1. Other information came from the following: Associated Press (12 August 2003), "Audit indicates millions in questionable expenses for former D.C. United Way leader," Associated Press, accessed through LexisNexis Academic; Berkshire, J.C. (31 May 2007), "Starting from scratch: How charities cope when their boards need a makeover." *The Chronicle of Philanthropy*, 19(16), pp. 2-4; Johnston, D.C. (17 July 2002), "Grand jury is investigating United Way in Washington," *The New York Times*; Strom, S. (6 September2002), "Director of the United Way in Washington steps down," *The New York Times*; Strom, S. (8 April 2003), "Usually resilient United Way now predicts a leaner year," *The New York Times*; and Taylor, G. (9 May 2002), "United Way audit clears managers," *The Washington Times.*

PROFESSIONAL INSIGHT

A HIGHER ETHICAL STANDARD FOR NONPROFITS

James E. Moody, president, Construction Suppliers Association

Because nonprofits enjoy tax-free status, we hold them to a higher standard. We expect them to operate in the public interest and to maintain the highest ethical standards. Yet nonprofits—charities, philanthropic organizations, and trade and professional associations—provide some of the most challenging ethical situations.

Some of these challenges arise simply because we expect them to be different than for-profit businesses. While we may not think it's fair for the CEO of a large corporation to make an exorbitant salary and enjoy rich "trappings of office," it's not an issue many of us feel viscerally. Yet when it was disclosed that William Arimony of the United Way was earning millions of dollars and jaunting around in limousines, many people who had sacrificed to give part of their salary to the United Way were justifiably angry.

Sometimes the ethical challenges are less obvious but perhaps more significant. Trade and professional associations make public statements that are often held with high regard because we perceive them to come from an unbiased source.

The board of directors generally makes the final decisions on what the association will say on any given topic. Every board member has self-interests that may color the member's feelings about the topic. And the association itself will almost certainly have a bias toward the group it represents. Dealing with these potentially conflicting interests is the key to maintaining a high ethical standard.

For example, we assume that statements from a medical association are issued in the interest of public health. Would that still be your assumption if you knew that the majority of the association's board members received significant income for being spokespersons for a drug company?

Even when self-interest is not an issue, decisions can be ethically challenging. Many nonprofits struggle to make ends meet. Nonprofit doesn't mean your goal is to lose money! Sometimes endorsement deals are an attractive way to increase revenue. Is it ethical for an association to endorse a product or service in exchange for money? What about when the association is aware that the product it endorses is no better than its competitors?

Many associations have adopted codes of ethics to help draw the boundaries. Additionally, many boards have conflict of interest policies that require members to disclose potential conflicts prior to their service on the board.

Of course, no code of ethics or conflict of interest policy can describe every potential ethical dilemma a nonprofit may face. And truly unethical people will not be troubled by breaking a code of ethics or "forgetting" to disclose a conflict. Ultimately, it is up to those with high ethical standards to rid their organization's leadership of those who cannot put their own interests aside.

Jim Moody is president of the Construction Suppliers Association, the trade association for suppliers of home-building products in Georgia and Alabama. He previously served as executive director of the Georgia Society of Association Executives, the trade association for staff members of associations and other nonprofits in Georgia. He graduated cum laude with a bachelor's degree in communication from Berry College and earned the certified association executive designation from the American Society of Association Executives.

8
Stakeholders: Governments and Regulators

Few organizations in the United States escape the scrutiny and influence of government regulators. From jetliners 35,000 feet above the earth's surface to miners 5,000 feet below it, most organized human activity attracts government attention. Some agencies, such as the Federal Aviation Administration (FAA), become as well known as the companies they monitor. Others, such as the Mine Safety and Health Administration, are seldom seen or heard outside their own industry.

Regulatory agencies exist because elected federal, state, and local officials create them to develop and enforce rules needed to carry out the law. In most cases, regulations focus on protecting human health and safety, the natural environment, and the free-market economic system.

THE ROLES OF PRACTITIONERS

Public relations practitioners must understand the regulations that govern their organizations' activities and anticipate how the rules might affect their own plans or those of competitors. Knowing the rules will help practitioners:

- Contribute effectively to discussion, analysis, and strategic planning.
- Understand the consequences of both compliance and noncompliance.
- Anticipate how regulations may affect customers, employees, investors, and others.
- Interpret the potential effects of newly proposed rules.
- Prepare to explain adverse regulatory decisions.

For example, the Federal Trade Commission (FTC) announced in 2003 that it would oppose Nestlé SA's acquisition of Dreyer's Grand Ice Cream Inc. because the combination would reduce competition in the gourmet ice cream segment. Despite the setback, the two companies publicly expressed their commitment to completing the deal. After three months of negotiations that were covered regularly in national media and watched closely by employees, they won FTC approval.

Another example was the Wall Street meltdown of 2008. Unprecedented shocks to the U.S. financial system led millions of Americans to press for a top-to-bottom overhaul of the regulatory structure that governed lending, investing, credit and securities.

REGULATORY COMPLEXITIES

Complex regulations and high stakes have made pharmaceutical public relations a demanding specialty. The FDA strictly enforces its rules concerning the language that drug companies must use in describing the testing, efficacy, and side effects of products. News releases or other materials that run afoul of FDA rules may lead to delay, embarrassment, fines, or other sanctions.

Occasionally, regulatory agencies have overlapping responsibilities. For example, both the FTC and the Federal Communications Commission (FCC) were involved in establishing the National Do-Not-Call Registry in 2003, responding to industry objections and subsequent lawsuits, and implementing the new rules.

When the federal government establishes a regulatory agency, state governments often create their own corresponding agency to govern intrastate activities, and strong state regulatory structures are common in public service utilities, such as power and telecommunications companies, and in the banking industry.

Some states have consistently adopted stricter rules than their federal counterparts in certain regulated activities, earning reputations as rule-making leaders and complicating the jobs of public relations professionals. For example, the California Air Resources Board has gained recognition for setting the nation's toughest auto emissions standards since it was established 40 years ago.

CRITICS OF REGULATION

Regulatory efforts have attracted a large number of critics who say they simply add to the costs of producing a product or service without providing an equivalent value in benefits. The operation of free markets, the critics say, would accomplish the same good effects that government rules do.

John Stossel, an investigative reporter and co-anchor for ABC-TV's "20/20" news program who's been honored five times for excellence in consumer reporting by the National Press Club and received 19 Emmy Awards, is a tireless critic of government regulation. He explained his reasons in 2001 at a Hillsdale College seminar:

> When I started 30 years ago as a consumer reporter, I took the approach that most young reporters take today. My attitude was that capitalism is essentially cruel and unfair, and that the job of government, with the help of lawyers and the press, is to protect people from it. For years, I did

stories along those lines—stories about Coffee Association ads claiming that 'coffee picks you up while it calms you down,' or Libby-Owens-Ford Glass Company ads touting the clarity of its product by showing cars with their windows rolled down. I and other consumer activists said, "We've got to have regulation. We've got to police these ads. We've got to have a Federal Trade Commission." And I'm embarrassed at how long it took me to realize that these regulations make things worse, not better, for ordinary people. The damage done by regulation is so vast, it's often hard to see. The money wasted consists not only of the taxes taken directly from us to pay for the bureaucrats, but also of the indirect cost of all the lost energy that goes into filling out the forms.

PROTECTING THE POWERLESS

Regulatory advocates respond that powerful corporations, highly motivated to minimize costs and well equipped with resources needed to prevail in disputes, would not adequately protect the health of workers or the environment if the government did not supervise them closely.

Here are brief descriptions of some of the most prominent federal regulatory agencies. The descriptions are adapted from materials the agencies have published.

Consumer Product Safety Commission

The CPSC protects the public against unreasonable risks of injuries and deaths associated with consumer products. The agency has jurisdiction over about 15,000 types of consumer products ranging from coffee makers to toys to lawn mowers.
CPSC activities include:

- Developing voluntary standards with industry representatives.
- Issuing and enforcing mandatory standards and banning products if no feasible standard would adequately protect the public.
- Obtaining the recall of products or arranging for their repair.

Environmental Protection Administration

The EPA mission is to protect human health and safeguard the natural environment on which life depends. In July 1970, the White House and Congress worked together to establish the EPA in response to growing public demand for cleaner water, air, and land. Before formation of the EPA, the federal government was not structured to make a coordinated attack on the pollutants that harm human health and degrade the environment.

Equal Employment Opportunity Commission

The EEOC coordinates all federal equal employment opportunity regulations, practices, and policies. The commission also interprets employment discrimination laws, monitors the federal sector equal employment opportunity program, and provides funding and support to state and local fair employment practices agencies and tribal employment rights organizations.

Federal Aviation Administration

The FAA is responsible for the safety of civil aviation. The FAA's major roles include:

- Regulating civil aviation to promote safety.
- Encouraging and developing civil aeronautics, including new aviation technology.
- Developing and operating the air traffic control system for civil and military aircraft.
- Developing and carrying out programs to control aircraft noise and other environmental effects of civil aviation.

Federal Communications Commission

The FCC operates bureaus that process applications for licenses, analyze complaints, conduct investigations, develop and implement regulatory programs, and take part in hearings. Some of the bureaus are:

- Consumer and Governmental Affairs, which educates and informs consumers about telecommunications goods and services and invites public input to help guide the work of the FCC.
- Media, which regulates AM and FM radio, and television broadcast stations, as well as cable and satellite distribution.
- Wireless Telecommunications, which oversees cellular and PCS phones, pagers, and two-way radios.
- Wireline Competition, which regulates phone companies that mainly provide interstate services through wire-based networks including corded and cordless phones.

Federal Reserve System

The Federal Reserve, the central bank of the United States, was founded in 1913 to provide the nation with a safer, more flexible, and more stable monetary and financial system.

The central bank's duties fall into four general areas:

- Conducting the nation's monetary policy.
- Supervising banking institutions and protecting the credit rights of consumers.
- Maintaining the stability of the financial system.
- Providing certain financial services to the government, public, financial institutions, and foreign official institutions.

Federal Trade Commission

The FTC works to ensure that markets are vigorous, efficient, and free of restrictions that harm consumers. Experience demonstrates that competition among firms yields products at the lowest prices, spurs innovation and strengthens the economy. Markets also work best when consumers can make informed choices based on accurate information.

To ensure the smooth operation of the free-market system, the FTC enforces federal consumer protection laws that prevent fraud, deception, and unfair business practices. The commission also enforces federal antitrust laws that prohibit anticompetitive mergers and other business practices that restrict competition and harm consumers.

Food and Drug Administration

The FDA is responsible for protecting the public health by assuring the safety, efficacy, and security of human and veterinary drugs, biological products, medical devices, commercial food supply, cosmetics, and products that emit radiation. The FDA advances public health by helping to speed innovations that make medicines and foods more effective, safer, and more affordable and by helping people get the accurate, science-based information they need to use medicines and foods to improve their health.

The FDA works to ensure that consumers have up-to-date, truthful information on the benefits and risks of regulated products. Its complementary roles are:

- Ensuring that the information companies provide about products is accurate and allows for their safe use.
- Communicating directly with the public concerning benefits and risks of products the FDA regulates.

Occupational Safety and Health Administration

OSHA's mission is to save lives, prevent injuries, and protect the health of America's workers. To accomplish this, federal and state governments work in partnership with the more than 100 million working men and women and 6.5 million employers covered by the Occupational Safety and Health Act. Nearly every working man and woman in the nation comes under OSHA's jurisdiction (with some exceptions such as miners and transportation workers).

National Highway Traffic Safety Administration

NHTSA is responsible for reducing death, injury, and economic loss resulting from highway accidents. The agency sets and enforces safety standards for motor vehicles and vehicle equipment. NHTSA investigates safety defects in motor vehicles, sets and enforces fuel economy standards, helps reduce the threat of drunk drivers, promotes use of seat belts, child safety seats, and air bags, investigates odometer fraud, establishes and enforces vehicle antitheft regulations, and provides consumer information on motor vehicle safety topics.

Securities and Exchange Commission

The primary mission of the SEC is to protect investors and maintain the integrity of the securities markets. As more first-time investors turn to the markets to help secure their futures, pay for homes, and send children to college, these goals are more compelling than ever.

The world of investing is fascinating, complex, and potentially fruitful. Unlike the banking world, where deposits are guaranteed, stocks, bonds, and other securities can lose value. There are no guarantees. The principal way for investors to protect the money they put into securities is to do research and ask questions.

The main purposes of the laws creating the SEC can be summed up in two propositions:

- Companies publicly offering securities for investment dollars must tell the public the truth about their businesses, the securities they are selling, and the risks involved in investing.
- People who sell and trade securities—brokers, dealers, and exchanges—must treat investors fairly and honestly, putting investors' interests first.

U.S. Department of Agriculture

The USDA's Food Safety Mission Area ensures that the commercial supply of meat, poultry, and egg products is safe, wholesome, and correctly labeled and packaged. The Food Safety and Inspection Service (FSIS) sets standards for food safety and inspects meat, poultry, and egg products produced domestically and imported. The FSIS inspects animals and birds at slaughter and processed products at various stages of production and analyzes products for microbiological and chemical adulterants. FSIS also informs the public about meat, poultry, and egg safety issues.

The cases in this chapter challenge you to explore the varied motivations and practices of communicating to and with governments. As you discuss these cases, address questions such as: How do the communication strategies and tactics described here indicate the priorities of these stakeholders? Do they encourage robust involvement in open, democratic action and processes? How might these strategies and tactics be understood in light of democratic principles and communication ethics?

ADDITIONAL READINGS

Downs, Anthony. (1994). *Inside bureaucracy.* Long Grove, IL: Waveland Press.

Jung, Donald J. (2002). *The Federal Communications Commission.* Lanham, MD: University Press of America.

Labaree, Robert V. (2000). *The Federal Trade Commission: A guide to sources* New York: Garland.

Wilson, James Q. (2000). *Bureaucracy: What government agencies do and why they do it.* New York: Basic Books.

CASE 31. HOSPITAL ADVOCATES FOR ITS
PROPERTY-TAX EXEMPTION

Provena Covenant Medical Center, in Urbana, Illinois, is a 254-bed regional facility that serves residents in east central Illinois and western Indiana with medical care provided by more than 250 physicians, and special services such as a cancer center, a physical rehabilitation center, a neonatal nursery, and cardiovascular care. It is part of a Catholic health system of six hospitals, 16 long-term care and senior residential facilities, and other health facilities in the two states.

It has also become the focus of an extended legal battle with local and state officials over its property-tax exemption status that provides an opportunity to observe how public relations, information and advocacy may directly impact the financial status of an organization. Throughout the state litigation, the hospital's federal tax-exempt status has been maintained without challenge.

Property-Tax Exemption is Denied

The legal issues began in 2002 when the hospital applied for property tax-exempt status. In January 2003, the Champaign County Board of Review recommended to the state Department of Revenue that the hospital's property-tax exemption be denied. The Board of Review argued that Provena's level of charitable care was not great enough to qualify for such an exemption.

Early in 2004, the Department of Revenue endorsed the county's proposal, and the hospital appealed that decision before an administrative law judge in December 2005. The judge ruled in favor of the hospital. The decision then went back to the state Department of Revenue for a final decision, and Director Brian Hamer denied the property-tax exemption. Provena appealed this decision in the circuit Court of Sangamon County.

The hospital responded with "An Open Letter to the communities and patients we serve" signed by David Bertauski, president and chief executive officer of Provena Central Illinois Region, that noted, "Stripping a hospital of its charitable status severely impairs its ability to fulfill the Provena Health mission and take care of those who truly need our care and compassion. We are not alone, as this decision presents a serious threat for every not-for-profit hospital in the state of Illinois and across the nation."

In a news release, the hospital indicated it would appeal the ruling. William T. Foley, the president and CEO of Provena Covenant, was quoted: "This decision is completely unsupported by legal precedent, or the facts we provided. The state's ruling flies in the face of our own charitable mission and challenges every Illinois hospital's ability to continue serving the poor and uninsured."

Provena enlisted the support of five hospital associations and a Catholic organization to help with its appeal. The Illinois Hospital Association, Illinois

Catholic Health Association, Metropolitan Chicago Healthcare Council, American Hospital Association, Catholic Association, and the Catholic Conference of Illinois filed a friend-of-the-court brief urging the state to restore the hospital's not-for-profit status.

The brief pointed to the potential impact of the tax ruling, arguing: "Denying Provena Covenant its property tax exemption will throw into question the exempt status of nearly every Illinois hospital. The resulting financial drain on hospitals will seriously jeopardize access to quality health services for every Illinois resident."

Since 2003, the hospital had paid $4.8 million in property taxes. The hospital reported it had committed more than $11.3 million in charitable benefits in 2005 alone.

The Exemption is Restored

The Sangamon County court restored the hospital's exemption in July 2007, saying the hospital deserved the exemption as it was both a religious and a charitable organization.

A July 27, 2007, announcement from the hospital noted its satisfaction with the ruling:

Provena Covenant Property Tax Exempt Decision

All of us at Provena Covenant Medical Center are extremely gratified that Circuit Court Judge Patrick J. Londrigan on Friday, July 20, reversed the State's decision to deny property-tax exemption to Provena Covenant, deeming it to be tax exempt on charitable and religious grounds, and entitling us to the return of property taxes paid since its tax exemption was removed in early 2004.

This judgment, based on the law and reached after full consideration of extensive briefing by the parties and a large record of evidence, reaffirms Provena Covenant's charitable and religious mission and will assist the Medical Center in continuing our commitment to providing for the needs of our community, our facility, and our dedicated team of employees.

As a faith-based and non-profit hospital, Provena Covenant, from its very beginnings, has existed for the purpose of caring for all regardless of their ability to pay. Despite the temporary loss of our property exemption, Provena Covenant continued to fulfill our commitment to providing quality health care to all we serve—a fact which has been long encouraged and supported by our Urbana-Champaign community.

We are very pleased the Court recognized this dedication to our charitable mission in its ruling handed down last week.

Provena Covenant Medical Center is very proud of its significant contributions to the community. It is also a pleasure to know that our restored property tax-exemption will allow us to continue to make further investment in our tradition of service and care for the benefit of generations of area residents to come.

After the ruling, the county returned the $6.1 million in property tax the hospital had paid since the original decision by the state.

More Appeals Follow

In turn, however, the Illinois Department of Revenue appealed the decision to the 4th District Appellate Court, which in August 2008, overturned the circuit court and upheld the Department of Revenue's decision to deny the property-tax exemption.

The appellate court wrote: "Just because Covenant never turns a patient away because of the patient's inability to pay, it does not follow that Covenant thereby provides charity. If, despite the patient's inability to pay, the patient is contractually liable to reimburse Covenant for the medical treatment, Covenant has extended no charity to that patient." The court also denied the hospital's claim that it deserved the exemption because it was a religious institution.

On September 9, 2008, the hospital announced it would appeal the decision to the Illinois Supreme Court. The county has asked that the hospital repay the taxes it had been refunded earlier.

Provena Covenant Provides Information

The hospital's Web site chronicles the legal struggle through news releases and announcements, but it also has additional resources. It highlights direct links to information about "Community Benefits & Tax Exemption." A statement on the site says: "Provena Health ministries are an integral part of their communities throughout Illinois. Providing high quality care to patients 24 hours a day, 7 days a week regardless of ability to pay tells only part of the story. We are committed to our communities' health in a number of ways, including fair and compassionate financial assistance and discount policies to help the uninsured, and partnerships and programs that address unmet health needs and promote community wellness. In 2006, Provena Health provided over $61 million in community benefit (according to the Catholic Health Association guidelines)."

Links pointed to:

- Extensive information about the programs and services the hospital offers its Provena Health Financial Assistant Policy
- Illinois Community Benefit Act: Report on Value to Illinois' Communities (IHA)
- AHA Report on Underpayment of Medicare and Medicaid
- MCHC Report on Hospital Benefits Provided in Metropolitan Chicago Area

- IHA on Charity Care.
- An annual "Community Benefit" report is linked from the site.

Pages on the Web site are also devoted to "advocacy." The landing page for this section explains the hospital's commitment to public affairs engagement and invites others to get involved:

> Provena Health's commitment to advocacy requires us to be active at the local, state and national level where health care policy decisions are made. Our various legislative bodies continually make decisions that impact health care coverage, financing and delivery in our communities. Our elected representatives may not know the impact of their decisions on the people we serve unless we tell them...Our involvement is essential to making legislators care enough about an issue to listen to the arguments—pro or con—and take a position...Effective advocacy is about building relationships and engaging our legislators in our mission and vision. It requires us to connect with others who share our policy goals and social justice values. It is hoped that the tools you find here will help you get involved in Provena Health's advocacy initiatives and that you will join us in building communities of healing and hope.

QUESTIONS FOR REFLECTION

1. Healthcare has been a focus of political and public discussions for years. In this environment, how might Provena seek to influence public and political opinion in its favor? What are the advantages and risks of taking its legal issues public, through such tools as advocacy ads?

2. How might not-for-profit hospitals publicize their missions and public-service activities effectively?

3. Evaluate the statement of advocacy Provena Covenant has posted. From what you understand about public relations and public affairs, what are its strengths? Would you suggest any revisions?

4. A number of trade and professional associations have joined with Provena in this legal battle. Why are these stakeholders important in such a political battle?

Information for this case was drawn from the following: Provena Covenant Medical Center Web site at www. Provena.org/covenant, a timeline and releases posted there, including (26 October 2008), "Provena Covenant Appeals Tax-Exempt Termination"; (29 September 2006), "Provena Covenant to Continue Tax-Exempt Fight"; (27 July 2007), "Provena Covenant Property Tax Exempt Decision"; (9 September 2008), "Provena Covenant to petition for Supreme Court review of decision."; and Chun, D. (15 February 2005), "Five leading hospital associations back property tax-exemption for Illinois hospital," Illinois Hospital Association Release, PR Newswire, www.prnewswire.com; (23 July 2007). "Late News: Judge backs Ill. Hospital's claims to tax-exempt status." *Modern Healthcare*, p. 4; Olsen, D. (4 March 2004), "Action against Catholic hospital casts pall on non-profit designation," Copley

News Service; Pressey, D. (28 August 2008), "Provena Covenant Medical Center loses tax exemption again," *The News-Gazette*, www.newsgazette.com/news/2008/08/28/provena_covenant_medical_center_loses_tax_exemption_again; Pressey, D. (10 September 2008), "Provena Covenant Medical Center stands pat on tax refund." *The News-Gazette*, www.newsgazette.com/news/2008/09/10/provena_covenant_medical_center_stands_pat_on_tax_refund; Shields, Y. (19 December 2007), "Illinois: Hospital sues state," *The Bond Buyer*, www.americanbanker.com.

CASE 32. NEW INTERNET COOKIE RECIPE GIVES
HEARTBURN TO DOUBLECLICK

Internet marketers have big appetites for cookies, but privacy advocates often find them not simply distasteful but dangerous. At DoubleClick Inc., a company that provides Internet services for advertisers, a new recipe for cookies caused so much indigestion that federal and state authorities decided to investigate DoubleClick's corporate kitchen.

On the Internet, a cookie is a small text file that's stored on your computer by many Web sites that you visit. The purpose? Like a serial number, a cookie can make your computer easily and uniquely identifiable to the Web site that created it—sometimes for marketing purposes and sometimes for access permission.

Web site operators hire DoubleClick to handle ad insertion and viewer measurement rather than do it themselves. Using computers called ad servers, DoubleClick inserts ads into the web pages of its clients, tallies usage of their Web sites, and analyzes usage patterns. DoubleClick technology can guarantee that the same ad isn't repeated for a Web site visitor, predetermine the order of ads in a series, and keep track of the number of unique visitors who access a Web site.

Recipe for Internet Cookies

Here's how the cookie process has generally worked:
1. You visit a Web site such as amazon.com or cnn.com. All types of organizations use cookies.
2. The Web site writes a small text file onto your hard disk. If your Internet browser is preset to accept cookies, you're not aware of this activity. (You can set browsers to refuse all cookies or accept only those meeting certain conditions.)

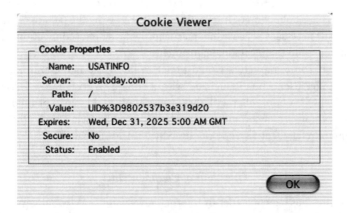

Figure 8.1 Magic cookies, written into a computer's memory by Web sites, contain a unique identifier and an expiration date. The cookie enables a Web site to recognize a computer each time it reconnects (Illustration by L. Lamb.))

3.   The text file contains both a unique number, assigned only to your computer, and an expiration date, which may be years away. The unique number could look something like iXxz@JB2ggkL…IvYN3BofhQl.
4.   Days or weeks later, you visit the same Web site again.
5.   The Web site checks the cookie files on your hard disk, finds the one it wrote, and recognizes that iXxz@JB2ggkL…IvYN3BofhQl is back for another visit.

As long as you don't erase the cookie and it hasn't reached its expiration date, the Web site that wrote the unique number will recognize your computer whenever it returns. A single Web site may write several cookies to your hard disk, depending on how many pages or features of the Web site you access, and multiple cookies might enable a Web site to catalog your interests.

This data collection makes some privacy advocates uneasy and alarms others because the potential for misuse of personal information grows as detailed profiles are built up. For this reason, most Web sites post privacy statements that outline their policies on confidentiality and the sale of information to third parties.

Sharing Data Collected With Cookies

Some Web sites hire DoubleClick under arrangements that allow the sharing of cookie data from multiple Web sites. Through sharing, DoubleClick collects information on your usage patterns and analyzes it to learn your preferences. Knowing your preferences, DoubleClick calculates marketing scores that rank your probable interest in purchasing certain kinds of products or services and then delivers ads to you that match your preferences. This analysis, scoring, ad selection, and ad delivery happen instantaneously as you browse the Web.

For example, cookie analysis may show that consumers who buy mysteries are likely to drink more tea than average. If you access an online bookseller's listing for the latest Patricia Cornwell novel, an ad may appear on the same web page offering a collection of international teas. Knowing the person's name and address isn't necessary because the Internet provides a direct connection between the marketer and the individual consumer.

Even so, some marketers would prefer to know the name and address of the computer user who's associated with a cookie. Who is iXxz@JB2ggkL…IvYN3BofhQl? A bookseller with that information could send a printed catalog of mystery novels to a computer user who accessed Patricia Cornwell titles but made no purchase. Intrusive? Undoubtedly. Ethical? Debatable.

Questions of Confidentiality

DoubleClick has been a leader in Internet advertising and technology services since the dawn of e-commerce, and for years its privacy statement had said that cookie data it collected would remain anonymous. Cookies inevitably become associated with individuals' names when computer users give personal information to Web sites to obtain free e-mail privileges, personalize news pages, gain access to password-protected Web sites, make purchases, and so on. When they do, they also consent to the Web site's policy concerning privacy—though most people never read it.

DoubleClick began reconsidering its policy after acquiring Abacus Direct, a database firm that sells buyer behavior information on 90 million identifiable U.S. households. With modifications to its privacy and consent statements, DoubleClick prepared to track the online habits of named—not anonymous— individuals and planned to sell the information to catalog marketers and others.

A tide of criticism swelled. A California woman sued the company in 2000, asking the courts to stop DoubleClick from collecting personal details without permission and to require it to erase any records it had accumulated, and 12 more lawsuits soon piled on.

The FTC notified the company that an FTC inquiry into its data-collection and ad-serving practices was under way, and the attorneys general of 10 states also began similar investigations.

Five-Point Initiative on Privacy

Apparently surprised by the ferocity of its critics, the company announced a privacy initiative a few days later. Under the five-point initiative, DoubleClick pledged to:

- Use its www.privacychoices.org Web site and full-page ads in *The New York Times* and other major newspapers to inform online users about privacy rights and the ability to opt out of cookies.
- Adopt a new policy requiring all Web site operators using DoubleClick technology to have a clear and effective privacy policy governing their sites.
- Engage independent auditors to verify the company's compliance with its privacy commitments.
- Establish an advisory board of consumer advocates, security experts, and online privacy authorities to guide the company in improving the clarity of privacy policies.
- Hire a chief privacy officer to ensure adherence to privacy policies.

Some privacy critics applauded the initiative as a good start, but others said that the changes were mostly cosmetic and left untouched the fundamental problem—surreptitious recording of user behaviors into a massive library of personal information.

DoubleClick insisted that it was doing nothing wrong and issued a statement by the company's president, Kevin Ryan, just three days after announcing its five-point initiative. "We are confident that our business policies are consistent with our privacy statement and beneficial to consumers and advertisers," he said. "The FTC has begun a series of inquiries into some of the most well-known web companies, including DoubleClick, and we support their efforts to keep the Internet safe for consumers."

Critics Pile On

Critics did not let up. The Electronic Privacy Information Center and the Center for Democracy & Technology complained that many privacy statements, even those of some prominent online retailers, were misleading and often ignored by Web site operators. Consumer advocates said that DoubleClick should directly ask Internet users for permission to record data.

Business Week warned in an editorial: "The hope that the Internet could police itself on privacy is quickly fading, as new invasive technology generates an ominous flood of intrusions…DoubleClick Inc., the biggest Internet ad placement company, unleashed a storm of controversy by profiling thousands of web surfers by name—without their explicit consent."

The editorial noted that some members of Congress were considering legislation to regulate the use of cookies and that the European Union already had imposed limits on the collection of personal data in its 15-member nations.

Doubleclick Acknowledges Mistake

After more than a month of complaints and castigation, the CEO of DoubleClick, Kevin O'Connor, acknowledged that the company had started down the wrong path and was ready to backtrack. He said on March 2:

> Over the past few weeks, DoubleClick has been at the center of the Internet privacy controversy. During this time, we have met and listened to hundreds of consumers, privacy advocates, customers, government officials and industry leaders about these issues. The overwhelming point of contention has been under what circumstances names can be associated with anonymous user activity across Web sites.
>
> It is clear from these discussions that I made a mistake by planning to merge names with anonymous user activity across Web sites in the absence of government and industry privacy standards.
>
> Let me be clear: DoubleClick has not implemented this plan and has never associated names, or any other personally identifiable information, with anonymous user activity across Web sites.
>
> We commit today that, until there is agreement between government and industry on privacy standards, we will not link personally identifiable information, to anonymous user activity across Web sites.

Over the next 30 months, the FTC closed its inquiry into the company's operations; a federal court approved a settlement that DoubleClick reached in the Internet users' lawsuits, and the company reached agreement with the attorneys general of 10 states, ending their investigation.

In none of the cases did DoubleClick admit any wrongdoing, and the company was required to do little beyond its original five-point initiative. In effect, the agreement with the states made the initiative legally binding rather than simply voluntary. DoubleClick continued to expand its business and was acquired by Google in 2007.

QUESTIONS FOR REFLECTION

1. Do you think that most people use the Internet with the expectation that their privacy—which sites they visit and how often—will be respected and protected? Is this protection a proper role for regulators?
2. Some Internet users like cookies because they can make the Internet easier to use if you repeatedly visit the same site. Others object to the invisible collection of data. Can the two viewpoints be reconciled?
3. Why was the FTC interested in Internet cookies?
4. What are the most recent controversies concerning Internet privacy? Do they resemble the DoubleClick issue?

Information for this case was drawn from the following: the DoubleClick Web site at www.doubleclick.com/us/about_doubleclick; Teinowitz, I., & Gilbert. J. (31 January 2000), "Online privacy disputes reach FTC panel, courts," *Advertising Age*, p. 92; Gray, D. (28 January 2000), "DoubleClick sued for privacy violations," IDG News Service; Miller, G. (3 February 2000), "Ad firm's practice seen as threat to net anonymity," *The Los Angeles Times*, p. A1; Dreazen, Y. (18 November 2002), "The best way to... guard your privacy," *The Wall Street Journal*, p. R4; Green, H. (23 April 2001), "Commentary: Your right to privacy: Going...Going..." *Business Week*, p. 67; Sullivan, B. (24 May 2002), "Privacy groups debate DoubleClick settlement," IDG News Service; Schwartz, J. (17 October 2002), "Consumers face tricky maze in guarding privacy," *The New York Times*, p. C1; Green, H., Alster, N., Borrus, A., & Yang, C. (14 February 2000), "Privacy: Outrage on the web," *Business Week*, p. 111; and (28 February 2000), "Time to move on Internet privacy," *Business Week*, p. 142.

CASE 33. "WORKING TOGETHER TO BRING PEACE": SAUDI ARABIA SEEKS TO IMPROVE ITS U.S. IMAGE

The commercial proclaimed: "We are separated by three oceans…one language… But we share the same desires…the same dreams…the same joy…the same pain…and the same hope that we can make our world a safer place. Together."

The advertisement, which aired in 14 American markets, was part of a multimillion-dollar public relations campaign financed by the Saudi Arabian government in an attempt to improve the image of the country among Americans and their leaders.

Post-September 11 Concerns

The image of Saudi Arabia had apparently been damaged by fears about terrorism and anti-U.S. sentiment. Fifteen of the 19 hijackers who attacked U.S. targets on September 11, 2001, were Saudi citizens. Reports that emerged following the attacks contained allegations that a Saudi princess had inadvertently given money to the terrorists. Security measures imposed following the attacks had led to the screening of visa applicants from the Middle East and intensive scrutiny of Arab charitable organizations within the United States; these actions heightened concerns about relations between the long-time allied countries. A Gallup opinion poll five months following the attacks found that negative opinion of Saudi Arabia was up to 64%, rising from the 46% of Americans who held unfavorable positions prior to September 11.

A Royal Public Relations Campaign

Since that time, the Saudi government has invested millions of dollars on an extensive public relations campaign to try to improve its image in the United States. Justice Department sources reported the Saudis hired several public relations firms and spent more than $5 million in the first year after the terrorist attacks, according to *The New York Times*.

Among the public relations firms employed were Patton Boggs, a firm known for its contacts among Democrats, and Akin, Gump, Strauss, Hauer & Feld, a firm headed by Robert Strauss, who once headed the Democratic National Committee. Lobbyists with Republican ties have also been employed, including James P. Gallagher, a former Senate staff member, and the media-buying firm of Sandler-Innocenzi.

Qorvis Communications is the public relations firm that produced the broadcast advertising campaign. It was being paid $200,000 a month for its services, garnering a reported $1.4 million from the Saudis from October 2002 to March 2003. The agency has prepared position papers that stress the positive relationship between the Bush administration and the Saudis. Reports said at least 10 other firms also had been hired to represent Saudi Arabia.

According to its Web site, Qorvis Communications is the largest independently owned public relations firm based in the Greater Washington, D.C., area. Formed in August 2000, Qorvis has offices in Washington and McLean, Virginia, and provides services to its clients in investor and financial relations, public affairs, grassroots campaigns, public and media relations, marketing communications, and research and opinion surveys. The Washington, D.C.-based law firm of Patton Boggs is an investor in and strategic partner with Qorvis.

Michael Petruzzello, the managing partner of Qorvis, was interviewed by the Associated Press in February 2003. He said negative American opinions about the Saudis can be changed. "After a year of a lot of high-profile attention, positive and negative, people in the United States are asking, 'Who are the Saudis?' ... So now, what we are trying to do is reintroduce the Saudi people."

The advertisements stressed the long-standing ties between the two countries. One spot featured black-and-white photos of Saudi leaders with U.S. presidents from Franklin Roosevelt to George W. Bush. Its voice-over says: "We've been allies for more than 60 years. Working together to solve the world's toughest problems. Working together for a world of prosperity. Working together to bring peace to the Middle East. Working together to create a better future for us all."

Another ad features quotes from Bush and Secretary of State Colin Powell commending the Saudis for their cooperation in the war on terrorism.

The campaign utilized more than television and radio advertisements. Adel al-Jubeir, a Saudi adviser, said the strategy for improving the Saudi image would include increasing press accessibility, sending officials on speaking tours, polling American public opinion, and cultivating research. Prince Bandar bin Sultan, the Saudi U.S. ambassador, wrote op-ed pieces for *The New York Times, Washington Post*, and *The Wall Street Journal*. The government has also purchased and run print ads in major magazines.

The Campaign Is Redesigned

But by December, *PRWeek* reported that the Saudis were displeased with the results of the campaign, and that it would be reshaped. Newly designed advertisements were to show a very modern Saudi Arabia. The royal family planned to travel to Washington and to meet with reporters, intending to discuss the common ideals of the United States and Saudi Arabia and to explain more about the Islamic faith.

An attack in Riyadh in May 2003 that killed 35, including 9 Americans, focused renewed attention on how the Saudi government was dealing with prospective terrorists. Results of the September 11 investigation released in summer 2003 led to more debate about the Saudi role and the public relations efforts concerning the country. The BBC reported that the 900-page report on the intelligence failings before the attacks said some Saudis had provided aid to the hijackers and had then failed to cooperate with the U.S. intelligence agencies. More than 20 pages were expunged from the report, leading to much speculation that it was the references to Saudi Arabia's alleged ties to terrorism that were omitted.

Referring to the secret section of the report, the Saudi Ambassador Prince Bandar bin Sultan told the BBC, "Twenty-eight blanked-out pages are being used by some to malign our country and our people." Saudi officials asked for 28 classified pages of a congressional report on the attacks to be made public, so the Arab kingdom can clear its name. But President Bush refused the official request on the grounds that it would compromise U.S. intelligence operations.

Some argued this request was a public relations gesture, because the Saudis knew that Bush had already decided not to release the document. *USA Today* reported that Saudi foreign minister Prince Saud defended Bush from charges that his refusal to release the information was motivated by a desire to protect a longtime ally. Anyone suggesting that Bush was engaged in a cover-up "must be out of touch with reality or driven by ulterior motives," the foreign minister said. "It is an outrage to any sense of fairness that 28 blank pages are now considered substantial evidence to proclaim the guilt of a country that has been a true friend and partner to the United States for over 60 years."

~

QUESTIONS FOR REFLECTION

1. What are the most effective communication practices for a nation seeking to build and sustain a positive image with the citizens and government leaders of other nations?

2. Was the use of broadcast commercials the most effective strategy to support the apparent goals for this campaign? What other media might you suggest for this campaign?

3. Identify some effective evaluation methods this campaign might have utilized.

4. Are there ethical considerations that should be examined when a public relations firm or counselor is asked to represent international clients

---

Information for this case was drawn from the following: Associated Press (27 February 2003), "When relations soured, U.S. and Saudi Arabia called in the PR professionals," Jefferson City (MO) News Tribune Online, www.newstribune.com; BBC News (25 July 2003), "Saudi Arabia denies terror links," http://news.bbc.co.uk; De la Garza, P. (27 April 2002), "Saudi Arabia ads part of campaign to clean up image," *St.Petersburg Times*, www.sptimes.com; Labott, E. (30 September 2003), "Saudi prince calls for end to U.S. tensions," CNN.com; Keen, J. (29 July 2003), "Bush refuses to disclose Saudi items in 9/11 report," *USA Today*, www.usatoday.com/news/washington.2003-07-29-saudis-bush_x. htm; Marquis, C. (29 August 2002), "Worried Saudis try to improve image in the U.S.," *The New York Times*, www.nytimes.com; Murawski, J. (13 June 2003), "Saudi Arabia's TV ads out to polish image in U.S.," *The Palm Beach Post*, p. A12; Orris, M. (6 July 2003), "Saudis sell image to a skeptical U.S.," *The Atlanta Journal-Constitution*, p.A15; and Quenqua, D. (16 December 2002), "Saudis rethink PR as $3m 15-month campaign stalls," *PRWeek*, p. 11

CASE 34. KICK ASH BASH SETS STAGE FOR
ANTISMOKING CAMPAIGN

Minnesota teenagers burned big tobacco companies with an antismoking program launched in April 2000 when 400 high school students from around the state gathered for a teen summit called the Kick Ash Bash. Organized by the Minnesota Department of Health (MDH) because of rising teen tobacco use, the summit decided to adopt the same tactics used by tobacco companies in attracting new customers to create a counter-effort fighting the habit.

Just before the summit, the health department had completed a survey of 12,000 randomly selected students in middle schools and high schools. Results showed that nearly 40% of high school students and more than 12% of middle school students were currently using tobacco. A "current user" was someone who had used tobacco on one or more of the preceding 30 days. Though cigarettes were most popular, cigars and smokeless products like chewing tobacco were used by more than 10% of high school students. Gender made no difference in cigarette smoking; boys were more likely than girls to use other tobacco products.

The proportion of Minnesota high school students using tobacco was slightly higher than the national average (38.7% vs. 34.8%), and the middle school rate (12.6%) was almost the same as the national figure (12.8%).

Seventeen percent of high school students were frequent cigarette smokers, defined as individuals who smoked on at least 20 of the preceding 30 days. The rate of tobacco use, which climbed steadily from 6th through 12th grade, reached 45% among seniors.

Shaping and Reshaping Attitudes

The health department's survey showed that students understood the dangers of smoking. More than 90% acknowledged tobacco's power to addict users, its threat to the health of regular smokers, and its risk for nonsmokers exposed to secondhand smoke. In addition, most students did not believe that smoking for a year or two and then quitting tobacco would be safe.

Teenagers who attended the Kick Ash Bash heard how tobacco companies studied new smokers, their motivations, and their potential as continuing customers to understand how to attract them. The teens saw that the companies used special events, advertising, and sponsorships to connect with the natural interests of young people. And they were told that nearly 90% of the cigarettes sold in the United States under about 50 different labels are produced by four large companies.

After learning how Big Tobacco divides consumers into segments and identifies critical characteristics on which brand appeal can be based, the teens formed an antismoking movement and gave it a name designed to tell Big Tobacco: "We know how you really see us." The name they selected for their movement was Target Market. From the start, the teens and the organizers decided that Target Market would depend on youth leadership supported by adult guidance.

Source of Funds

Funding for Target Market and its anti-tobacco campaign came from an endowment from the Minnesota legislature, using a portion of the state's $6 billion settlement with the tobacco industry. The settlement stemmed from a lawsuit that the state had filed to recover some costs of tobacco's past harms. Endowment interest of $17 million in 2001 was earmarked for support of Target Market and other tobacco control initiatives, and the interest amount was expected to rise in succeeding years.

Teen interest in Target Market was strong from the outset, and membership reached 20,000 within a year. Looking for an organization to guide Target Market after its first year, the MDH issued a public request for proposals. The MDH request said that the selected organization would need significant experience in youth empowerment and grassroots organizing, knowledge of the state's youth market, and skill in motivating behavior change among the young.

The MDH said Target Market's mission was to "expose the marketing tactics the tobacco industry uses to target teens to become lifelong customers and to target the tobacco industry back with their own campaign."

A Specific and Measurable Objective

The objective of the endowment-supported programs was to reduce tobacco use among youth by 30% by the year 2005. The MDH was very explicit in spelling out this goal in its report on the Minnesota Youth Tobacco Survey (YTS).

"To meet the state's five-year goal, current tobacco use would have to fall from 38.7 to 27.1 percent among high school students and from 12.6 to 8.8 percent among middle school students when the YTS is conducted in 2005," the report stated.

In Minnesota, people under age 18 may not legally purchase tobacco products. Target Market's critical public included all individuals from age 12 through age 17, smokers and nonsmokers alike. The YTS specifically recommended that prevention efforts should focus on the 18% of middle school students and the 9% of high school students who had never smoked but had no firm commitment to avoid the habit.

Strategy for Action

The health department said studies had shown that teenagers resented adult control and attempts to manipulate them. Teens knew that tobacco use was harmful but didn't want to hear lectures or nagging on the subject. Although their familiarity with tobacco's dangers was high, knowledge of the industry's use of the social sciences to analyze and influence behavior was lower. Target Market's strategy was to open teenagers' eyes to the manipulation that lay at the heart of tobacco marketing and to give them the tools to create a campaign of their own to counter Big Tobacco.

Broadly, the tools included advertising, public relations, grassroots organizing, and an interactive Web site. In addition, Target Market had partners, also funded by the endowment, with whom it would need to coordinate its efforts. One partner's role was the creation of a media campaign—using television commercials, outdoor advertising, and more—that would carry the messages of Target Market throughout the state. Other partners included about 50 local coalitions addressing public health concerns.

The MDH established a $1.5 million annual budget for the organization chosen to guide Target Market in the second and third years of the program and indicated that the arrangement might be renewed for another three years if results were satisfactory.

Evaluation Based on Logic Model

Under contract terms, the organization would be required to apply 10% of the budget to the evaluation of results. The health department said that a "logic model" for the program was an essential precondition to development of an evaluation plan.

The department said in its request for proposals:

> Before you plan your evaluation, you need to develop a program "logic model." The logic model lays out what the program is expected to achieve and how it is expected to work, based on an expected chain of events.
>
> The chain of events that links inputs to outputs to outcomes in response to a situation is your "logic model." It articulates what you hope to achieve and how. It is based on a series of ordered actions that are logically linked. All begin with a clear specification of the situation—the problem or issue— being addressed in order to indicate the most appropriate chain of events.

The department offered an example of a seven-part logic model:
1. Goals. What do you expect to achieve?
2. Strategies. What services and activities do you plan to use?
3. Intensity and duration. How often and for how long do you plan to use them?
4. Target group. Who will participate in and be influenced by the program?
5. Theory of change. How will the strategies produce the outcomes?
6. Short-term outcomes. What immediate changes are anticipated?
7. Long-term outcomes. What changes will occur over time?

Discouraging alteration of the original program, the department made its expectations clear: The selected organization would "continue the mission and momentum that is already underway at Target Market."

Tactics for Influence

In its first year after the Kick Ash Bash, Target Market had gained widespread visibility and thousands of new members through a variety of activities:

- A Web site at www.tmvoice.com went online in June 2000 to provide background on the movement and give teens an opportunity to exchange ideas.
- Special anti-tobacco teen events were scheduled at the Back-to-School Lounge at the Mall of America in Bloomington, 15 minutes from St. Paul and Minneapolis, and at the Minnesota State Fair.
- Sponsoring a statewide Battle of the Bands contest, the movement built awareness of its goals by associating Target Market with music popular among teens.
- A compact-disc compilation of emerging Minnesota musicians was conceived and created by movement members to promote Target Market.
- The TM Cruiser, a walk-in panel truck, traveled to Minnesota's beaches, festivals, parades, fairs, malls, and concerts to recruit the young into the movement.
- Members appeared in TV and radio commercials, produced by the movement's media campaign partner, offering unscripted comments on Big Tobacco.

To offer evidence of the industry's manipulation, Target Market took copies of tobacco marketing reports right to the schoolhouse. The TM Document Tour, a traveling exhibit of tobacco industry documents, visited middle schools across the state. Installed in a tractor-trailer combination, the exhibit included examples of industry analysis and marketing reports. They contained statements like this excerpt from Philip Morris in 1981:

> Today's teenager is tomorrow's potential regular customer, and theoverwhelming majority of smokers first begin to smoke while still in their teens. In addition, the ten years following the teenage years is the period during which average daily consumption per smoker increases to the average adult level. The smoking patterns of teenagers are particularly important to Philip Morris.

With the traveling exhibit and other tactics, Target Market not only attained a high profile in its first year but also earned a number of awards, including Silver Anvils from the PRSA and Bronze Quills from the IABC.

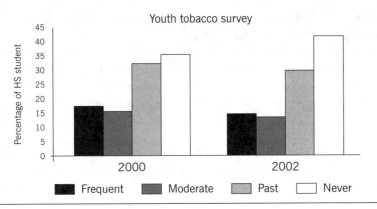

Figure 8.2 The use of tobacco among Minnesota high school students showed a decline after introduction of the Target Market antismoking campaign (Source: Minnesota Department of Health. Chart by L. Lamb)

Comparison to Benchmark

In early 2002, the MDH repeated the survey of middle school and high school students that it had first conducted in early 2000. About 11,500 randomly selected respondents were represented, and the results showed solid progress over the two years.

The proportion of high school students who were currently using tobacco had dropped to 34.4% from 38.7%, and the middle school rate went down to 11.2% from 12.6%. In both categories, the number of current tobacco users per thousand students had dropped 11.1%. The number of frequent smokers per thousand students declined 40% in middle schools and went down 13% in high schools.

The department also published ad measurements provided by Target Market's media campaign partner. They indicated that 92% of teens had seen at least one of the movement's ads. Six of every 10 were able to recall specific details of the ad, and among this 60%, 8 of 10 indicated that they understood Big Tobacco's marketing approach.

Critics and Complaints

Despite the popularity and apparent success of Target Market, the movement had its critics, embarrassments and scrapes. When it said that 40,000 teenagers had joined the movement, some observers said only 3,000 were active. The two-year decline in teen tobacco use was welcome, but critics said it simply paralleled declines in national figures.

Minnesota legislators expressed concern about the lyrics and messages of a Chicago band that had performed at a Target Market concert. The lyrics referred approvingly to heavy drinking and used obscenities profusely.

For a few months, a Duluth teen named Matt Hannula maintained a Web site, www.antitargetmarket.com, questioning the tactics of Target Market and the organization's influence. A cross-country runner and nonsmoker, Mr. Hannula told the *Duluth News-Tribune*, "Skateboarding and rock concerts never helped anyone quit or kept them from starting."

Eventually, the major threat to Target Market came not from critics but from a $4.5 billion deficit in Minnesota's budget. When the state administration made its budget plan public at midyear 2003, the endowment funding Target Market was gone. Recessionary forces drained budgets not just in Minnesota but in most states and led many to reallocate tobacco settlement funds for essential government services.

Protests of Target Market teens and public health professionals could not overcome the arguments of those who said the tobacco prevention program was nice to have but not a need.

QUESTIONS FOR REFLECTION

1. Organizations that submitted proposals to guide the Target Market antismoking campaign were required to outline their "logic model." What's the purpose of a logic model?

2. How do the results of the Minnesota survey of teen smoking habits compare to your personal perceptions of your high school experiences?

3. Was the choice of the movement name, Target Market, a wise and effective choice?

4. Which Target Market tactics offered the best combination of creativity and potential effectiveness?

Information for this case was drawn from the following: the Minnesota Department of Health Web site at www.health.state.mn.us/; its teen smoking Web site at www.tmvoice.com/index.asp; (2002), Minnesota Youth Tobacco Survey, Center for Health Statistics, Minnesota Department of Health; Phelps, D. (9 May 2003), "Advocates criticize use of tobacco settlement money to fight deficit," *The Star Tribune* (Minn.), p. B1; Stawicki, E. (31 March 2003), "Target Market targeted to disappear," Minnesota Public Radio; (2001). Target Market organization: Request for proposals, Minnesota Department of Health; (August 2000), "Teens and tobacco in Minnesota," Center for Health Statistics, Minnesota Department of Health; and (Accessed 11 July 2003), "What's TM been up to?" The Tobacco Initiative, www.mntobacco.net.

CASE 35. "WHAT HAPPENED": FORMER PRESS SECRETARY'S MEMOIR SPARKS CONTROVERSIES

The publication of the memoir of former George W. Bush press secretary Scott McClellan in 2008 prompted a furor of discussion about the Bush White House, and it also drew attacks from those who doubted the motives of the writer and questions about the loyalties needed to serve as a political spokesperson.

Scott McClellan served as the White House press secretary from 2003 to 2006; before then, he had been the principal deputy press secretary in the White House and traveling press secretary for the 2000 Bush-Cheney campaign. Earlier, he had served as deputy communications director for Mr. Bush when he was Texas governor.

"What Happened: Inside the Bush White House and Washington's Culture of Deception"

The book begins with McClellan's account of his role in the Valerie Plame leak scandal, during which he steadfastly defended the administration as having played no role in the matter. He writes that he had been assured that this was the truth; when the investigation revealed otherwise, he learned that he had been knowingly misled.

He uses this incident and others from the Bush administration—from the September 11 attack to the Iraq War to the 2004 campaign, even the management of Hurricane Katrina relief—to describe an environment in which politics has become a "permanent campaign," in which "governing becomes an offshoot of campaigning rather than the other way around" (p.64). He argues that in such a climate, virtually all initiatives, from legislation to budgeting to international affairs, are all designed to "reward political loyalists, punish enemies, and win votes." A "scandal culture" has emerged since Watergate, McClellan argues, fostering a defensive attitude, "a destructive culture" of cynicism. These factors lead to what he describes as the third element of contemporary national politics, an "increasingly ruthless, win-at-all-costs attitude" he calls "the philosophy of politics as war" (p. 66).

However, he notes that political leaders must be aware of public opinion and must have popular support. Yet seeking those, he says, should not lead politicians to the excesses of deception and the misuse of political offices.

McClellan notes in the book that he continues to admire George W. Bush.

What Happened After the Book Was Published

The book was a bestseller. But political and media reaction to the book was as heated as its sales. The May 29 *Los Angeles Times* cited appearances by Dan Bartlett, a former counselor to President Bush, on CNN, and Karl Rove, former

White House strategist, on Fox News in which McClellan was criticized. Dana Perino, who was the current Bush press secretary, was quoted as telling reporters that McClellan was "disgruntled" about his time in the White House. The May 30, 2008 *Washington Post* noted, "It has also prompted many of McClellan's oldest friends and colleagues to brand him, among other things, a turncoat and a fraud." On June 2, Howard Kurtz, writing in the *Post*, reported that the "White House called McClellan 'disgruntled,' Matt Drudge branded him a 'snitch,' and National Review Online ran six pieces on Friday trashing him as 'pasty,' 'maladroit,' 'plodding' and 'shameful.'" Some asked why he had not articulated his misgivings while working in the White House.

McClellan was asked to testify in June 2008 before the House Judiciary Committee investigating the Plame leak. The June 21 *New York Times* cites statements from Rep. Lamar Smith from Texas, the ranking Republican on the committee, that were sharply critical of McClellan. The *Times* reported that Rep. Smith said "that with his book Mr. McClellan had raised the question of why he went from 'a loyal and trusted staff member to an embittered person who makes biting accusations.' Mr. Smith then said, 'Scott McClellan alone will have to wrestle with whether it was worth selling out the president and his friends for a few pieces of silver.'"

Some public relations practitioners discussed the impact of the book in the June 9 *PRWeek*, noting that spokespeople generally disclose what they know, but that they should ask questions or express disquiet during situations and not wait until afterward.

What Happened Before

McClellan is not the only former White House insider to write a critical book after leaving office. Other Bush officials and supporters have done so while Bush was in office. And during the Clinton administration, George Stephanopoulos, who had served as a communications director and policy advisor for the Clinton White House, published a memoir in 1999 shortly after leaving his work at the White House. The book, *All Too Human*, provided an insider's look at the power struggles, political successes and personal lives of those within the White House. He, too, faced sharp criticism for providing the candid information. One example: Writing in the March 8, 1999 *Washington Post*, John F. Harris quotes an unnamed "veteran Clinton aide" as saying: "This is such a betrayal. George was family, he was that close."

Certainly, many insiders have written books about the presidents they served. Even Franklin D. Roosevelt had such a book written. Aides to Eisenhower, Kennedy, Johnson and Nixon also published memoirs—but not during the administration. However, during the post-Watergate era, articles or books detailing accounts of administrative actions and strategies have appeared while the presidential subjects were in office.

Such timing may explain some of the tensions and uneasiness about the communication and public relations advisors who opt to share information while it may still influence political outcomes. One is left to wonder whether the drive for personal vindication or economic gain—or even a sense of serving the public interest by revealing what they believe should be known—were more important than loyalty to their former employers.

~~✦~~

QUESTIONS FOR REFLECTION

1. What options are available to spokespersons who may disagree with the policies or actions of the organization or cause they represent?
2. What public-relations counsel would you have offered the Bush White House in dealing with the publication of the book? What advice would you have offered McClellan about dealing with the criticisms and praise of the book?
3. If McClellan is correct in his assessments of the nature of presidential governance, what implications do these suggest for the practice of public relations in a democracy? How might public-relations practitioners make a difference?
4. One of the PRSA values says: "We are faithful to those we represent, while honoring our obligation to serve the public interest." Do you think that Mr. McClellan observed this value?

Information for this case was drawn from the following: McClellan, S. (2008). What happened. Inside the Bush White House and Washington's culture of deception. New York: Public Affairs; Harris, J.F. (8 March 1999). "Stephanopoulos book tests loyalty." *Washington Post*, A3; Kurtz, H. (2 June 2008). "McClellan, a tad late correcting the story." *Washington Post*, C1; Lewis, N.A. (21 June 2008), "Former Bush aide testifies about CIA leak," *The New York Times*, accessed at www.nytimes. com; Eggen, D., & Weeks, L. (30 May 2008), "McClellan says book's tone evolved," *Washington Post*, p. A1; McKenna, T. (9 June 2008), "Book row puts spotlight on spokespeople," *PRWeek*, p. 6; Schmitt, R.B., & Gerstenzang, J. (29 May 2008), "Political world abuzz over McClellan's book," *The Los Angeles Times*, p. A1; Stephanopoulos, G. (1999). All too human: A political education. Boston: Little, Brown & Co.

PROFESSIONAL INSIGHT

IS SAYING "NO" AN OPTION FOR THE GOVERNMENT?

Gene Rose, communications director, National Conference of State Legislatures

Don Hewitt, the former executive producer of "60 Minutes," tells audiences that the success of the program is based on four words: "Tell me a story."

A few corporations and government agencies do a good job of telling their stories. Others, though, have a lot to learn. Take the typical "60 Minutes" piece that takes on a government agency. How many times have we heard a reporter say that an agency representative "declined to be interviewed" for a story? On the other hand, how many times have we seen a government official agree to be interviewed, only to be embarrassed?

Which raises the question: Does a government agency have the right to say "no" to an interview request?

Every person employed in government communications has had to argue this point with their superiors at least once in their careers. Those who understand how media relations works know that every request for an interview presents an opportunity. Sometimes the interview requests are not opportunities worth pursuing, and there is a valid reason for saying "no" since there are no benefits and no consequences. (More often than not, a government communicator is trying to convince an official to not react publicly and inflame a one-day story.)

For agencies or public officials under the microscope, the tendency is to avoid the media and hope the story dies away. If legal counsel becomes part of the equation, then the communication director's case to cooperate with the press rarely wins.

While the battlefield is lined with those who did not survive the "let's meet the media head-on" strategy (think former Congressman Gary Condit and radio talk show host Don Imus), there are more success stories from those who had a credible story to tell combined with the ability to tell it well. Ronald Reagan and Bill Clinton certainly had plenty of excuses to stop talking with the media, but they took their lumps and kept pressing their message. That's why they have reputations as effective communicators.

Public officials and government agencies often fail to take into consideration the public's perception. The Gallup Honesty and Ethics Poll published in late 2006 reveals public trust of local officeholders and state office holders was only 26% and 24% respectively. Senators and congressmen came in at 15% and 14%, edging out insurance salesmen, HMO managers and car salesmen. (It should be noted that journalists only scored 26%.)

Saying "no" only reinforces the public's perception that government is not effective and, more importantly, is hiding secrets. The 2007 release of historic CIA documents that revealed covert operations is an example where documents—when viewed through the public's eyes—reveal that the government does keep secrets.

Promoting government transparency—the ability for the public to see how it operates—is difficult, challenging, and in some cases, nearly impossible. Agencies that listen to their government communicators on strategies and efforts to tell their story will not only be better served but will better serve the public.

Gene Rose served as president of the National Association of Government Communicators in 2007. He also is director of communications for the National Conference of State Legislatures and is a former newspaper reporter.

9
Stakeholders: Activists

Activists are saints, sinners, and sometimes both. It depends on your perspective of the public issue on which activists have focused. Because issues seldom have only two sides, several activist organizations may get involved in a public discussion or controversy and try to influence its eventual outcome. Not only would the groups voice a range of viewpoints, but they also might use a variety of methods to grab attention and get support for their preferred outcome.

Activist groups generally adopt conventional behaviors, conforming to public expectations because there's little reward in intentionally annoying people. Some groups are more colorful or aggressive, especially if they have a hard time getting noticed. A small number are deliberately destructive and engage in illegal acts.

PURPOSES OF ACTIVISM

In democracies, activism contributes the process of public life. Activists have influenced social acceptance of diverse lifestyles, social restraints on tobacco use, popular attitudes on animal rights, public debate on gun control, reproductive rights, alcohol consumption, and much more. So prevalent is the role of activists that a 322-page *Encyclopedia of American Activism: 1960 to the Present*, by Margaret B. Dicanio, was published in 1998.

Activist groups, often called special-interest groups or advocacy groups, usually try to:

- Influence popular opinion.
- Promote changes in public policy.
- Exert pressure on corporations.
- Remedy social problems.
- Affect personal behavior.

By owning shares in public corporations, activists gain the right to make statements and offer resolutions at annual meetings attended by investors. Shareholder resolutions proposed by activists not only draw public attention to the group's central concern, but also affect corporate decision making on sensitive issues. Even when the resolutions are voted down, corporate officers may later modify the practices that antagonized critics to avoid future confrontations.

FOCUSING ON SOCIAL PROBLEMS

In big cities and small towns around the world, community activism has been used successfully to spotlight social problems and propose solutions. Activists have organized campaigns against drug abuse, teen pregnancy, neighborhood deterioration, domestic violence, and homelessness. They have formed programs to promote mass transit, historical preservation, youth activities, and fairness in hiring and housing.

The Annie E. Casey Foundation of Baltimore funded production of the Making Communications Connections toolkit for community activists so that they could learn how to use strategic public relations in solving social problems. Since 1948, the foundation has been working to create better futures for disadvantaged children and their families through public policies, human services reforms, and community supports. Written by the FrameWorks Institute, the kit's recommendations reflect research into more than 50 community campaigns that covered a range of issues and localities. The strategic approach is familiar to almost everyone who studies or practices public relations, beginning with a clear definition of the problem and ending with an evaluation of the campaign's impact.

FRAMING A MESSAGE

To explain message development, the toolkit offers advice on framing messages and suggests six elements of the frame: context, numbers, messengers, visuals, metaphors, and tone.

The recommendations:

- *Context:* Include details about trends affecting the problem, and describe the broader social system in which the problem persists; focus on community efforts rather than individual or family responsibilities; present a solution.
- *Numbers:* Tell what your numbers mean; don't overwhelm narrative with numbers; state your message first, and then support it with numbers.
- *Messengers:* Use speakers whom the public will accept as knowledgeable and trustworthy; if possible, use unlikely allies.
- *Visuals:* Avoid conventional images already associated with the issue; avoid close-ups of a child alone or with parents because it may suggest a family, rather than community, problem; use public and community situations.
- *Metaphors:* Check metaphors in language and visuals to confirm that they will support rather than undermine your message.

- *Tone*: Avoid rhetoric that polarizes; present the problem in human scale; don't over-dramatize a problem, making it appear beyond community control.

The kit also tells community activists that they should look for program partners in the local business community. Sympathetic businesses may include a group's messages in promotional materials or sponsor group events.

AN UNDER-EXAMINED ROLE

Some public relations scholars have said that the study and practice of public relations have focused too much on examining the discipline from the standpoint of a practitioner working in or for a large organization. More work is needed, they've said, to understand relationships from the activists' perspectives and to listen to voices in the community that have been completely left out of discussions on public issues. In some circumstances, arriving at a win-win solution may simply mean that the quiet voices of small groups or unaffiliated individuals have been ignored.

In contrast, some critics have said that carefully orchestrated activist campaigns often distort the true dimensions of popular opinion. Some campaigns, critics say, hijack the public agenda by using conflict to lure the news media to a shallow pool of controversy and then claim it's the mainstream of public thought.

The chief executive officer of DaimlerChrysler's Chrysler Group said, "You might call it the difference between natural public opinion and synthetic public opinion."

As you consider these cases, seek to identify the public relations problem or opportunity, the methods and tools used to resolve the situation, and how one might evaluate the success or failure of the public relations efforts. Explore these questions: What would characterize a mutually beneficial relationship between an organization and an activist group in this circumstance? How would you define the objectives of the activists in each case? Those of the business or organization? Could better communication practices have helped resolve this situation more quickly? And if so, what should have been done, and when? What are the most appropriate ways to evaluate the success of an activist campaign? What ethical principles should underlie communication among activists, organizations and their other stakeholders?

ADDITIONAL READINGS

Alinksy, Saul. (1989). *Rules for radicals: A practical primer for realistic radicals*. Vancouver, WA: Vintage Books.

Best, Joel. (2001). *Damned lies and statistics: Untangling numbers from the media, politicians, and activists*. Berkeley: University of California Press.

Keck, Margaret E., & Kathryn Sikkink (1998). *Activists beyond borders: Advocacy networks in international politics*. Ithaca, NY: Cornell University Press.

Shaw, Randy. (1999). *Reclaiming America: Nike, clean air, and the new national activism.* Berkeley: University of California Press.

CASE 36. PETA SERVES UP "HOLOCAUST ON
YOUR PLATE" CAMPAIGN

Eight panels, each six feet high and ten feet long, paired bigger-than-life photographs of holocaust victims with images of livestock to support the "Holocaust on Your Plate" campaign created by People for the Ethical Treatment of Animals. A typical panel showed a five-foot-square photo of concentration camp inmates, crowded into three-tiered bunk beds, and a same-sized image of chickens in cramped cages. Across the panel's top, big block lettering said, "To animals, all people are Nazis."

PETA sent sets of the panels for public display across the nation and around the world in 2003 to raise awareness of animal rights.

The campaign also sought to include television ads as part of the media plan. PETA reported that one TV station in Richmond, Virginia, did agree to air a commercial in October that had been rejected by stations in other states. The ad showed someone looking through slits in the side of a truck with a voice-over using the tagline: "Each age has its own atrocities. End the animals' holocaust. Please become a vegetarian."

The Advocates Face Protests

The United States Holocaust Memorial Museum protested the exhibit, as did the Anti-Defamation League. The museum had sold copies of the photos to the group unknowingly, it said. Spokeswoman Mary Morrison told the *N.Y. Daily News* that the request to use the photographs came from a private e-mail account. The project was described as one that would be "comparing the atrocities of the Holocaust to other forms of oppression throughout history."

The Anti-Defamation League denounced the project. In a February 24 release, Abraham H. Foxman, the ADL national director and a survivor of the Holocaust, said: "The effort by PETA to compare the deliberate systematic murder of millions of Jews to the issue of animal rights is abhorrent. PETA's effort to seek 'approval' for their 'Holocaust on Your Plate' campaign is outrageous, offensive and takes chutzpah to new heights."

PETA Responds

PETA defended its use of the photographs in the exhibits and ads. An October 9, 2003, PETA release announcing the exhibition's display in New York City explained its purpose this way:

> PETA wants to stimulate contemplation of how the victimization of Jews, Gypsies, homosexuals, and others characterized as 'life unworthy of life' during the Holocaust parallels the way that modern society abuses and

justifies the slaughter of animals. Just as the Nazis tried to 'dehumanize' Jews by forcing them to live in filthy, crowded conditions, tearing children away from their mothers, and killing them in assembly-line fashion, animals on today's factory farms are stripped of all that is enjoyable and natural to them and treated as nothing more than meat-, egg-, and milk-producing 'machines.'

Campaign Coordinator Matt Prescott, who PETA explained had family members who had been murdered by the Nazis, was quoted as saying:

The very same mindset that made the Holocaust possible—that we can do anything we want to those we decide are 'different' or 'inferior'—is what allows us to commit atrocities against animals every single day. We are asking people to allow understanding into their hearts and compassion onto their tables by embracing a nonviolent, vegan diet that respects other forms of life.

Despite criticism, PETA maintained the campaign. For almost two years, the exhibit traveled throughout the United States and into other countries and was frequently met with protesters.

A Sudden Apology

Then, on May 5, 2005, PETA President Ingrid Newkirk sent an e-mail message to many Jewish media outlets and Jewish rights groups. The message read: "I have decided to apologize for the pain caused by the 'Holocaust on Your Plate' campaign."

In response, the Anti-Defamation League said while it "would have preferred that the apology had come earlier, it welcomes the letter and expressed hope that PETA would no longer engage in efforts to compare the slaughter of animals to human suffering in the Holocaust."

Another Controversial Campaign

However, soon PETA unveiled a new campaign composed of 12 large panels that showed pictures of animals next to images of African-American men and women being abused as slaves or former slaves. The photos were graphic and horrifying. One panel in the exhibit showed a black civil rights protester at a lunch counter being beaten next to a photo of a seal being bludgeoned. Another panel paired the photograph of a lynching with that of a cow hanging in a slaughterhouse. Another panel showed a photograph of a chained slave's foot next to a photo of the chained foot of an elephant. The title of the exhibit: "Are Animals the New Slaves?"

PETA had planned a 10-week, 42-city national tour. However, reaction to the exhibit was quick and heated. Newspapers wrote editorials criticizing the campaign. Groups such as the National Association for the Advancement of Colored People and the American Jewish Congress protested.

On August 15, 2005, PETA said it would suspend the campaign. Dawn Carr, a PETA spokesperson, told the Associated Press: "We're not continuing right now while we evaluate. We're reviewing feedback we've received—most of it overwhelmingly positive and some of it quite negative."

QUESTIONS FOR REFLECTION

1. What would motivate PETA to plan such extreme exhibits?
2. How would you have advised the groups, such as the ADL and the NAACP, to respond to the exhibits they opposed?
3. Identify the ethical issues raised by these two campaigns. How might these campaigns have been more persuasive in fostering a commitment to vegetarianism?
4. PETA has been criticized for some past campaigns as well as its holocaust and slavery efforts. Why would PETA favor campaigns that shock and offend?

Information for this case was drawn from the following: Anti-Defamation League (24 February 2003; updated 5 May 2005), "ADL denounces PETA for its 'Holocaust on Your Plate' campaign; calls appeal for Jewish community support 'the height of chutzpah.'" ADL release, www.adl.org/PresRele/HolNa_52/4235_52; Center for Consumer Freedom (1 September 2005), "PETA flops with race card," www.consumerfreedom.com; Katz, C. (4 March 2003), "D.C. Holocaust Museum outraged by PETA pix," *New York Daily News*, p. 15; Mnookin, S. (10 March 2003), "Ads: A plate of controversy," *Newsweek*, p. 10; Morgante, M. (28 February 2003), "Animal-rights comparison to Holocaust draws fire," The Associated Press; Prescott, M. (9 October 2003), "Grandson of celebrated Jewish author brings giant graphic display to show how today's victims languish in Nazi-style concentration camps," PETA release, www.peta.org/mc/NewsItem.asp?ie=3021; Prescott, M. (30 September 2003), "Group asks Holocaust Museum to consider today's victims of factory farming," PETA release, www.peta.org/mc/NewsItem.asp?id=2946; Smith, W.J. (6 May 2005), "PETA's non-apology apology," National Review Online, www.nationalreview.com; Tolerance.org Staff (6 May 2005), "PETA apologizes for Holocaust on your plate campaign," www.tolerance.org/news/article_tol.jsp?id=1207; Tolerance.org Staff (15 August 2005), "PETA rethinks 'slavery' exhibit," www.tolerance.org/news/article_tol.jsp?id=1266; Walker, D. (13 August 2005), "PETA reconsiders campaign after complaints of racism," Associated Press; Willoughby, B. (7 March 2003), "PETA turns Holocaust into Pig Pen," Teaching Tolerance, www.tolerance.org/new/article_hate.jsp?id=724.

CASE 37. GREENPEACE PRESSURES CHEMICAL
PRODUCERS TO REDUCE RISKS OF CHLORINE GAS

Greenpeace environmentalists and American Chemistry Council (ACC) members have skirmished for a generation, but the terrorist attacks of September 2001 reshaped the dispute and sharpened anxieties.

Central issues have included the use or misuse of earth's resources, risks to human health near chemical plants, public access to information about plant hazards, and security against criminal intrusions and sabotage. In the debate, Greenpeace USA represents its 250,000 members, and the ACC speaks for chemical producers.

Seven months before al-Qaeda terrorists hijacked four airliners, Greenpeace activists organized a surreptitious visit to a Dow Chemical plant in Plaquemine, Louisiana, to test its security. They scaled an unguarded fence and entered an unlocked pump house, where they had access to a control panel regulating the discharge of wastewater into the Mississippi River. To provide journalists with proof of the unauthorized tour, the visitors took photographs and passed them out to news media in Baton Rouge upstream and New Orleans downstream.

The 1,500-acre Plaquemine operation, with nearly 3,000 workers at the site, produced 50 basic chemical products, including a large volume of chlorine.

The Dangers of Chlorine

Chlorine has been a chief concern of Greenpeace because the chemical is so common and so toxic. Most people are familiar with chlorine's beneficial uses: water purification, manufacture of pharmaceuticals, production of household bleach and PVC (polyvinylchloride) pipe, and more. However, it also is potentially dangerous.

Normally stored under pressure as a liquid, chlorine is a greenish-yellow gas at standard temperature and pressure with a strong unpleasant smell. Because it's heavier than air, it stays near the ground and spreads when released. In the trench warfare of 1915 and later, Germans used the same gas to disable and kill British troops.

The rate at which it dissipates, or mixes with surrounding air, depends on whether there's a breeze. Lab tests indicate that concentrations of 900 parts per million may be lethal to animals. Human response to chlorine gas depends on duration of exposure and concentration of the gas. Because chlorine combines with water to form hydrochloric and hypochlorous acids, it attacks moist tissue first—the eyes and upper respiratory tract. Soon after exposure, people notice irritation in the nose, throat, and lungs, and tears flood the eyes.

In the United States, deaths from chlorine exposure have been rare—averaging fewer than one fatality per year in the 1990s. In most cases of exposure, the symptoms were uncomfortable but posed no threat of long-term damage. Some records indicate that about 1 in 10 incidents resulted in moderate or severe injury. The potential for serious accidents exists not only near plants but along rail lines as well. Nine people died in Graniteville, South Carolina, in 2005 after a rail car containing chlorine ruptured and leaked 90 tons of the gas following a collision between two trains.

The Threat of Terrorism

Greenpeace has cited an elevated threat of terrorist attacks in insisting that companies producing and using chlorine should do more to lower the risks for communities near plant facilities. Safer substitutes exist for many applications that use the gas. For example, some water treatment facilities kill microbes with ultraviolet light.

Greenpeace also criticizes companies that store large quantities of the gas. The activist organization has said that releases, whether caused by sabotage or accident, could threaten the health and lives of hundreds of thousands.

To support its position, Greenpeace referred to disaster scenarios prepared by chlorine producers themselves under requirements of federal law. The Emergency Planning and Community Right-To-Know Act of 1986 compelled companies to account for the release of hazardous materials into the environment. It was enacted two years after 27 tons of methyl isocyanate spilled from a Union Carbide pesticide plant in Bhopal, India, killing 4,000 or more in neighborhoods surrounding the facility. Later, a 1990 amendment to the Clean Air Act obliged producers to describe worst-case scenarios of industrial accidents and their prevention plans. Summaries of the scenarios were made public.

Scaling Back on Access

In the months following the al-Qaeda attacks, the chemical industry persuaded the federal government to limit access to the accident scenarios, arguing that terrorists could use them in planning new attacks. Greater secrecy might deter or discourage terrorists.

Greenpeace countered that it was the producers themselves who were endangering communities by continuing to produce and store hazardous chlorine when substitutes were available. The environmentalists said that communities were entitled to know the risks imposed on them by industrial neighbors. Greater secrecy would relax pressure on the producers but handicap communities' power to protect the health and safety of residents.

To dramatize its concerns, Greenpeace sponsored a five-kilometer footrace— under the banner "Run for Your Life"—in Jersey City, New Jersey, in May 2003. The organizers distributed a news release that said the purpose of the race was to focus attention on the nation's vulnerability to a catastrophic release of toxic gas.

The environmentalists chose Jersey City for the race because it lies within the worst-case disaster scenario sketched out by Kuehne Chemical Company for its plant in nearby South Kearny. Kuehne (pronounced KEE-nee) stores chlorine at the facility for bleach production.

Worst-Case Scenarios

Greenpeace posted a map on its Web site showing cities and landmarks that lie within a 14-mile radius across which a chlorine cloud could drift if the Kuehne plant experienced a worst-case accident. Twelve million people live in the area and might face death or lung damage from exposure.

A year before the race, *The Wall Street Journal* reported that a Kuehne executive voiced concern about terrorism and criticized the activists' intention to publish the disaster map, saying, "I don't think someone who wants to do us harm has a right to know this."

In a subsequent letter, Greenpeace complimented Kuehne on steps it has taken since September 2001 to reduce the risks posed by chemicals at the New Jersey plant but suggested that more should be done:

In practice, we see three stages of progress toward disaster-free, safer technologies. First are immediate and permanent steps to reduce storage. Second is the use of easier, drop-in substitution of less hazardous chemicals. Third is the conversion to safer materials and processes that eliminate the production and use of chemicals, such as chlorine, which can be turned into a weapon of mass destruction. We think that is the wave of the future for smart "green chemistry" oriented companies.

Despite industry complaints, Greenpeace has published disaster maps not only for the Kuehne facility but also for plants operated by Dow Chemical, DuPont, and others in Michigan, Delaware, Texas, and West Virginia. Copies went to journalists as well.

Chemical industry representatives say that the worst-case scenarios fuel fears unnecessarily. In an imagined worst case, all safety systems would fail, and no one would try to flee the unfolding doom. In one of these nightmare scenarios, a 90-ton railcar loaded with chlorine would spill its entire contents within 10 minutes. A harmful cloud of gas then would roll along the ground for 14 miles in all directions. Anyone who was near the accident and unprotected would die; those at the 14-mile-distant perimeter would suffer mild respiratory irritation.

A Spill in Missouri

In an actual accident that occurred in Festus, Missouri, in August 2002, the chlorine leak was slower, smaller, and less damaging. Workers were using two hoses to transfer chlorine from a railcar into 1-ton and 150-pound containers.

One of the hoses burst, and an automatic shut-off valve failed to actuate. When a manual override device also failed, employees evacuated the site immediately, and emergency response personnel went door to door in the surrounding neighborhoods, warning people to leave. U.S. Highway 61, adjacent to the facility's property, and nearby Interstate 55 were closed.

The chlorine continued to escape from the hose for three hours, discharging about 24 tons of gas. After donning protective equipment, hazardous-materials personnel entered the area near the railcar and measured lethal gas concentrations above 1,000 parts per million. They walked through a waist-high greenish-yellow cloud and climbed the tank to close the valves.

Sixty-three people, workers and local residents, received medical treatment for nausea, respiratory distress, and coughing, and no one was seriously injured. Residents returned to their homes seven hours later.

After the accident, activists said that the leak, its lethal concentration, and failure of safety systems underscored the need for public access to information on the chemical industry's use of hazardous materials. The industry's efforts to scale back its availability might raise risks to public health and lower trust in producers' operations.

Chemical Week magazine reported that the ACC's own random survey of Americans nationwide in early 2002—before the Festus leak—found that more than half were worried about chemicals or the chemical industry and that 48% described themselves as "distrustful" and 62% as "suspicious." The magazine said about two-thirds of the respondents, when asked to indicate their overall assessment of the industry, held a largely neutral view, and the remaining third were almost evenly divided between positive and negative assessments.

QUESTIONS FOR REFLECTION

1. Greenpeace and chemical producers have quarreled about public access to information concerning health risks in neighborhoods surrounding chlorine plants. What is most convincing about the positions they have staked out?
2. Chlorine producers have said that they are concerned that terrorists might obtain and use the information that Greenpeace wants to publish. Should regulators restrict the availability of disaster maps?
3. *Chemical Week* magazine said that about half of all respondents to an ACC survey said they were "distrustful" of chemicals and the chemical industry. What might account for this response?
4. Greenpeace organized an unauthorized visit to an unattended chemical plant pump house in 2001. Was this entry unethical?

Information for this case was drawn from the following: the Greenpeace USA Web site at www.greenpeaceusa.org; the American Chemistry Council Web site at www.accnewsmedia.com; (October 2002), "Chlorine leak provokes fears," *Occupational Hazards*, p. 42; Cone, M. (17 April 2003), "Chemical plants said to pose risk," *The Los Angeles Times*, p. B1; Davis, A. (30 May 2002), "Toxic cloud: New alarms heat up debate on publicizing chemical risks," *The Wall Street Journal*, p. A1; (2 May 2003), "Investigators recommend steps to prevent future chlorine leaks," *The Jefferson City News Tribune*, p. 5; Pianin, E. (12 November 2001), "Toxic chemicals' security worries officials," *The Washington Post*, p. A14; (15 August 2002), "Rail car leak sends 28 to hospital in Missouri," *The Los Angeles Times*, p. A23; Schmitt, B. (3 July 2002), "Industry's critics make respect an elusive goal," *Chemical Week*, p. 42.

CASE 38. ACTIVIST CAMPAIGN IN INDIA EXAMINES
SOFT DRINKS

India's Centre for Science and Environment (CSE) managed to unite the two top rivals in the soft-drink industry as perhaps no one has done ever before. Coca-Cola and PepsiCo temporarily suspended the cola wars in August 2003 to stand shoulder-to-shoulder in condemning CSE laboratory tests that showed high levels of contaminants in beverages sold by the two companies in India.

CSE said that tested samples of 12 soft-drink brands sold in and around New Delhi contained pesticide residues that far exceeded limits adopted in the United States and European Union. The Coca-Cola Company and PepsiCo Inc. said the test results were just plain wrong.

The CSE is a nonprofit, nongovernmental organization that has functioned as a self-appointed public watchdog for the one billion people who live on the Indian subcontinent. Established in 1980, CSE aims to raise awareness of issues in science, technology, environment, and development that affect the lives of ordinary Indians. Here's how the center has described itself:

> Centre for Science and Environment is considered one of India's leading environmental NGOs [nongovernmental organizations] specialising in sustainable natural resource management. Its strategy of knowledge-based activism has won it wide respect and admiration for its quality of campaigns, research and publications. CSE promotes solutions for India's numerous environmental threats – of "ecological poverty" and extensive land degradation on one hand, and rapidly growing toxic degradation of uncontrolled industrialisation and economic growth on the other.

CSE Tackles Public Policy Issues

Through activist campaigns, CSE has focused attention on innovations in rainwater harvesting, protecting groundwater from pesticide invasion, air pollution caused by diesel fuels adulterated with kerosene and naphtha, and pure food regulations. In February 2003, the organization said it found potentially dangerous contaminants in most samples of bottled water sold at retail in Mumbai (formerly known as Bombay) and New Delhi.

In August 2003, CSE made headlines around the world when it announced that its lab tests had detected insecticides in Coca-Cola, Pepsi, Mountain Dew, and nine other popular soft drinks.

"All samples contained residues of four extremely toxic pesticides and insecticides: lindane, DDT, malathion and chlorpyrifos," the CSE news release said. "In all samples, levels of pesticide residues far exceeded the maximum residue limit for pesticides in water used as 'food,' set down by the European Economic Commission (EEC). Each sample had enough poison to cause – in the long term – cancer, damage to the nervous and reproductive systems, birth defects and severe disruption of the immune system."

Pesticide Levels Compared

According to CSE, the average pesticide levels in the Coca-Cola brands and the PepsiCo brands were similar—at least 30 times higher than acceptable European levels. The organization said that it also tested samples of Coca-Cola and Pepsi-Cola sold in the United States and found that they contained no pesticides.

Without excusing the soft-drink giants, the organization laid much of the blame at the doorstep of India's legislators and regulators, indicating that government has neglected its responsibility to protect public health and safety. CSE said that the rules governing bottled water were stricter than those applying to the soft-drink industry, which it described as "virtually unregulated."

Sunita Narain, director of CSE, acknowledged to the *Hindu Business Line* that milk and other foods in India often contain traces of pesticide. The country's environmental-protection laws generally do not match those in Europe or the United States.

Miss Narain told the financial daily that: "Just because others violate the law, it does not give the right to global corporates such as Coke and Pepsi to do the same. They are market leaders and need to set an example. Ground water here does contain pesticide, but companies should invest more in cleaning up the water, which is the raw material for soft drinks. Water accounts for more than 80 percent of the soft drink."

According to *The Washington Post*'s account of the controversy, Miss Narain said she was not trying to pick a fight with either of the soft-drink giants. The newspaper quoted her as saying: "Our battle is not with Pepsi or Coca-Cola; it is with the Indian government, whose norms are a vague maze of meaningless definitions."

Soft-Drink Executives Rebut Claims

On the same day that CSE disclosed its lab results, the chairman of PepsiCo's operations in India and the president of Coca-Cola India said that the quality of their companies' products is the same worldwide. They dismissed the CSE complaints as baseless and invited inspections by independent and accredited authorities. Appearing together at an unusual joint news conference, Coke and Pepsi executives said that any impurities in their soft drinks were well below the European thresholds of safety, which are stricter than those generally applied in the United States.

Despite the reassurances, the reaction in the Indian Parliament and on the street was immediate and harsh. In New Delhi, Parliament suspended sale of the soft drinks in its cafeteria, and demonstrators smashed bottles of the beverages on pavements in cities across the country. India's health minister promptly promised an investigation, as samples of the soft drinks were sent to government labs for independent analysis.

Soft-drink consumers reacted harshly, too. Within 10 days of the initial announcement, daily sales of Coke and Pepsi products had dropped about one-third. The controversy represented a significant setback for the two companies because the soft-drink market in hot, humid, and huge India appeared to offer so much potential for growth.

Soft-Drink Market in India

India's annual per-capita consumption of soft drinks was nine eight-ounce servings; just nine per year for each person in India's population of 1 billion. The comparable figure for the United States was 848 per capita and for Germany was 341, according to *Beverage Digest* magazine's global profile for 2001. (Mexico was the world champion at 1,500 servings per capita per year.)

India's weather seems ideal for selling soft drinks. New Delhi's average daily high temperature in July is 101° Fahrenheit (38° Celsius) and in January is 68° Fahrenheit (20° Celsius).

In 2002, the total sales of all soft drinks in India reached about $2.3 billion. The Coca-Cola Company's brands together accounted for about 60% of the total, but the Coke brand itself, market leader almost everywhere else, is third in sales in India. Pepsi is No. 1, and Thumbs Up, a local cola that Coca-Cola acquired in 1993, ranks second.

Producers Fight Fears

The soft drink companies acted quickly to stem August's decline in sales. Giving consumers reasons to reject the fears stirred by the CSE report, the soft-drink companies talked with reporters, issued news releases, and created advertising that detailed their quality assurance programs.

Coca-Cola India created a special section on its Web site with individual pages describing its quality commitment, testing procedures, filtration systems, and more. It also included a section identifying what the company called false statements, or myths, that had been circulating since the CSE announcement and paired each myth with an explanation to refute it.

In the Myths and Facts section, Coca-Cola India addressed one of the statements that had inflamed passions the most. Here is the pair from the Web site:

The myth: Coca-Cola has dual standards in the production of its products, one high standard for western countries and another for India.

The fact: The soft drinks manufactured in India conform to the same high standards of quality as in the USA and Europe. Through our globally accepted and validated manufacturing processes and quality management systems, we ensure that our state-of-the-art manufacturing facilities are equipped to provide the consumer the highest quality beverage each time. We stringently test our soft drinks in India at independent, accredited and world-class laboratories both locally and internationally.

Process for Purification

In a joint statement to editors, Coca-Cola and Pepsi described the multiple-barrier filtration process that both use to purify water contained in soft drinks. The four-step process is as follows:

1. Chlorination disinfects the water.
2. Filtration at the molecular level removes dirt, clay, suspended materials, microbial matter such as bacteria and viruses, and heavy metals and compounds.
3. Activated carbon filters absorb organic compounds, which include pesticides and herbicides.
4. Finally, the water passes through a high-efficiency 5-micron filter that removes any trace of activated carbon.

The joint statement also explained that the companies buy high-grade sugar from mills in India and treat it to remove impurities before converting it into sugar syrup for use in soft drinks.

Health Minister's Report

On August 21, India's health minister gave Parliament a report on results obtained by government labs in their tests of soft-drink samples. She said that all 12 brands were safe to drink and met Indian standards for bottled water. However, she noted that several were not completely free of pesticide residue and some exceeded the limits set for contaminants by the European Union. Among the 12 brands, the labs found pesticide residue in 9 that were one to five times higher than European standards.

Soft-drink executives expressed delight that the government had declared the beverages safe to drink. The headline of a joint news release read: "Coca-Cola and Pepsi-Cola welcome Indian Government's endorsement on safety of soft drinks."

CSE officers also found some vindication in the health minister's report and continued their call for stricter regulation of bottled water, soft drinks, and the use of pesticides. The central government opened an inquiry into standards for soft-drink purity, and state governments began testing samples as well.

To some extent, individuals on all sides of the issue appeared to agree with some of the sentiments expressed in the Myths and Facts section of Coca-Cola India's Web site: "The situation calls for the development of national sampling and testing protocols for soft drinks, an end to sensationalising unsubstantiated allegations, and cooperation by all parties concerned in the interests of both Indian consumers and companies with significant investment in the Indian economy."

The Changing Role of NGOs

As the soft-drink controversy was unfolding in India, *The Economist* newspaper noted that the role of nongovernmental organizations (NGOs), such as the CSE, has been expanding beyond disaster relief campaigns and advocacy for human rights and environmental issues.

NGOs have performed better than government agencies in some poor nations and in areas of conflict such as Afghanistan and Iraq, the newspaper said. In other cases, the expanding role of NGOs has produced mixed results:

Campaigns against corporations often focus on the targets most likely to capitulate, rather than the worst offenders. The politicisation of many NGOs has led rich-world governments (such as that of Britain) to eschew them in favour of less effective governmental networks for delivering aid. The campaign against globalisation, which involves many NGOs, is a focus in the wrong direction (as some NGOs are coming to realize). In fact, measures such as water privatisation are likely to benefit the poor. And, the bullying of corporations pursuing compensation claims against poor countries may deter investment in the developing world.

QUESTIONS FOR REFLECTION

1. NGOs, such as the CSE, often tackle social problems when poor governments can't or won't. How can NGOs overcome claims that they are too political?
2. Why would CSE focus on brands like Coca-Cola and Pepsi-Cola when other foods in India, such as milk, contain pesticides?
3. Do you agree with the strategy adopted by Coca-Cola and Pepsi-Cola to combine efforts in refuting CSE's claims?
4. What advice would you give to the CSE concerning its future efforts to get chemicals out of India's food chain?

Information for this case was drawn from the following: the Centre for Science and Environment Web site at www.cseindia.org; the Coca-Cola India Web site at www.myenjoyzone.com/press1; (5 August 2003), "Coke, Pepsi contain pesticide residues," *The Hindu Business Line*; (7 August 2003), "Non-governmental organizations," Economist.com, www.economist.com/background/displayBack-ground.cfm?story_id1982550; Kripalani, J., & Clifford, M. (February 10 2003), "Finally, Coke gets it right," *Business Week*, p. 18; Lakshmi, R. (10 August 2003), "Soda giants battle public panic in India,"

The Washington Post, p. A17; Slater, J. (15 August 2003), "Coke, Pepsi fight product-contamination charges in India," *The Wall Street Journal*, p. B1; Slater, J. (22 August 2003), "Coca-Cola, Pepsi pass India's test on pesticides," *The Wall Street Journal*, p. B5; Slater, J. & Terhune, C. (25 August 2003), "Coke, Pepsi still face issues in India," *The Wall Street Journal*, p. B4; and Waldman, A. (23 August 2003), "India tries to contain a tempest over soft drink safety," *The New York Times*, p. A3.

CASE 39. ACTIVISTS KEEP NIKE ON THE RUN

Nike knows how to compete. It won its position atop the world's shoe industry a generation ago and remains the leader. It received acclaim twice as Advertiser of the Year (in 1994 and 2003) at France's Cannes Lion festival, sometimes called the Olympics of Advertising. It's the company whose 1996 ads said: "You don't win silver. You lose gold." Nike has repeatedly bested rivals like Adidas, New Balance, and Reebok in the athletic-shoe footrace. In the United States, its market share is about 40%.

Yet, clear-cut victory has eluded Nike in its marathon contest with activists and media critics who have run the company ragged on the issue of worker abuse in overseas production facilities. Even when Nike asked the U.S. Supreme Court in 2003 to affirm the company's First Amendment right to speak publicly on the issue, the court refused to take a position on the question. No gold, no silver, no bronze.

Code of Conduct

Nike, headquartered in Beaverton, Oregon, doesn't own or operate shoe production plants overseas. Instead, it hires subcontractors in low-wage countries such as China, Indonesia, South Korea, and Vietnam to produce shoes to Nike specifications. To assure workers' rights there, Nike requires its subcontractors to adopt Nike's Code of Conduct and allow unannounced visits by inspectors chosen by Nike. Adopted in 1992, the code requires compliance in four areas of employee welfare:

- Health and safety.
- Pay and benefits.
- Terms of work.
- Management-workers relations.

Yet, some critics have said that Nike's worker-protection program is little more than window dressing for sweatshop operations, and others say that the company's public statements on the issue have been misleading and incomplete. Complaints about overseas labor abuse began plaguing Nike in the 1980s, and the reports reached a wide audience in the 1990s in media such as *The Economist* and *The New York Times*. CBS News reported in 1996 that workers making Nike shoes in Southeast Asia were poorly paid, exposed to hazardous chemicals, and mistreated by managers.

Columnist Provokes CEO Letter

In a single week in June 1996, *New York Times* columnist Bob Herbert twice used his commentary to take a swipe at Nike, its cofounder and chief executive,

Philip H. Knight, and the famous professional athletes making millions from Nike contracts. Citing Indonesia as an example, Mr. Herbert said thousands of workers producing Nike products earned $2.20 a day.

"Philip Knight has an extraordinary racket going for him," the columnist wrote on June 10. "There is absolutely no better way to get rich than to exploit both the worker and the consumers. If you can get your product made for next to nothing, and get people to buy it at exorbitant prices, you get to live at the top of the pyramid."

Four days later, Mr. Herbert added: "Nike is the most vulnerable to criticism of the athletic footwear corporations because it is the biggest, the most visible and by far the most hypocritical. No amount of charitable contributions or of idealized commercial images can hide the fact that Indonesia is Nike's kind of place. The exploitation of cheap Asian labor has been a focus of its top executive, Philip Knight, for more than three decades."

Mr. Knight, in a letter to the *New York Times* 1 week later, responded:

Nike has paid, on average, double the minimum wage as defined in countries where its products are produced under contract. This is in addition to free meals, housing and health care and transportation subsidies.

Underdeveloped countries must trade or see deeper declines in living standards. History shows that the best way out of poverty for such countries is through exports of light manufactured goods that provide the base for more skilled production.

Nike continued to answer its critics with information on its inspection and enforcement program as well as economic arguments about international trade, comparative advantage, and global competition.

Tongue-Tied Public Relations

The Wall Street Journal, under the headline "Nike Inc.'s Golden Image Is Tarnished As Problems in Asia Pose PR Challenge," asked in 1997: "How has Nike, a brand renowned for its global marketing finesse, found itself in this situation? It's because the athletic-shoe maker has remained tongue-tied, public relations experts say, in the face of a loose-knit but efficient attack that combines the speed of the Internet with good old-fashioned rabble-rousing."

On college campuses, student activists were questioning deals arranged by Nike and its competitors to provide big universities not just with footwear and apparel for varsity teams but also logo-licensed products for sale to the public. The activists said that, through the multiyear contracts, university administrators were complicit in the abuse of foreign laborers because universities assured a future market for goods produced under exploitation. To coordinate anti-exploitation campaigns emerging on more than 100 college campuses, activists formed the United Students Against Sweatshops.

At the University of North Carolina (UNC) at Chapel Hill, student activists tried to persuade administrators to cancel a Nike contract in 1997 with a campaign featuring "Just Don't Do It" leaflets that accused the shoe company of unfair labor practices.

According to *The Wall Street Journal*, "In 1997, Nike signed an $11.6 million deal with UNC's athletic department to outfit most of its sports teams and to manufacture UNC-logo sweatshirts and T-shirts, which in turn would generate $6 million to $8 million in annual sales for the company."

Nike's Campus Visit

As the activist campaign gained attention at UNC, Nike responded with a combination of ads in *The Daily Tar Heel* student newspaper, campus visits by a public relations team, and personal contact by Nike representatives with the members of the activist group. Before the fall semester ended, the company had offered an expense-paid trip to Southeast Asia for a faculty member and three students, including a *Daily Tar Heel* reporter. Under the plan, the four would tour facilities to see for themselves the conditions in which Nike shoes were made.

The plan was scrapped when some UNC faculty members objected, and a regular undergraduate course on environment and labor in the global economy was established instead. Nike executives were invited to attend the class, and one who did in April 1998 was Nike chief executive Philip Knight.

An Activist Sues

Marc Kasky, a San Francisco activist interested in humanitarian causes, watched the give-and-take between the company and its critics, and he grew angry over Nike statements that he considered misleading or downright false. At about the same time that Mr. Knight visited the Chapel Hill classroom, Mr. Kasky filed a complaint in California Superior Court, accusing the company of unfair business practices, negligent misrepresentation, fraud, and deceit.

In his lawsuit, Mr. Kasky cited nine instances in which Nike issued positive statements about its labor practices that conflicted with information from other sources. The nine instances included:

- A letter from Nike to university presidents and athletic directors.
- A 30-page brochure on Nike labor policies.
- A news release on its labor practices.
- Material on the Nike Web site concerning its code of conduct.
- A document offering Nike's perspective on the labor controversy.
- A news release responding to sweatshop allegations.
- A letter from Nike to the YWCA of America.

- A letter from Nike to the International Restructuring Education Network Europe.
- Mr. Knight's letter to *The New York Times*.

Facts in Conflict

For example, Mr. Kasky challenged Nike's claim that it paid double the minimum-wage rate in Southeast Asian countries. He said that Ernst & Young, an auditing firm that Nike hired to inspect a Vietnamese factory, found that workers received an average wage of $45 monthly, $5 above the minimum wage. He called Nike's claim "deceitful."

Noting that Nike's Code of Conduct forbids the use of corporal punishment or harassment of any kind in worker discipline, Mr. Kasky said the CBS News "48 Hours" program reported that 45 Vietnamese workers were forced by supervisors to kneel with their hands held in the air for 25 minutes. The same program, he said, reported that a supervisor hit 15 Vietnamese women on the head as a penalty for poor sewing.

Nike's letter to university officials included assurances of compliance with health and safety regulations, according to Mr. Kasky, but the Ernst & Young inspection found that thousands of women between the ages of 18 and 24 were exposed to high levels of toluene fumes and chemical dust in a Vietnamese plant.

In his lawsuit, Mr. Kasky said a central purpose of Nike's Code of Conduct was "to entice consumers who do not want to purchase products made in sweatshop and/or under unsafe and/or inhuman conditions." He said that the letters and other communications were marketing tools used by the company to attract customers.

Public Debate or Commercial Speech?

Nike disagreed. The company told the court that it was engaged in a public discussion of controversial issues, such as globalization and international trade, that had sparked comment in a number of quarters. The letters, news releases, Web pages, and other communications represented the company's voice in an open debate on matters of public policy, according to Nike, and its participation in public discussion was protected absolutely by the First Amendment.

The decision of the California Superior Court favored Nike. When Mr. Kasky appealed to the California Court of Appeal, his argument was rejected again. Mr. Kasky persisted, and the California Supreme Court reversed the earlier decisions in May 2002.

"Because the messages in question were directed by a commercial speaker to a commercial audience, and because they made representations of fact about the speaker's own business operations for the purpose of promoting sales of its products, ...[Nike's] messages are commercial speech," the California judges said.

The court did not say that Nike had misled anyone, deceived consumers, or misrepresented its practices. In fact, such an evaluation had not been attempted by the lower courts because they judged that Nike's statements were entitled to full protection of the First Amendment.

Breathing Space in Public Debate

In public policy discussions, the courts generally say that the First Amendment protects the expression of views, even if incorrect or exaggerated, as long as they contain no deliberate or reckless falsehoods. Full and robust debate flourishes when speakers have the liberty to voice ideas, however unconventional or unpopular, without fear that they may be hauled into court to explain errors, misstatements, misinterpretations, or shades of meaning.

Commercial speech is a different animal, the courts say, and the First Amendment affords it limited protection because its fundamental purpose is to promote a transaction rather than to contribute ideas to public debate.

The California Supreme Court explained, "Our holding in no way prohibits any business enterprise from speaking out on issues of public importance or from vigorously defending its own labor practices. It means only that when a business enterprise makes factual representations about its own products or its own operations, it must speak truthfully."

Five months after the California court ruled that Nike's statements were commercial speech, the company filed an appeal with the U.S. Supreme Court, asking it to review the decision. Nike's attorneys said the California verdict would curtail businesses' participation in public discussion and deprive the general public of a full spectrum of views.

U.S. Supreme Court Accepts Case

In January 2003, the high court agreed to hear Nike's appeal. Many First Amendment scholars, news organizations, and others supported Nike and filed friend-of-the-court briefs to oppose California's apparent expansion of the commercial-speech umbrella. Among the briefs was one filed by the PRSA.

"Those of us who assist companies in gathering and disseminating information related to their businesses have always relied on the same First Amendment protections as those who openly criticize Nike and other corporations," PRSA president Reed Byrum said. "Without that protection, there will be a serious impact on all aspects of corporate communications from business, to corporate crisis communications and even to philanthropic and community-outreach programs."

Sonia Arrison, a First Amendment Fellow of the National Press Club, wrote a newspaper commentary that said, "Laws that were meant to stop false claims such as 'orange juice cures cancer' should not be distorted and used as political weapons. And surely in an established democracy, the government does not allow one side in a debate to summarily stifle its opponents' viewpoints."

A Mix of Debate and Marketing

When the Supreme Court heard attorneys for Kasky and Nike in April 2003, several justices seemed to see elements of both commercial speech and noncommercial speech in the Nike communications.

According to a *New York Times* account of the hearings, Justice Stephen G. Breyer told the attorneys, "The truth of the matter is, I think it's both," and later he added, "I think the First Amendment was designed to protect all the participants in a public debate, and a debate consists of facts. Once you've tied a party's hands behind his back with respect to the facts, you've silenced him."

The Supreme Court handed down its order in June 2003 and left many who had looked forward to a landmark ruling in stunned silence or heated indignation. "Improvidently granted," said the court, meaning that it had changed its mind about taking the case. Six voted to dismiss, and three would have rendered a verdict.

Nike faced the prospect of returning to the California court system, where it would have to defend its communications as commercial speech. The company would be going back in 2003 to the future it had first faced in 1998.

Settlement Reached

Less than three months after the U.S. Supreme Court decided not to decide, Nike and Marc Kasky settled their differences out of court. Nike agreed to give $1.5 million to programs of the Fair Labor Association (FLA). With the funds, the FLA planned to support:

- Improvements in independent monitoring of workplace conditions in manufacturing countries.
- Worker development programs that focus on education and economic opportunity.
- Collaboration to formulate a global standard for measuring and reporting corporate responsibility performance.

The FLA was formed in 1999 by a diverse group, including Nike and other apparel manufacturers, colleges and universities, human rights organizations, and activists. It promotes its code of conduct, monitors practices in factories that make products for Nike and other brands, and coordinates public reports on monitoring results.

In the Bloomberg news service reports on the settlement, a law professor at George Washington University said Nike's payout was a sensible alternative to further litigation.

The professor, Jonathan Turley, said, "Any trial in this case would have been a bloody nightmare – the type of press that a company like Nike would never welcome."

Attorneys for Mr. Kasky issued a statement saying that their client was "satisfied that this settlement reflects Nike's commitment to positive changes where factory workers are concerned."

QUESTIONS FOR REFLECTION

1.   In what ways did Nike's communications focus on marketing and sales? In what ways did they focus on public debate about international trade and economic growth?

2.   Nike doesn't operate shoe production facilities in the United States or elsewhere. Why would some consumers hold the company responsible for working conditions in facilities where its shoes are made?

3.   Most footwear companies hire subcontractors in developing countries to make their shoes. Why would Nike attract a lion's share of the criticism?

4.   Nike has said it will refrain from public debate about overseas working conditions in the future. Is this a good idea or a bad idea?

Information for this case was drawn from the following: the Nike Web site at www.nike.com/nikebiz/ nikebiz.jhtml?page=0; Arrison, S. (22 January 2003), "Letting Nike speak," *The News & Observer*, p. A25; Carter, R. (30 April 2002), "ABC: Athletics, business & Carolina," *The Daily Tar Heel*, p. 1; (20 April 1998), Complaint, Kasky v. Nike, Superior Court of the State of California; Herbert, B. (14 June 1996), "In America: Nike's bad neighborhood," *The New York Times*, p. 25; Herbert, B. (10 June 1996), "In America: Nike's pyramid scheme," *The New York Times*, p. 27; Knight, P. (21 June 1996), "Letter: Nike pays good wages to foreign workers," *The New York Times*, p. A29; Marshall, S. (26 September 1997), "Nike Inc.'s gold image is tarnished as problems in Asia pose PR challenge," *The Wall Street Journal*, p. B1; McCarthy, M. (15 June 2003), "Wake up consumers? Nike's brash CEO dares to just do it," *USA Today*, p. B1; (26 June 2003), Opinion, Nike v. Kasky, U.S. Supreme Court; (3 March 2003), "PRSA presses Supreme Court to protect free speech right for American business," PRSA news release; Savage, D. (11 January 2003), "Justices to hear Nike free-speech claim," *The Los Angeles Times*, p. C1; Stancill, J. (15 November 1997), "Nike offers tour of Asian factories to UNC critics," *The News & Observer*, p. B1; Tkacik, M. (10 January 2003), "High court may decide to hear whether Nike's PR statements to media, others are protected," *The Wall Street Journal*, p. B1.

PROFESSIONAL INSIGHT

THREE KEY CONCEPTS FROM A PR PIONEER TURNED CRITIC

Larry Pfautsch, vice president, corporate communications, American Century Investments

When Edward L. Bernays died in 1995 at 103, he was eulogized as "the father of public relations." The Austrian native and nephew of Sigmund Freud has long been credited with transforming public relations from press agentry into a social science. For that reason alone, those who aspire to a public relations career would do well to understand how Bernays shaped and defined the profession and why, later in life, he became one of its harshest critics.

His most famous quote: "Public relations today is horrible. Any dope, any nitwit, any idiot can call him or herself a public relations practitioner."

If Bernays didn't like what he saw in the evolution of public relations, his indictment clearly had as much to do with how it's practiced as how it's defined. Bernays defined a practitioner as "a special pleader before the court of public opinion." While he would no doubt object to pejorative terms like flak or spinmeister to describe how public relations practitioners are sometimes viewed, he preferred to use the more noble-sounding term "counsel on public relations."

One can argue that this voice from the distant past is no longer relevant in a world of instant communication and the continually broadening scope of activities under the umbrella of public relations. Yet in some important respects, the concepts Bernays espoused might actually be more relevant today than in the previous century.

First among these is the notion of public relations as a noble profession. Bernays advocated licensing of practitioners, much as lawyers and doctors are licensed. Short of that, public relations and communications organizations like PRSA and IABC provide standards, ethics codes, continuing education, sharing of best practices, research, recognition and accreditation, and lend considerable credibility to the profession.

But noble? Think about that. When a crisis puts a client's reputation at stake, the counselor who can show the wisdom of taking the high road—doing the right thing in the face of intense pressure to cover up or mislead—is performing a noble service. The practitioner who can help a client see the wisdom of finding common ground with adversarial groups instead of suing them performs a strategic and noble service. The public relations professional whose relationships with reporters, expertise in the use of new media, or well-placed story builds third-party credibility for the client's product or service achieves a noble goal for both the client and the public.

The second concept worth calling out is that of the public relations practitioner as social scientist. In simple terms, this is all about understanding human behavior, sometimes called knowing one's audience. How many times do practitioners write public relations plans or recommend a course of action without doing an ounce of research? This is the second big sin of public relations practitioners, superseded only by the first big sin: failure to understand the client's business.

The third concept that bears mention has to do with the fundamental job of any public relations professional—to build trust. Call it credibility, reputation management, corporate positioning or even marketing, the thing clients most value is the operating freedom that derives from public trust and good will. Such an environment is only achieved when a client's actions match its words. The irony, of course, is that too many public relations practitioners advise clients on how to build trust but don't behave in a trusting manner themselves, effectively negating any counsel they might provide.

Think about someone you have admired or voted for, and chances are it comes down to trust. When each of us takes personal responsibility for being trustworthy, we do a great service to our clients, our profession and ourselves.

Larry Pfautsch is vice president, corporate communications, at American Century Investments, a leading manager of investment funds with an expanding range of products and services, including fixed income, growth, international and value strategies for institutions, investment professionals and individuals.

10
Stakeholders: Global Citizens

China has been the biggest market outside the United States for KFC fried chicken and has sometimes produced more profit for the restaurant chain than its U.S. operations. KFC was the first foreign fast-food operation to open stores in China.

The world's busiest McDonald's restaurant is on Pushkin Square in Moscow, a 10-minute walk from the Kremlin. McDonald's opened its first Russian restaurant in 1990 and now operates more than 130 throughout the country.

More than 70% of the Coca-Cola Company's net operating revenues come from outside the United States. Coca-Cola is available in more than 200 countries.

Evidence of globalization is visible within the United States, too. Most of the U.S. market for super-premium ice creams, such Haagen-Dazs and Ben & Jerry's, is controlled by two European companies—Nestlé SA of Switzerland and Unilever of the Netherlands. Americans think first of Japan's Sony or Korea's Samsung in consumer electronics and use more cell phones from Finland's Nokia than from any other producer. Toyota sold more cars in the United States than Ford for the first time in 2006.

Figure 10.1 Globalization of American institutions creates new challenges for public relations practitioners. For example, McDonald's has many restaurants in Russia, including this one on Prospekt Mira in Moscow

249

PRACTITIONERS' ROLE IN A GLOBAL MARKET

As markets for products and services connect countries and cultures around the world, organizations with multinational operations need public relations practitioners who can manage communication programs across borders, who can understand the risks of dynamic situations and who can adapt quickly to either opportunities or problems.

Most of the time, public relations professionals in the United States have taken for granted the predictability and convenience of life in a free-market economy with political stability. Of course, several nations match the U.S. standard of living, and a few others are rapidly closing the gap. Many are far behind.

Where living standards approach America's norm, differences in culture and media may complicate a public relations process that would seem simple in the United States. Even nations that share as much as the United States and Great Britain still contain remarkable differences.

Language is one example. Though English is spoken by almost everyone in both countries, the meaning of the same word may differ depending on where it's said. In Great Britain, businesspeople commonly use the word "turnover" to mean total revenues for a financial period, but Americans use the word "sales" to express the same idea. Americans often expect the noun "scheme" to mean a cunning or devious plot, but in Great Britain it's commonly used as a synonym for plan or program (or programme, as it would be spelt in London).

CULTURAL DIFFERENCES

Almost as variable as language, attitudes toward the use of time vary widely from culture to culture. To many in other nations, Americans appear to rush everything, even leisure. A business dinner that might last 75 minutes in a United States restaurant could take twice as long in some European cities.

The meals themselves—the food, when it's eaten, how it's eaten—also change from country to country. An English breakfast is large and varied, and afternoon tea remains a tradition. In Italy, the first meal of the day may be a bun and espresso, and other meals are likely to include pasta as a side dish but not a main dish. In Russia, breakfast foods—meats and cheeses—resemble what some Americans eat for lunch. Evening meals in many nations are later than they would be in the United States.

For public relations professionals, arranging media receptions or special events that feature food involves meticulous planning and selection to please guests. In an unfamiliar culture, only local expertise can ensure that an important event will succeed rather than embarrass.

GET LOCAL HELP

Respected authorities in international public relations strongly advise practitioners working in cultures other than their own to:

- Avoid the ethnocentrism that overvalues American habits and methods.
- Get advice and assistance from established public relations consultants in the locations where goodwill is needed.
- Allow more time to complete arrangements and obtain delivery of needed materials.

Americans sometimes believe that what works at home will surely work in other countries. Adapting tactics that have worked famously in U.S. cities, they plunge ahead, expecting similar results. Sometimes they are lucky and get what they want, but often they confuse, mystify, or offend their target publics or miss them altogether.

Local consultants can provide help with language, customs, regulations, media contacts, local transportation, and last-minute supplies or modifications. They can identify stakeholders and opinion leaders whose views will count the most. By including on-site consultants in early planning for an international program, practitioners can save time and money and achieve a better outcome.

OVERCOMING LANGUAGE BARRIERS

In international efforts, language often represents the single most troublesome challenge. Not only are the words and sentence structure different, but also the alphabet may be entirely unfamiliar or misleadingly similar. In Russia, the Cyrillic alphabet is used, and the letters *BP*, the name of the petroleum giant, would sound like *VR* if strict pronunciation were used.

Sometimes, the problem is a common phrase in one language that conveys the wrong message when spoken in another. According to *The New York Times*, an expensive Italian restaurant gave Shanghai residents reason to smile when it opened under the name Va Bene, which means "go well" in Italian. In the Shanghai dialect, it sounded like "not cheap."

Translation is essential, but it often slows things down. When a speaker and translator take turns, the speaker's remarks double in length, risking both boredom and misunderstanding. To avoid the need for clumsy sequential translation of a speaker's remarks through a translator, a practitioner might team up with a local consultant who learns the intricacies of a public relations program's platform and key messages well enough to handle media interviews and similar tasks independently.

Some multinational corporations are large enough to have full-time public relations professionals in countries where they operate, or they train managers in other departments to handle public relations as needed. In either case, the staffers should come from the local population.

Executives at corporate headquarters also should listen carefully to public relations advice they get from consultants or qualified staff working in another country and adjust plans or responses to issues accordingly. Listening to local voices is essential regardless of where the headquarters might be.

PARALYSIS OR HUBRIS?

In 2000, *Business Week* reported that Firestone's public relations crisis in the recall of 6.5 million tires resulted, in part, from executive paralysis at its parent, Bridgestone Corporation, in Tokyo.

"Bridgestone's behavior speaks volumes about the huge gaps that still exist between U.S. and Japanese management," the magazine said. "All the Tokyo executives...seem unable or unwilling to respond to pleas from investors and the media for explanations and reassurance."

A year earlier, the Coca-Cola Company suffered a series of embarrassing recalls in Europe that seemed to cascade from one country to another. First, about 200 consumers in Belgium and France complained of illness after drinking Coke products. Critics said the company was slow to respond to the concerns, and authorities in Belgium, France, and Luxembourg ordered 65 million cans of Coke products off the shelves. Days later, Coca-Cola issued a small recall of soft drinks in Portugal when specks of charcoal from a filtration system were found in cans. A week later, the company recalled bottled water in Poland because of the presence of mold.

In Coca-Cola's hometown, an *Atlanta Business Chronicle* columnist said Coke's "combination of marketing and legal muscle has made the company extraordinarily successful and perhaps left it feeling a tad omnipotent. Enter the dust-up in Belgium and France over supposedly contaminated Coca-Cola products. The company's culture didn't allow it to respond as quickly as it should have, and the result was a crisis."

CRITICS OF GLOBALIZATION

Although globalization probably ranks as the leading economic force of the new century, it has attracted its share of critics. Some say globalization is a movement that exploits poor workers in weak and underdeveloped countries to provide inexpensive consumer goods for individuals who are privileged to live in prosperous countries.

Activist groups like the Mobilization for Global Justice have held rallies and marches to draw attention to the poverty of many workers in Latin America and Asia. The groups have performed street-theater skits outside offices of Citibank, the International Monetary Fund, Monsanto, Occidental Petroleum, and The World Bank. Radical protesters resorted to violence and vandalism at demonstrations in Seattle and Geneva.

Business Week pointed out that "Anti-globalization groups speak in the name of Third World countries, but democratically elected governments in countries such as Mexico and India often disagree with them. They want more corporate investment, not less; freer trade, not more restricted markets; and the enforcement of local labor laws, not the imposition of foreign ones."

ADJUST TO GLOBAL THREATS

The global practice of public relations has gained new urgency with the increase in geopolitical tensions between the United States and other nations. Fears of terrorism and anti-American violence have caused U.S. companies to add more security at overseas operations, re-examine relationships in vulnerable locations, and rely more on operational leadership chosen from local populations.

Reviewing the anxious situation, *PRWeek* magazine said that multinational companies should:

- Step-up employee communications activities for workers in stressful regions.
- Emphasize long-term relationships and high-ranking local managers.
- Focus on the company's local history, employment, and contributions.

"Stick to talking about who your company is and what its products offer," the magazine recommended, "and don't get caught up in political issues or side-taking."

The cases in this chapter will ask you to consider how organizations, citizen groups and governmental agencies can best respond to the opportunities and challenges posed by a global system. As you read each one, ask yourself: How can this organization best achieve mutually beneficial relationships with its critical stakeholders despite cultural, language or economic differences?

ADDITIONAL READINGS

Tilson, Donn J., & Emmanuel C. Alozie (2004). *Toward the common good: Perspectives in international public relations.* Boston: Pearson Education.

Casmir, Fred L. (1997). *Ethics in intercultural and international communication* Mahwah, NJ: Lawrence Erlbaum Associates.

Higgins, Richard. (2000). *Best practices in global investor relations.* Westport, CT: Greenwood.

Kruckeberg, Dean, & Katerina Tsetsura. (2003). *A composite index by country of variables related to the likelihood of the existence of "cash for news coverage."* Gainesville, FL: Institute for Public Relations.

CASE 40. "OUR WEAPON IS OUR NAKEDNESS": NIGERIAN WOMEN USE CULTURAL TABOO TO FIGHT BIG OIL COMPANY

Dr. Marcie L. Hinton, assistant professor of journalism, Middle Tennessee State University

In the Nigerian Delta, in the shadow of a multinational oil facility, 600 women threatened to strip bare in order to gain schools, medical treatment, pay and environmental protection from rich companies using Nigeria's natural resources to line deep pockets in the western world.

"Our Weapon is Our Nakedness"

"Our weapon is our nakedness," cried Helen Odeworitse, one of the protesters and now a global symbol of what serious, thoughtful protesting can accomplish. So impressive was the protest and what it accomplished that women from Australia to America disrobed to demonstrate for everything from peace to animal rights. But what does such a protest accomplish when it is taken out of the original cultural context in the Nigerian Delta?

The idea behind the threat of the collective disrobing of 20- to 90-year-old women was to shame Chevron and others into hiring (and then fairly paying) more Nigerian men, and providing electricity and other economic and environmental improvements to the surrounding villages, as was promised when the likes of Chevron, Shell and Exxon moved into the region in the early 1980s.

The protest was not a spontaneous gathering of the 600 women. It was a combined effort of several different regions and women of all ages, who had endured years of environmental damage and community hardship. There were villagers who had endured a five-year gas flare when the Shell Oil Company set oil on fire to contain a spill in the area's water supply, who joined the Ogonis, who had faced the companies before and saw all their leaders hung for their efforts. The highly organized group brought together historically uneasy ethnic divisions to protest the Nigerian government and the multinational oil firms.

The 2002 protest was a month-long, all-female demonstration that ended with the 10-day siege of ChevronTexaco's offices in Escravos. Analysts said the protest by the women had a large impact because they forced U.S. multinational oil companies operating in Africa to be a catalyst for social improvement, when governments did not have the means or the motivation to make those improvements or compel the companies to do so before building their facilities.

Sokari Ekine, the international coordinator of the Niger Delta Women, explained: "The stripping off of clothes particularly by married and elderly women is a way of shaming men—some of whom believe that if they see the naked bodies they will go mad or suffer some great harm. The curse extends not just to local men but also to any foreigner, who it is believed would become impotent at the sight of 'the naked mother.'"

The 600 women blocked docks, helicopter pads and airstrips of the Escravos oil facility—all its entry and exit points—for 10 days in 2002, trapping 700 workers and bringing international attention to their unconventional protest. The sit-in and the threat of nudity were enough to enable talks between government officials, Chevron administrators and the protesting women.

Peaceful "Weapon" Brings Results

Nigerian men, including those in the government, understood the seriousness of the threat to disrobe. The women never actually had to impose the cultural taboo on ChevronTexaco. The corporation entered into talks with the women and conceded to many of their demands for new jobs, schools, and electrical and water systems for the communities without the women disrobing. While many would say the multinational companies should do more for the people of the Niger Delta, they did respond to the gravity of the demonstrators.

The peaceful protest was monumental in at least four ways. First, most earlier protests in the oil-rich delta had included machetes, guns, kidnapping and sabotage by young men, while this protest was obviously a departure from past practice. Second, women were organizing to gain voices and rights after years of degradation and inhumane treatment. Third, it offered a prime example of the need for cultural understanding by big business. Fourth, it was linked to a cultural phenomenon that was lauded by women's rights groups and poorly translated by protestors from other cultures.

Just 70 years prior to the Escravos facility protest, Nigerian women in Calabar waged what is known in the Niger Delta as the "women's war." While under British colonial rule in 1929, villagers from the Owerri province protested a tax assessment from a mission teacher. The women notified others by sending folded palm leaves to one another to begin attacks against structures that were symbols of what the *Christian Science Monitor* in 2002 called the "imperial presence."

International Companies and Local Communities

The people in the Niger Delta are among the poorest in Nigeria, despite living on the oil-rich land of the world's sixth-biggest oil exporter and the fifth-biggest supplier of U.S. oil imports.

Activists throughout the twentieth century, feeling powerless against the Nigerian government's lack of development, focused demands for roads, water and schools on the multinational oil companies with the means and the obligation to do something about it.

In the 1990s, oil companies and local communities drew international attention when violent protests by the small but fierce Ogoni tribe forced Shell to abandon its wells on their land. The late Nigerian dictator Gen. Sani Abacha responded in 1995 by hanging nine Ogoni leaders, including Ken Saro Wiwa, a writer and academic known for his nonviolent environmental campaign.

The Curse as Cultural Taboo and Valuable Communication Tool

By 2002, living conditions called for a new kind of protest that summoned a cultural weapon. Anthropology scholar Terisa Turner said the curse is summoned only under extreme circumstances. In fact, women usually take a formal vow to honor the enormity of its symbolism. According to Turner, when women expose their genitalia, it is about taking back the life that was brought forth from the womb—a form of social execution. Men who view the nudity, especially of married or elderly women, are considered dead to society. No one will cook for them, marry them, or do business with them.

Some say the activism of women in the Niger Delta is firmly rooted in religious and commercial practices. Experts find the ethnic composition of southern Nigeria helps, as women do participate in commerce and there are fewer Muslims than in other parts of the country. Therefore, they are not thwarted by Islamic traditions regarding women's place in society.

Nakedness is Relative: Baring Witness

When news of the effectiveness of the Niger Delta protest spread around the world, it was interpreted outside of its cultural context. One group, called Baring Witness, claimed on its Web site to honor the protesting women of Nigeria by "using the greatest weapon women have, the power of the feminine, the power of our beauty and nakedness to awaken our male leaders and stop them in their tracks...by risking with our nakedness—our charm and beauty and vulnerability—in service of peace we are exposing the flesh all humans share. We are casting off the old dominant paradigm of aggression and restoring the power of the feminine to its rightful place as the protector of life."

Led by the group's founder, Donna Sheehan, 40 women got naked in West Marin County, California, for pro-peace demonstrations. Pictures of these naked women were flashed on television shows and in newspapers around the Western world, catching the eye of some, not in an act of shame, but of bemusement. In Byron Bay, Australia 750 women—inspired by Baring Witness—disrobed for peace in 2003. PETA members regularly "bare skin to save skins" of animals.

Nude protests in cultures without societal and spiritual repercussions are spectacles, not statements. Somewhere in the translation of the Nigerian Women's protest "in the shadow of paradise" where they threatened nudity as an ultimate act of shame and cultural shunning, people in more westernized cultures may have trivialized the actions of mothers, grandmothers, sisters and daughters of the Nigerian Delta by actually stripping nude to promote peace.

The Nigerian women built their protest on historical precedence (the women in the "women's war" in 1929), regional factors (more powerful women, with fewer religious restrictions), cultural phenomena (nudity of the woman shaming the man) and unique means (something other than men with machetes), which combined to create a powerful communication strategy. When the consequence of such a protest is taken out of context, it may become a weak communication instrument or simply a cultural curiosity.

～

QUESTIONS FOR REFLECTION

1. What is an American cultural taboo that could be a useful communication tool in a protest?

2. When working for a global company, how can public relations professionals prepare employees for the variety of symbols and symbolic actions found within different cultures?

3. How may human rights groups use and translate cultural phenomena as communication tools in the global village? Can you think of any examples?

Information for this case was drawn from the following: the Baring Witness Web site, www. baringwitness.org/vision.htm; International Museum of Women Web site, www.imow.org/wpp/ stories/viewStory?storyId=1098; Bolt, A. (6 March 2003), "Stunt stripped bare," *Herald Sun* (Melbourne, Australia), p. 21; Curtin, P., & Kenn T. Gaither. (2007). *International Public Relations: Negotiating Culture, Identity and Power.* Sage Publications: London; Doran, D. (14 July 2002), "Nigerian women take over four more pipeline stations," *The Gazette* (Montreal, Quebec), p. A17; Peel, M. (12 August 2002), "Peacefully, Nigerian Women Win Changes from Big Oil," *Christian Science Monitor*, p. 7.

CASE 41. BAYER DRUG RECALL STRAINS
INTERNATIONAL RELATIONSHIPS

The Bayer name means aspirin to most consumers, but production of the pain reliever represents a small fraction of the German company's global business. Headquartered north of Cologne in Leverkusen, the Bayer Group is a chemical industry giant, producing products in three business areas: healthcare, crop science, and plastics and polymers. Its worldwide 2007 revenues exceeded €32 billion (about $47 billion), and employees numbered about 106,000.

The company's health care products include over-the-counter medications such as Bayer aspirin and Alka-Seltzer tablets as well prescription drugs such as Cipro antibiotic. Cipro gained attention in 2001 when it was used to treat U.S. Postal Service workers and others who had been exposed to anthrax in acts of bioterrorism.

Fighting High Cholesterol

In 1997, the U.S. FDA approved a new Bayer drug, Baycol, that physicians could prescribe to help patients lower their cholesterol levels. High cholesterol levels can cause the formation of plaque in arteries and lead to heart attacks.

In Europe, the same drug, under the name Lipobay, received approval in 1997 from the British Medicines Control Agency, whose licensing authority was accepted by countries in the European Union through a process called mutual recognition.

Baycol was a member of a class of drugs called statins, a popular therapy for individuals with high cholesterol. Other pharmaceutical companies, such as Merck and Pfizer, already were producing statin drugs.

Because heart disease is the leading cause of death in industrialized nations and high cholesterol contributes to heart disease, the market for drugs that lower cholesterol has attracted pharmaceutical companies. It is a big and profitable category.

Though four or more therapies are available, the statin class of drugs is widely used. According to some sources, the number of individuals using statins exceeds 8 million in the United States alone. Depending on an individual's prescription, a one-month supply of Baycol might cost about $75.

Bayer was pleased with the results of its new drug from the outset. The number of physicians prescribing it grew rapidly, suggesting that it had the potential to reach blockbuster status—generally regarded as annual sales of $1 billion.

Bayer Issues Warnings

However, problems began to mount two years after Baycol's approval. Bayer told the FDA in December 1999 that it had detected a troubling rate of rhabdomyolysis among Baycol users in the United States. Rhabdomyolysis (often called "rhabdo") is a disorder involving the release of toxins from muscle deterioration into the bloodstream. Symptoms include muscle pain and weakness. In some cases, rhabdo can lead to kidney damage and even death.

Baycol users were more likely to develop rhabdo if they were taking the prescription in combination with Lopid—a cholesterol drug made by Pfizer—or were using the highest approved Baycol dosage (0.8 milligrams). In January 2000, the first rhabdo death of a Baycol user in the United States was reported.

Bayer changed Baycol's label to warn against concurrent use with Lopid and sent a letter to physicians outlining the risk. In June 2000, Bayer changed the label again to limit use of the highest approved dosage. About one year later, Bayer shared information with European regulators about rhabdo risks with Lipobay, and they acted in June 2001 to require the same warnings adopted earlier in the United States.

Deaths From Side Effects

On August 8, 2001, Bayer announced that it had decided to voluntarily withdraw Baycol from the market in the United States and Europe. By that date, Bayer had learned of 31 deaths among Baycol's 700,000 American users.

Lipobay users had died in Europe as well, but no tally was immediately available because no single European agency was responsible for monitoring the safety of drugs once they were licensed for use. In Spain, health officials said that three people had died from rhabdo; in Germany, the total was five. Later in August, Bayer confirmed 52 deaths worldwide and 1,100 cases of rhabdo side effects. In Japan, the drug remained available until September because Pfizer's Lopid was not distributed there.

Some European government officials were highly critical of Bayer's procedures for sharing information on the discovery of risks linked to Baycol/Lipobay. Seven weeks before withdrawing the drug, Bayer had given the British Medicines Control Agency (MCA) a study on severe side effects in Baycol users who also took Lopid. After the drug's withdrawal was announced, the German health ministry in Berlin, about 350 miles from Bayer's world headquarters, complained that it had not received the study given to the British MCA in London. It called Bayer's information-sharing policies unacceptable.

A *New York Times* article quoted an official at the Federal Institute for Medicine and Medical Products, Germany's counterpart to the FDA, as saying: "It isn't the job of the MCA to be postman for the European Union."

When journalists raised questions about the year-long delay in warning European health care authorities about the risks, a Bayer spokesman explained that Europeans were less likely to combine the cholesterol drugs, and fewer problems were detected.

Reactions to the Withdrawal

In the United States and Europe, the withdrawal of the Bayer drug triggered three distinct reactions:

1. Pharmaceutical companies promptly produced public relations programs to assure physicians and patients that the statin class of drugs was safe.
2. Public policy advocates called for improvements in systems to track drug safety and alert health care officials and their patients to problems.
3. Plaintiffs' attorneys began seeking compensation for Baycol/Lipobay users who suffered the side effects of rhabdomyolysis.

As cardiovascular patients learned about the Baycol withdrawal, competing pharmaceutical companies feared that their statin drugs would lose users to other types of medication. With Bayer's drug out of the picture, the makers of Lipitor, Pravachol, Zocor, and other statin drugs acted to protect their existing statin business and to appeal to Baycol users. According to *Pharmaceutical Executive* magazine, Pfizer teamed up with the American Heart Association and *Prevention* magazine in a public relations campaign to reassure statin users and their physicians about safety and efficacy; and Bristol-Myers Squibb offered Baycol users a month's trial supply of its statin drug.

Some individuals and organizations were alarmed that drug safety problems could go undetected for years and unresolved for an even longer period. Baycol was on the market for more than four years and had millions of users worldwide. Advocates called for changes in the systems used in the United States, Europe, and other nations to find pharmaceutical problems more quickly. Commenting on the issue, *Business Week* said:

> The system for tracking the safety of prescription drugs after they hit the market is inadequate. The FDA spots those problems mainly through voluntary reporting by physicians when patients have bad reactions. But by the FDA's own estimate, no more than 10 percent of these reactions ever get reported. "We know how many suitcases were lost last year by the airlines," says Dr. Raymond L. Woosley, vice president for health sciences at the University of Arizona. "But, we don't know how many people have been harmed by prescription drugs."

For Bayer, the biggest immediate threat following the withdrawal announcement came from a flood of litigation filed by plaintiffs' attorneys on behalf of Baycol users who said the drug had caused them to suffer rhabdomyolysis. By the time the first case came to trial in February 2003, the number of lawsuits had reached 7,800. A Bayer attorney insisted that most of the plaintiffs had not experienced any adverse effects from using Baycol.

Even so, investors' fears about the potential liability had helped push the price of Bayer common stock down to $13.37 on February 25, 2003, as the trial began.

The price had been $33.09 on January 24, 2002, when Bayer shares first began trading on the NYSE as American depository receipts (securities issued in the United States to represent shares of a foreign company).

The First Trial Begins

The initial case, heard in Nueces County Court in Texas, involved an 82-year-old resident of Corpus Christi and began with Bayer committing an embarrassing public relations faux pas. On the day before jury selection was to begin, the public relations vice president for Bayer's U.S. health care operations sent a letter about the impending proceedings to 2,100 local residents. The letter reminded residents that Bayer employed 2,000 people at its Texas operations.

"As you hear and see reports of the trial," the letter said, "I hope that you will keep an open mind to the efforts that Bayer made to give fair redress to this gentleman and, on a much broader scale, the tremendous contributions that our company has and continues to make to the health and welfare of millions of people worldwide."

A Bayer attorney told the Nueces County judge that the letter had been intended for members of the Corpus Christi Chamber of Commerce, and its wider distribution was a mistake that resulted from miscommunication within Bayer. At least one prospective juror received the letter. The district attorney considered filing jury-tampering charges against the Bayer public relations executive but decided against it.

At trial, the plaintiff's attorneys tried to show that Bayer had known about the risks of Baycol long before withdrawing it and failed to adequately warn physicians and patients of the dangers. The plaintiffs suggested that the drug's success and profitability interfered with the corporation's conscience. At the time of withdrawal, Baycol was Bayer's third-best-selling drug.

Bayer countered that it met its responsibilities to the regulatory authorities, health care professionals, and patients. It pointed out that it forwarded data on side effects to the FDA promptly, strengthened the warnings in the prescribing information, and eventually withdrew the drug voluntarily.

Jury Clears Bayer

The jury verdict cleared Bayer in the Corpus Christi case on March 18, 2003. The company had been working to resolve other cases out of court and had already paid $125 million to settle about 450 of these when it received the verdict.

Following the decision, the company issued this statement from its headquarters in Leverkusen:

> Bayer said it is pleased that the jury in the Corpus Christi, Texas, USA, Baycol trial reached a verdict in its favor. The verdict validates Bayer's

assertion that the company acted responsibly in the development, marketing and voluntary withdrawal of Baycol.

Bayer will now turn its attention to the other pending Baycol cases to analyze the specific circumstances of each case and the nature of the claims. It is Bayer's intention to pursue its policy of seeking to fairly compensate anyone who experienced serious side effects from Baycol, regardless of whether we have valid legal defenses to such claims. At the same time, where an examination of the facts indicates that Baycol played no role in the patient's medical situation, or where a settlement is not achieved, Bayer will continue to defend itself vigorously as it did in the Corpus Christi case.

QUESTIONS FOR REFLECTION

1.   Bayer notified government regulators in the United States and Europe about unexpected reactions to its high-cholesterol drug, but the company provided the warnings at different times. How would you justify the difference?

2.   In Europe, no single agency has been responsible for monitoring a new drug's safety after it's licensed for use. How does this situation affect a pharmaceutical company's risk profile?

3.   Bayer's competitors scrambled to attract Baycol users once the Bayer drug was withdrawn. What public relations methods would you have recommended to reach former Baycol users?

4.   A Bayer public relations executive's letter to the Corpus Christi Chamber of Commerce accidentally got wider distribution. How would you explain the purpose of sending the letter to its originally intended audience?

Information for this case was drawn from the following: the Bayer Web site at www.press.bayer.com/News/News.nsf/id/010005; Andrews, E. (22 August 2001), "Drug's removal exposes holes in Europe's net," *The New York Times*, p. C1; Barrett, A. (10 September 2001), "Commentary: Drug safety needs a serious overhaul," *Business Week*, p. 61; (8 August 2001), "Bayer voluntarily withdraws Baycol," Bayer news release; (4 September 2001), "Bayer faces Baycol probe," CNN; Breitstein, J. (October 2001), "Baycol fallout," *Pharmaceutical Executive*, p. 96; Fuhrmans, V., & Harris G. (9 August 2001), "Bayer withdraws major cholesterol drug," *The Wall Street Journal*, p. B2; Fuhrmans, V., Harris G., & Winslow, R. (10 August 2001), "Bayer recall spurs Europe to wide review," *The Wall Street Journal*, p. A3; Fuhrmans, V. (19 March 2003), "Jury rules Bayer isn't liable in closely watched drug case," *The Wall Street Journal*, p. B2; Petersen, M. (22 February 2003), "Judge criticizes letter from Bayer," *The New York Times*, p. C14; and Simmons, M. (21 August 2001), "Left holding the pill bottle," *The Washington Post*, p. F3.

CASE 42. BREWING INTERNATIONAL RELATIONSHIPS: DOES STARBUCKS C.A.F.E. PROGRAM SERVE SOCIAL RESPONSIBILITY TO ETHIOPIAN COFFEE FARMERS?

Dr. Marcie L. Hinton, assistant professor of journalism, Middle Tennessee State University

The name around the mermaid insignia stamped on every eco-friendly cup and exotic bag of Starbucks coffee was meant to recall seafaring coffee traders who might have been contemporaries of the company's namesake, Starbuck, first mate in the epic novel *Moby Dick*. Coffee farmers in distant lands also were destined to earn a role in the history of Starbucks Coffee Company along with the first mate.

The company's Web site says Starbucks is "wholeheartedly committed to making a positive difference in the lives of farmers and their communities [by] promoting the sustainability of coffee production." To make that positive difference and participate in the international fair trade conversation, in 2001 the company began a program called "Coffee and Farmer Equity Practices" (C.A.F.E.) to promote mutually beneficial relationships with farmers, workers and communities, protect the environment and guarantee the production of high-quality coffee.

C.A.F.E. Program

The C.A.F.E. program encourages suppliers and, in most cases, their countries to adhere to "critical social, environmental, economic and quality aspects of growing, processing and selling coffee for Starbucks." Farmers in countries such

Figure 10.2 Starbucks has grown to include more than 7,000 U.S. and 1,700 international coffee shops, with more than 6,000 other licensed locations in the United States and across the globe (Photo by Lauren V. Wright)

as Guatemala, Tanzania, Colombia, Kenya and Ethiopia must meet minimum requirements, which include 28 specific tenets in five areas: product quality, economic accountability (transparency), social responsibility, environmental leadership in coffee growing, and in processing. High scoring suppliers are rewarded with contracts that will guarantee higher prices for their beans and better contract terms altogether.

Concentrating its social responsibility efforts on coffee growers around the world, Starbucks buys coffee directly from local farmers in 27 third-world countries. Of the approximately 312 million pounds of coffee the company buys each year, 18 million pounds are from fair trade farmers. As of November 2007 fair trade contracts guaranteed a price of $1.26 per pound (organic coffee went for $1.31 per pound), as opposed to free market prices that have fallen as low as $.04 to $.05 per pound.

Starbucks is no doubt the largest international purveyor of fair trade coffee. Through the C.A.F.E. program, Starbucks built its brand on a commitment to its well educated, middle class customer base as the "coffee that cares" about economic, social and environmental justice in the world. So why did NGOs like Oxfam International (who are also committed to such ideals) question the company's commitment to coffee farmers in Ethiopia and other third-world countries?

The Brew-ha-ha

In 2006, Ethiopian coffee growers and the Ethiopian government wanted to trademark coffee in the United States, as it had in Canada and the European Union, so as to be bigger players in the coffee marketplace. Rumor had it that Starbucks was opposing that effort. Starbucks denied the rumor. While Starbucks and the Ethiopian government brokered an understanding that Starbucks was not the one blocking the trademarks, Starbucks was still called upon to clarify and reinforce its commitment to coffee farmers around the world.

Starbucks said it didn't block Ethiopia's trademark bid and claimed the dispute was between Ethiopia and U.S. regulators. However, America's National Coffee Association (NCA), the industry lobby group, opposed the trademark. NCA exists to represent the interests of the big coffee marketers, and there is no coffee marketer bigger than Starbucks. Furthermore, the chair of the NCA's Government Relations Committee, happened to be Dub Hay, Starbucks' senior vice president of Coffee and Global Procurement.

So, an international discussion ensued. Starbucks' reinvention of the populist coffeehouse morphed into a symbol of imperialistic corporate bad guy for anti-globalization groups. Media chatter suggested that Starbucks had a heart of darkness and Ethiopian coffee farmers and their government had hearts of gold. Oxfam's public relations blitz accused Starbucks of depriving farmers of $90 million a year by opposing the Ethiopian's cooperative plan to trademark its products. More than 85,000 Starbucks customers listened to Oxfam's messages and complained with an impressive fax, e-mail, snail mail and postcard campaign, prompting the coffee company to defend itself by distributing material, including a podcast showing its contributions to clean water and farming families in Ethiopia.

The discussion also prompted NCA to post a position on its Web site, which read:

> ...the NCA clearly communicated to the Ethiopian government the association wanted to work with them to develop effective and constructive solutions to the challenges they are facing, including enhancing market access and value through brand building.
>
> The NCA is committed to supporting sustainability and a socially responsible industry...To avoid any further inaccuracy in this context, the NCA also reiterates that this matter was not brought to the attention of the NCA by any of its members. Contrary to statements made by Oxfam International and their purported sources, NCA president [and] CEO Robert F. Nelson never told Ethiopian government staffers at any meeting that an NCA member brought this issue to its attention.

As the issue gained a higher profile in the media, Starbucks had to do more than say "we aren't involved." Starbucks defended its position, arguing that the farmers would be better served under a certification mark, a lesser regulated intellectual property protection than a trademark. Opponents rebuffed this claim by saying that a certification mark only protects traditional regional foods against copycats and ensures a traditional way of producing products. It does not offer any avenue for economic growth, which is the purpose of an actual trademark. Starbucks countered that the issue was never about royalties. It was about protecting coffee quality and Ethiopian farmers.

Decaffeinating the Debate

In mid-2007, Starbucks and Ethiopia signed a distribution, marketing and licensing agreement, which gives some preferential treatment to Starbucks as a buyer but allows Ethiopia to trademark three of its regional "coffee brands," thus claiming the coffee as intellectual property and gaining more control over the brand to improve profits.

Oxfam declared the agreement a "win-win" situation. Raymond C. Offenheiser, president of Oxfam America, said the agreement "...represents a business approach in step with 21st-century standards in its concern for rights rather than charity and for greater equity in supply chains rather than short term profits." Ethiopian Prime Minister Meles Zenawi praised the agreement and said the campaign against Starbucks was meant to help producers obtain their rightful share of the profits.

In the agreement, Starbucks offered to open a center in Ethiopia to help coffee farmers improve productivity and profitability. Skeptics scoffed, saying Ethiopian farmers "invented" quality coffee and didn't know what Starbucks had to offer farmers in the birthplace of coffee. However, the Ethiopian government defended Starbucks, conceding that the center will offer modern production and marketing techniques, which will aid the farmers in being more competitive in the complex and intricate world markets.

Neither the prime minister nor the Starbucks chairman disclosed how much Ethiopian coffee the company buys, but since 2004, Starbucks increased its purchases of Ethiopian coffee by 400%, and would double that amount by 2009-2010.

Brewing the Right Blend

For all its good intentions, Starbucks C.A.F.E. program alone is not capable of leading the world's coffee growers out of poverty. By positioning itself as the savior of the impoverished third-world farmer, Starbucks could not help coffee producers participate in a fair trade marketplace and then expect them to not become entrepreneurs themselves.

In an era of globalization where business-to-business relationships mean a populist coffeehouse proprietor from Seattle finds himself negotiating with foreign governments, public relations is increasingly important. As Starbucks former CEO Howard Shultz wrote in his 1997 autobiography, *Pour Your Heart Into It*: "Running a company, while keeping to high ethical standards presents [a] dilemma: Sometimes you can't figure out how to live up to them."

QUESTIONS FOR REFLECTION

1. Did Starbucks "brew the right blend of global ambition and ethical trade?"
2. Discuss the ethical dilemma posed when the National Coffee Association's mission of representing all coffee marketers may be in conflict with a clear leader among its internal activist publics.
3. What is the role of corporate philanthropic strategies? Is this changed when it may be used to counter negative media messages?
4. Is there a point when social responsibility may have to take a backseat to profitability and vice versa?
5. What advantages and disadvantages does the development of an international, socially responsible program pose for practitioners?

Information for this case was drawn from the following: (15 February 2007), "Oxfam-Starbucks needs to change," Africa News; Bain, S., & MacDermid, A. (28 August 2007), "The coffee may be hot and sweet…but do you know if it is fair?: Starbucks defends plan to promote African farms," *The Glasgow Herald*, p. 3; Clark, T. (2007), Starbucked: A double tall tale of caffeine, commerce and culture. New York: Little, Brown and Company; O'Rourke, P.J. (15 December 2007), "The frothy side of a corporate behemoth," *The International Herald Tribune*, p. 8; Pagnamenta, R. (11 December 2006), "Starbucks seeks the right blend of global ambition and ethical trade," *The Times*, p. 44; Schultz, H., & Jones-Young, D. (1997), Pour your heart into it. New York: Hyperion; and the National Coffee Association Web site, www.ncausa.org; Oxfam Web site, www.oxfam.org; Starbucks web site, www.starbucks.com; and the Voice of America Web site, www.voanews.com.

CASE 43. PUBLICIS AND THE EUROPEAN CENTRAL BANK INTRODUCE "THE EURO, OUR MONEY" TO THE WORLD

Money talks, or so the cliché says. Imagine if the money in question has to speak at least 12 different languages, be accepted by citizens used to different currencies and conversion rates, and be "heard" within a few months. In essence, this was the task faced by the European Union (EU) nations who moved in January 2002 to adopt the euro as their official currency as they phased out their traditional bill and coin systems. Introducing the new bills and coins to members of the public so they would be familiar enough with their values for them to be used in daily commerce would require a coordinated communication campaign across the 12 EU nations that had adopted the euro.

Adopting the Euro

The euro became the official banking currency of 12 EU nations: Austria, Belgium, Denmark, Finland, France, Germany, Greece, Ireland, Italy, Luxembourg, the Netherlands, and Spain, on January 1, 1999. By January 2002, the national currencies were to be phased out and the euro was slated to become the united currency. After the initial creation of the euro notes, member nations continued to use their traditional national currencies such as the mark, franc, and lire. Converting to the new single currency, among those nations that had chosen to do so, was no simple task, involving more than designing and printing new bills and minting new coins.

The value of the euro had to be fixed against the national currencies of the participating nations. Prices in stores and calculations in registers and ATMs had to be converted to euros.

By January 2002, more than 14.5 billion euro banknotes were printed and ready for distribution. Then, the national notes and coins of the participating

Figure 10.3 The new currency featured distinctive designs for its bills and coins. (Photo by Lauren V. Wright).

countries had to be withdrawn before they became illegal some two months after the introduction of the euro.

A European Central Bank (ECB) news release from December 28, 2001, described the adoption process:

> On 1 January 2002, the 306 million citizens of the euro area will begin to use the euro banknotes and coins. The euro cash changeover operation has been advancing according to plan, thanks to the thorough preparations and firm commitment of the hundreds of thousands of people directly involved in the cash changeover process.
>
> As a complement to the euro-related information activities conducted by the governments, the European Commission and other private and public entities, the European Central Bank (ECB) and the 12 national central banks of the euro area have conducted the Euro 2002 Information Campaign in order to familiarise citizens with their new money.
>
> Over the last few weeks of 2001 some 200 million copies of a leaflet providing information on the euro banknotes and coins, their security features and the changeover modalities in the eleven official Community languages have been distributed to European households. This leaflet has also been translated into 23 other languages, in co-operation with the respective national central banks.
>
> To keep the media and the general public informed of the progress of the euro cash changeover, the ECB will publish daily updates on its website from 2 January to 11 January 2002, and weekly updates on 18 and 25 January 2002.
>
> More than 15 billion euro banknotes, worth more than EUR 630 billion, have been produced, as have well over 51 billion coins worth almost EUR 16 billion. Of these 15 billion euro banknotes, less than 10 billion will enter circulation initially. The rest will be held as logistical stocks to accommodate any changes in demand.

Celebrating the Euro

So, who would help make the new currency "talk" by designing and coordinating the cross-national communication campaign? Some 40 firms initially sought the account. After the list of agencies was narrowed, the ECB chose Publicis, a French-based firm, to manage the multimillion "Euro 2002" campaign over J. Walter Thompson/Hill & Knowlton, and Young & Rubicam/Burson Marsteller. Publicis is a full-service agency, with units offering advertising, media relations, direct marketing, and consultancy. Joanna Baldwin, head of business development at Publicis Worldwide, was quoted in the November 11, 1999, *Marketing Week*: "We aim to make people feel good about the euro—that it is a cause for celebration."

Publicis worked with the European Commission, the executive body for the EU. Publicis was charged with "gradually preparing the general public for the introduction of the euro banknotes and coins, so that they are favorably received," according to the ECB. The agency faced some major challenges: different languages, different cultures, differences among the traditional currencies used, and the vast numbers of people who needed to be informed, ranging from the 302 million residents of the euro-using nations to the millions outside the EU who needed to understand the currency. It chose the theme, "The euro. Our money," to introduce the euro as the official currency of the 12 participating EU countries.

The total budget for the campaign was estimated at between $30 million and $50 million. The campaign had two phases: one designed to build recognition for the new currency, and a second designed to teach cashiers and clerks how to recognize counterfeit currency. This second phase spread beyond the immediate EU nations into the United States, Japan, and Eastern Europe.

Understanding the Currency

The saturation campaign was launched in September 2001 to prepare for the launch of the euro in January 2002. The strategy was based on the belief that the public would be more receptive to information about the notes and coins right before they were issued. A survey conducted in February 2001 suggested that about half the public might not receive or understand the messages about the euro. Therefore, the campaign's messages were designed to be simple and clear.

ECB president Wim Duisenberg told the *Financial Times* of London in March 2001: "We aim to provide very broad access to information, to communities and individuals, to old and young, to people in towns and the countryside, to the disabled and the able-bodied."

The campaign was launched simultaneously with the unveiling of the look of the new currency. Television commercials, newspaper ads, posters, and leaflets were used in the campaign. The initial television ad, in an appeal to unity, stressed that the euro would be used by 300 million people across the continent. Three more commercials announced the seven different denominations of the notes and stressed their security features. The fourth advertisement listed the coins' denominations. The advertisements were produced in all the languages of the countries involved in the euro conversion.

The ECB and the European Commission worked together to distribute 28,000 kits with dummies of the euro banknotes for use with trainers of those with physical or learning disabilities. The ECB set up a Web site with extensive information on the currency and how it was developed. The site added a "children's zone" where children could play games using the euro.

QUESTIONS FOR REFLECTION

1. What obstacles might be faced when planning a multi-language information campaign?

2. What obstacles might be encountered when asking key stakeholders to change nationally accepted symbols such as currency?

3. What obstacles might be encountered when your key stakeholders groups are composed of a variety of age groups?

Information for this case was drawn from the following: (31 October 2000), "Ad campaign aims to ease euro's arrival," *The Wall Street Journal*, p. B24; Barber, T. (2 March 2001), "Euro publicity blitz to be launched in September," *Financial Times* (London), p. 7; Barber, T., & Brown, K. (30 August 2001), "Design of euro banknotes unveiled today," *Financial Times* (London), p. 8; Bentley, S. (11 November 1999), "Publicis lands GBP30m euro task," *Marketing Week*, p. 11; Geary, J., & Sautter/Bonn, U. (16 March 1998), "Europe: The euro as child's play," *Time International*, p. 27; (5 November 1999), "Publicis wins $30M-$50M account to launch the euro," Euromarketing via E-mail, III (6) accessed at http://newfirstsearch.oclc.org, 4 June 2003; and (6 December 2000), "Publicity campaign in Italy to take the sting out of the euro," European Report, accessed at http://newfirstsearch.oclc.org, 4 June 2003.

CASE 44. RED, WHITE, AND BLUE—AND GOLDEN?
MCDONALD'S RESPONDS TO INTERNATIONAL PRESSURES

The golden arches of the McDonald's logo may help make it the most recognizable company in the world. The company, which, at one time, operated about 30,000 company-owned and franchised outlets in more than 120 countries, has found in recent years that the arches may just as well have been depicted as red, white, and blue as the company has become the focus of anti-American sentiment or animosity toward its international economic power in many locations around the world.

McDonald's expanded rapidly internationally during the 1990s and early 2000s, even opening a franchise in 1994 inside Mecca, Saudi Arabia, the most sacred site for Muslims, who are required to visit Mecca on pilgrimage at least once during their lives, if able. The *International Herald Tribune* said McDonald's had opened as many as 1,000 restaurants a year worldwide during the boom. In 2001, it reported international system sales of $7.8 billion. Its Web site says its vision is "to be the world's best quick service restaurant experience."

Violence and Protests Rock the Arches

One research study found that the most frequent target of corporate terrorism was the McDonald's Corp., which had 10 restaurants attacked between 1998 and 2003. The *Toronto Star* reported that since 1990, franchises in France, Belgium, Mexico, London, Chile, Serbia, Columbia, South Africa, Turkey, and Greece have been bombed. Violence against the fast-food chain has escalated. In December 2001, a restaurant in China was bombed, and in September 2001, a McDonald's in Istanbul was destroyed. In September 2002, a restaurant in a suburb of Beirut was bombed, and a month later, a Moscow restaurant was bombed. On November 20, 2002, a franchise in Riyadh, Saudi Arabia, was burned. Then, in December 2002, a bomb killed at least three in a McDonald's in Makassar, Indonesia.

French farmer Jose Bove led protests against "mal bouffe," or what he called junk food, that destroyed a McDonald's under construction in Millau in 1999. A new McDonald's in Grenoble, France, was burned in November 2002 following protests.

Although there may have been no link, the corporation announced in late 2002 that it was closing 175 of its overseas restaurants and all its outlets in Bolivia and two Middle Eastern countries it did not identify. In four international markets in the Middle East and Latin America, ownership would be transferred to licensees. At the same time, some 200 to 250 jobs were cut in the United States, and another 200 to 350 jobs were eliminated internationally. The fast-food chain had seen its earnings drop in the previous seven quarters.

The cutback in the number of restaurants did not halt the attacks, however. In February 2007, a McDonald's restaurant in St. Petersburg, Russia, was bombed.

At least six people were injured in the attack that broke windows and destroyed the ceiling.

Harvard anthropology professor James Watson, who studies McDonald's, told *The Toronto Star*: "In many parts of the world if people can't reach the embassy, there's always McDonald's...McDonald's represents an entire packaged cultural system. The fact that it's food makes it even more dangerous and more powerful; there's nothing more powerful than food in any society as a symbol of identity."

Benjamin Barber, author of *Jihad vs. McWorld*, agreed. He told the newspaper: "Attacking McDonald's is not a surrogate for attacking America's foreign policy. They're attacking McDonald's because it directly stands for things they oppose."

Growing evidence suggests that Barber's assessment is accurate. McDonald's and other American corporations such as Starbucks and Coca-Cola that either operate in or support Israel have faced boycotts. Some Muslim fundamentalists have called for attacks on McDonald's, according to reports on Salon.com, which said that in October 2001, an article in the online Islamist magazine *Khilafah* identified McDonald's and McDonnell-Douglas as "two devices that are used for ensuring American global reach." The fast food chains have become imperial fiefdoms, sending emissaries far and wide.

Sometimes, it is not anti-Americanism that leads to involvement in conflict, however, but other issues of culture and faith. The corporation was sued in 2001 by a group of Hindu vegetarians and others who charged in a class-action lawsuit that McDonald's French fries had used beef extract not listed in the ingredients. When in 1990 the company replaced beef fat in its deep fryers with 100% vegetable oil, it didn't reveal that it added beef essence to the oil. McDonald's paid a $10 million settlement, apologized, and altered the way it reports ingredients in its foods.

The Corporation Seeks to Adapt

McDonald's CEO Jack Greenberg participated in a panel discussion at the February 2002 World Economic Forum with the secretary general of the League of Arab States, Amr Moussa. Moussa said there were "deep grievances" against U.S. policies around the world. Greenberg said his restaurants offered a "model of how a corporation has to behave" through dialogue, facts and solutions, *The New York Times* reported.

McDonald's has responded to protests by trying to stress that its golden arches are grounded in local soil. It has allowed employees to close for prayers during the day, to alter its menu to meet religious requirements, and to separate male and female diners, according to *Franchise Times* magazine. Salon.com reported that McDonald's has incorporated other local and cultural requirements into its menu, offering a vegetarian McNistisima menu in Cyprus, a kosher McDonald's in Israel, and wine in France. In Japan, the children's playgrounds have been replaced by computer play centers.

Reuters described the McDonald's in Jakarta, Indonesia, in an October 2001 article, as an example of an adapting restaurant. Customers are served by women in veils and men in prayer caps. Islamic posters inside point out that "McDonald's Indonesia is owned by an indigenous Muslim Indonesian." Some posters are in Arabic, and others are in English. Some of the restaurants play religious music.

The company's annual *Worldwide Corporate Responsibility Report*, first published in 2002, pointed to its international charitable works. Posted on the company Web site in both English and Spanish, the report gave information about the $60.9 million raised to support children's charities, its sponsorship of the Olympics, the FIFA World Cup and the UEFA championship games, and country-specific programs, such as a soccer initiative for Korean children and a Canadian Go Active! Fitness Challenge. The idea for an annual report grew out of an internal social-responsibility audit carried out by the Business for Social Responsibility NGO based in San Francisco.

McDonald's also offers a "Best of Green: McDonald's Best Environmental Practices in Europe" e-booklet on the Web at http://apps.mcdonalds.com/bestofgreen. The report details case studies of particular environmentally sensitive practices in restaurants across the globe and highlights how the restaurants are cooperating with local interest groups to achieve common environmental goals.

A Golden Day for Children

McDonald's launched a major public relations campaign in 2002 to support the November 20 World Children's Day, which sought to raise millions in support for the Ronald McDonald House Charities and other children's services, such as support for orphanages in Russia, Estonia, and Kuwait, for children's hospitals, and for children's health organizations. The event commemorated the 100th birthday of McDonald's founder Ray Kroc and was timed to commemorate the anniversary of the Convention on the Rights of the Child, which was held on November 20, 1989. A portion of the proceeds from all sales on November 20 were donated to the causes.

Golin/Harris International coordinated public relations for the event, but McDonald's also worked with local agencies. Internal communication support began in April, and public announcement of the World Children's Day came in July after CEO Greenberg met with the secretary general of the United Nations and the executive director of UNICEF.

International musicians Celine Dion and Enrique Iglesias and 125 Olympic athletes were recruited to serve as spokespeople for the day. International events included a day-long concert in Mexico City where more than 40 celebrities were slated to appear. In Auckland, New Zealand, the prime minister made an appearance. In Hong Kong, a local musician was to cook breakfast for area children, and in Moscow, a McDonald's hosted orphans. Cathy Nemeth, senior director for worldwide communications with McDonald's, told *PRWeek*, "It's a global public relations program that is community based."

QUESTIONS FOR REFLECTION

1. What principles should characterize community relations and social responsibility practices on an international scale?

2. Discuss the role of research in the development of public relations campaigns and programs for multinational corporations.

3. How might corporations such as McDonald's and Kentucky Fried Chicken differentiate themselves from their home country? What possibilities and what dangers does that differentiation pose for practitioners and managers?

Information for this case was drawn from the following sources, including the McDonald's Web site at www.mcdonalds.com, and (23 March 2007), "Authorities detain five in connection with St. Petersburg McDonald's restaurant bombing," Associated Press Worldstream; Associated Press (15 December 1994),"New mecca for burger with fries," *Newsday*, p. A22; Chabria, A. (22 April 2002), "McDonald's shows off CSR credentials in debut report," *PRWeek*, p. 3; Elam, S. (23 October 2002), "McDonald's pledges to refocus on core locations," *National Post*, p. FP18; Frank, J. N. (11 November 2002), "McDonald's starts PR push for global kids fundraiser," *PRWeek*, p. 9; Goldberg, M. (6 December 2002), "Falling arches," Salon.com; Goldberg, M. (8 December 2002), "Fires of anti-Americanism burn McDonald's," *The Toronto Star*; Jung, H. (19 April 2003), "Starbucks risks a backlash with international growth; overseas dissent is reminiscent of some of the problems faced by McDonald's," *London Free Press*, p. C5; Pfanner, E. (20 November 2002), "Diet awaits the giant of fast food; McDonald's to trim its expansion plans," *International Herald Tribune*, p. 11; Prewitt, M. (18 February 2002), "Chains look for links overseas," *Nation's Restaurant News*, p. 1; Schmemann, S. (2 February 2002), "Forum in New York; workshops; where McDonald's sits down with Arab nationalists," *The New York Times*, p. A10; Simon, E. (11 September 2006), "Can fear be quantified? Specter of terrorism has hurt stocks, but no one knows how much," Associated Press Worldstream; Soetjipto, T. (12 October 2001), "U.S. icon McDonald's embraces Islam in Indonesia." Reuters Business Report; Valkin, V. (9 November 2002), "McDonald's to close 175 overseas outlets." *The Financial Times*, p. 19; Weiss, J. (8 July 2002), "McDonald's fries fracas simmering," *The Dallas Morning News*, p. A1.

CASE 45. MARITIME TRAGEDY COMPOUNDED BY
CULTURAL DIFFERENCES

People throughout Japan angrily condemned the U.S. Navy when a submarine accidentally rammed and sank a Japanese fishing vessel in the open ocean off Hawaii on Friday, February 9, 2001. Over the weekend, anger over the collision and relief at the rescue of 26 aboard paled beside anxiety over 9 still missing, including 4 teenagers.

As Navy officers and Japanese survivors provided more details, people everywhere were astonished to learn that the sub's maneuvers had been arranged to impress 16 civilian guests on board and that some guests had handled critical controls before the accident.

"It's outrageous and unforgivable," one resident of Uwajima, the fishing vessel's home, told BBC News. "It sounds like they were fooling around. It's very upsetting for the people in this town."

Additionally, Japanese survivors said the submarine had rescued no one but instead waited for the U.S. Coast Guard to arrive and lift them from their life rafts. Confirming their tale, the Navy said waves had been too high to risk opening the sub's hatches or approach the small rafts.

The Navy began investigating the collision immediately and relieved the sub's commanding officer. As he prepared for a court of inquiry, he asked to testify under immunity and initially declined to speak publicly about the incident. In the United States, high rates of litigation and gigantic jury awards have conditioned people to proceed cautiously as the facts of an accident are collected and assessed, especially when criminal charges might result.

The *Yomiuri Shimbun*, Japan's largest daily newspaper, expressed disapproval: "In Japan, the person responsible for such an accident would be bound to personally apologize for their actions and accept full responsibility."

Figure 10.4 U.S. Navy divers swim alongside the Ehime-Maru during recovery operations off Honolulu (USN photo by Andrew McKaskle)

Pieces of the Puzzle

Eventually, investigators pieced together events that led to the collision. The *Ehime-Maru*, a 180-foot trawler, was heading south at 11 knots on February 9 with the open Pacific ahead and the coastline of Oahu just visible nine miles off the stern. It had departed Honolulu 90 minutes earlier, at noon, carrying a crew of 20 as well as 13 students and 2 teachers from the Uwajima Marine Products High School. Skies were overcast, and haze made visibility no better than fair, but it was a warm day; the air was 78 degrees and the ocean temperature was 77. The surface was choppy, rolling with swells of 4 to 6 feet.

Built in 1996 and weighing 500 tons, the *Ehime-Maru* functioned as a floating classroom, with accommodations for up to 45 students, where Japanese teens could learn the skills they'd need in the maritime trades. The trawler was bound for a fishing area 435 nautical miles distant. High above the white hull and bridge, surface search radar scanned the vicinity for traffic.

Four hours before the trawler left Honolulu, the USS Greeneville had put to sea at 8 a.m. from the Naval Station at Pearl Harbor, just a few miles to the west. On board were 106 officers and enlisted men.

Distinguished Civilians Aboard

Also on the Greeneville were 16 civilians—men and women who were the Navy's guests for the day, expecting to return to port before nightfall. The Navy arranged such visits to the Greeneville and other ships as part of its community relations program. The purpose was to demonstrate:

- The Navy and Marine Corps team as a unique and capable instrument of national policy.
- Resource requirements for the nation's maritime security strategy.
- Prudent stewardship of taxpayer investments in naval platforms and systems.
- The proficiency, pride, and professionalism of sailors and Marines and the need to recruit and retain them.

"The Greeneville's sole mission on 9 February," according to a Navy document, "was to conduct a public affairs 'distinguished visitor' (DV) embark for 16 civilian guests."

Assigned to a large operations area south of Oahu, the 362-foot sub proceeded on the surface for the first two hours, with the commanding officer taking groups of guests up to the bridge. Then, the Greeneville submerged at 10:17 a.m. During this maneuver, guests operated some of the dive controls under close supervision of the crew, and the sub continued south until noon and then reversed course. The sub's sonar array first detected the *Ehime-Maru* at about 12:30 p.m. Due to error, initial calculations showed that the distance between the two vessels was increasing rather than closing.

Demonstration of Maneuvers

As the Greeneville continued north, the commanding officer put the 6,000-ton submarine through a series of up-and-down angles and high-speed turns to demonstrate its tactical maneuverability. He also planned to execute a rapid dive to a depth of 400 feet as well as an emergency surfacing drill. Navy rules require a submarine to rise to periscope depth before an emergency surfacing maneuver so that officers can look in all directions to eliminate any danger of collision. Only after this inspection of the surface is complete will a submarine descend to practice the rapid ascent.

As prescribed, the Greeneville scanned the surface through its periscopes, but the officers and crew saw nothing. The seas were high; a white haze reduced visibility; the trawler's hull was white; its angle of approach reduced its profile; and the sub's surface search procedure was short. At the time, the *Ehime-Maru* was less than two miles away from the Greeneville, and the sub's detection equipment confirmed the trawler's presence, its distance, its speed and its course. Because of earlier miscalculations and inadequate crew communications on the sub, the danger went unnoticed.

Approaching the Fatal Moment

After 66 seconds at periscope depth, the Greeneville began its dive and reached 400 feet about two minutes later. The commanding officer invited one visitor to sit at the helm, another to operate ballast actuator valves, and a third to sound a klaxon horn during the emergency drill. All three guests were under close crew supervision. The *Ehime-Maru*, unnoticed and unsuspecting, was less than a mile away.

It took the Greeneville less than a minute to get from 400 feet to the surface. As it shot out of the waves, its rudder sliced the fishing boat from starboard to port. The trawler captain gave immediate orders to get everyone on deck for a headcount. Even before the count could be completed, waves washed across the deck and began sweeping people into the sea. The vessel was gone in less than 10 minutes.

The trawler's life rafts deployed automatically, and the crew and students struggled through waves, diesel fuel and flotsam to reach them. Within minutes, the rafts held 26 survivors. Missing were four 17-year-old students, three crew members, and both teachers.

On the Greeneville, the officers and crew were surprised by the noise and shudder caused by the collision. Using the periscopes, they examined the surroundings and were surprised to see a fishing vessel sinking and its people tumbling into the water. The sub itself had suffered some damage but nothing that would threaten its seaworthiness.

The Greeneville immediately called the U.S. Coast Guard for rescue assistance, but the high seas prevented the submarine itself from taking survivors on board. Water washing across the deck would have poured into any open hatch as the cylindrical hull rolled with the waves. The officers also were concerned that the sub's rolling motion might swamp or capsize the rafts if the vessel got too close.

Survivors Evacuated to Honolulu

Coast Guard watercraft arrived at the scene about one hour later and by 4:15 p.m. had moved all survivors to Honolulu. Surface vessels and aircraft from the Coast Guard and Navy continued to search for the nine missing Japanese for days but had no success.

Tragic as the collision was, the Navy's embarrassment grew as it acknowledged over succeeding days, first, that the sub was impotent in the rescue efforts; second, that a sizeable guest contingent was aboard; third, that civilians handled controls in the drills; and then, that the sole purpose of the cruise was public relations.

By Sunday, apologies and condolences had been extended to Japan by the commander in chief of the U.S. Pacific Fleet, the Ambassador to Japan, the Secretary of State, and the new U.S. President, inaugurated less than a month earlier. The Japanese Prime Minister lodged an official protest and warned that the United States might have to raise the trawler from the ocean floor, 2,000 feet beneath the waves, if the missing nine were not found.

In Japan, people were far from satisfied by the expressions of regret, and the news media there kept insisting that the United States and the submarine's commander should extend "sincere" apologies.

Figure 10.5 USS Greeneville sits atop blocks in dry dock at Pearl Harbor Naval Shipyard following a collision at sea with the Japanese fishing vessel (DoD photo)

A Contrast in Cultures

Japanese writer Shin-ya Fujiware, commenting in *The New York Times*, said: "The nonappearance of the commander of the Greeneville—his failure to meet the families of the victims to express his feelings of apology and mourning—is shocking, even incomprehensible to a people whose culture stresses decorum and form. Such decorum is not merely 'formal' in the American sense; it is the shape in which common humanity finds expression."

One month after the accident, the sub commander arranged to meet face to face with relatives of the victims who were lost. In a closed-doors gathering in March, he bowed formally before them and tearfully expressed his regrets.

In June, the Navy acceded to the wishes of the missing victims' families and began a salvage effort to lift the trawler from the ocean floor and move it to shallower waters where divers could search the vessel's interior for bodies. All but one of the missing nine were found by November.

Navy Gets Cultural Guidance

During the salvage operations, the Navy turned to a professor of religion at the University of Hawaii for guidance in observing cultural norms to show proper respect in the recovery of remains. Professor George J. Tanabe, Jr., reflecting on the entire episode for *The New York Times*, said: "You couldn't have constructed a better scenario for the uncorking of the darker side of Japan's love-hate relationship with the United States…It was one humiliation after another for Japan, a reinforcement of deeply resented stereotypes of the relationship between the two countries as tough guys versus wimps."

Cultural differences represent more than the manners and preferences of peoples. They represent perceptions of what is right and wrong, what deserves

Figure 10.6 U.S. Defense Secretary Donald Rumsfeld (center) confers with Japanese Senior Vice Minister of Foreign Affairs Seishiro Eto (right), Ambassador to the U.S. Shunji Yanai (left) and Chief of Naval Operations Veri Clark (DoD photo by R.D. Ward)

Figure 10.7 During final ceremonies for the Ehime-Moru aboard JDS Chihaya, representatives from three families threw flowers into the sea to honor their lost relatives (USN photo by Keith W. DeVinney)

respect and how to show it, the power of symbols, the need for dignity, and the expectation of truth revealed promptly and thoroughly.

QUESTIONS FOR REFLECTION

1. Some reporters said that the Navy's slow release of details in the first week after the accident provided a steady flow of damaging news. What were the alternatives?
2. Was the Navy obligated to shield the "distinguished visitors" from the media's intrusiveness?
3. What steps were available to the Navy to address the anger in Japan and make sincere apologies?
4. How would you balance the concerns about litigation in the United States with demands in Japan for full accountability and openness?

Information for this case was drawn from the following: the U.S. Navy Web site at www.cpf.navy.mil/greeneville; Cushman, J. (11 February 2001), "Sub in collision was conducting drill, Navy says," *The New York Times*, p. A1; French, H. (5 November 2001), "U.S. makes amends to Japan for sinking of ship," *The New York Times*, p. A6; Jehl, D. (12 February 2001), "Clues sought in sub accident; some Japanese fault rescue," *The New York Times*, p. A1; Kakuchi, S. (7 March 2001), "Apologies do little to ease grief over sea tragedy," *Asia Times*, p. 7; Marquis, C. (10 February 2001), "9 are missing off Pearl Harbor after U.S. submarine collides with Japanese vessel," *The New York Times*, p. A16; Shin-ya, F. (17 February 2001), "In Japan, waiting for the captain to appear," *The New York Times*, p. A17; (16 February 2001), "Sub tragedy leaves Japanese town bitter," BBC News, www.bbc.co.uk/1/hi/world/asia-pacific; (13 April 2001), Transcript of USN Court of Inquiry into circumstances of collision.

PROFESSIONAL INSIGHT

GLOBAL CONNECTIONS, DISTINCTIVE DIFFERENCES

Julie Freeman, ABC, APR; president, International Association of Business Communicators

Students in marketing classes learn that one strategy companies can use to increase sales is to sell their products to new customers in new markets. Many companies have successfully followed this strategy for quite some time. U.S. consumers can drive Audis, talk on Nokia cell phones or listen to their Yamaha stereos. And when they travel abroad, they can drink Starbucks coffee, eat McDonald's hamburgers and watch news on CNN.

Public relations firms are no different from manufacturing or consumer products companies. They wish to grow their revenue by capitalizing on the opportunities that the new global marketplace offers. Furthermore, if an existing client is expanding into new markets, the firm wants to broaden its global reach as well.

Yet, to conclude that global expansion can be supported by a one-size-fits-all global public relations strategy is a huge mistake. Wise companies know that while their brand must remain faithful to its core attributes, they also must adapt to local customs and preferences. The pastries that are sold in Starbucks in Beijing are much different from pastries that are sold in Starbucks in Boston.

So, too, must public relations campaigns adapt to local attitudes, customs, laws and lifestyles. Golin/Harris Taiwan demonstrated that principle when it conducted a marketing campaign for Kimberly Clark's paper towels. They chose the period prior to Ghost Month, when ghosts of deceased relatives are allowed to return to earth and enjoy lavish meals with their families. Golin/Harris hired a folklore specialist to help design towels with designs appropriate for the month and launched them right before Ghost Month to highlight their value as a cleaning helper and a magic weapon for luck.

A successful HIV/AIDS prevention program in Tanzania focused its message on counseling rather than testing to sidestep the local stigma associated with testing. The key message was "Come, let's talk." That message was spread, through both mass media and by counselors who wore "Come, let's talk" t-shirts at public events and by others who gave talks at bridal showers.

These are but two examples of successful adaptation to local customs and attitudes. If communicators are going to be successful as they enter new markets, these kinds of stories need to be the rule, not the exception.

Given the increasing connections between people around the world, it is very likely that practitioners will work on projects targeted to markets outside their own communities. But they should not make the mistake of thinking that what works at home will work somewhere else. Just because we have all become more connected does not mean that we have all become the same.

Julie Freeman, ABC, APR, is president of the International Association of Business Communicators. She has worked in communication and nonprofit management for almost 20 years. What Julie enjoys about working with nonprofits is the opportunity to perform a variety of functions, including strategic planning, crisis management, media relations, publishing, special events planning and employee communications.

Index